LEARN
BASIC
NOW

LEARN
BASIC
NOW

Michael Halvorson & David Rygmyr
Foreword by Bill Gates

PUBLISHED BY
Microsoft Press
A Division of Microsoft Corporation
16011 NE 36th Way, Box 97017
Redmond, Washington 98073-9717

Library of Congress Cataloging in Publication Data
Halvorson, Michael.
Learn BASIC now.
          p.   cm.
Includes index.
1. BASIC (Computer program language)
I. Rygmyr, David, 1958– .   II. Title.
QA76.73.B3H335   1989   005.13'3   89-13234
ISBN 1-55615-240-X   CIP

Printed and bound in the United States of America.

1 2 3 4 5 6 7 8 9   FGFG   3 2 1 0 9

Distributed to the book trade in Canada by General Publishing Company, Ltd.

Distributed to the book trade outside the United States and Canada by Penguin Books Ltd.

Penguin Books Ltd., Harmondsworth, Middlesex, England
Penguin Books Australia Ltd., Ringwood, Victoria, Australia
Penguin Books N.Z. Ltd., 182–190 Wairau Road, Auckland 10, New Zealand

British Cataloging in Publication Data available

IBM®, PC/AT®, and PS/2® are registered trademarks, and PC/XT™ is a trademark
of International Business Machines Corporation.
Microsoft® and MS-DOS® are registered trademarks of Microsoft Corporation.

Project Editor: Megan E. Sheppard   **Technical Editor:** Dail Magee, Jr.

For Kimberly,
who believes that dreams come true.
M.J.H.

For my parents, Chester and Odlaug,
who taught me the value of an honest day's work.
D.L.R.

Note to the Reader

If you are using an IBM PS/2 or another computer without a 5¼-inch disk drive, you'll need to convert the *Learn BASIC Now* disks or order 3½-inch disks from Microsoft Press. See Appendix A for conversion and ordering information.

Contents

Foreword

It's been said thousands of times that what separates us from all other animals is our ability to create and manipulate tools to effect change around us. And rapid progress is most easily achieved when tools are standardized. When your friend throws you the keys to her car and says "You drive," you don't wonder: "Where do I put the key? Where is the gas pedal? Where is the brake?" You know where to find and how to manipulate the major tools in any car. The same should be true when you sit down at your computer, whether you're an artist, a student, a programmer, or an accountant. You should be able to concentrate on the problem or task at hand and avoid spending time learning the fundamentals.

One reason that modern technology has come so far, so fast, has been a willingness on the part of manufacturers to standardize tools. Standardization allows us to maximize our investments—both in education *and* in technology—at the same time that we minimize our effort and expense.

So why should you learn BASIC? BASIC has been the "standard" programming language on microcomputers since 1975, when Paul Allen and I wrote the original microcomputer version to run on the then-revolutionary Altair computer. For the next six years, Microsoft convinced virtually all personal-computer manufacturers to build our BASIC into their hardware. For the first time, one unifying language cut across all hardware, and a huge community of programmers and users grew up around BASIC. This proliferation occurred not only because BASIC came free on millions of micros sold each year but also because BASIC's English-like simplicity and features made it an easy language to learn. Plus BASIC offered the versatility required to solve even the most complex problems.

Our research shows that four million personal-computer users now program in BASIC. They do so to build professional applications and for a wide range of other reasons, including education, personal challenge, and enjoyment. And they choose to use BASIC three times more frequently than they choose the next-most-popular programming language.

In recent years, machine capabilities have grown dramatically, allowing us to improve BASIC by adding rich new features in QuickBASIC that simply were not possible on the earlier hardware. This increase in power, coupled with a drop in computer hardware costs, is changing forever the way computers are used.

No longer are computers the exclusive domain of programmers. New operating systems and excellent applications software (for word processing, spreadsheets, databases, and more) are now affordable and widely available, and they allow millions of personal-computer users to accomplish an enormous amount of work with ease on micros.

That's today, but what does the future hold for microcomputers and for BASIC? Through the use of a standardized screen interface such as Microsoft Windows, we are now coming to a new level of consistency between varying types of software. Using a universal BASIC-like language, you will one day be able to embellish or alter the performance of your computer's software both from within your application (where you could use this language to streamline repetitive tasks) and among different applications (allowing you to combine the power of varied products). My belief is that by providing one simple yet common language, we will ensure that the microcomputer becomes more and more accessible to the typical user.

BASIC figures prominently in my vision for future standards. It is the best choice as a "learning" language, and *Learn BASIC Now* offers an easy entry into the fun and challenge of programming on your computer. Authors Michael Halvorson and David Rygmyr have expertly applied their years of experience at Microsoft Press, our book-publishing division, to create a text that demystifies the process of learning to program while at the same time showing some of the power and features you can expect from this modern evolution of BASIC using the QuickBASIC Interpreter.

My hope is that, after learning how enjoyable writing programs can be with the tools now available, you will continue to pursue new and better ways to use the microcomputer. Continued innovation on microcomputers requires that not only computer science graduates embrace this technology and apply it to their daily lives—we need a diverse community of users creating tools and solving problems to fully achieve the potential of the microcomputer. We need you to learn BASIC now!

Bill Gates

Acknowledgments

It never ceases to amaze us how much time and effort go into making a quality computer book, and how many people are involved in the process. The following individuals deserve specific mention for their outstanding efforts on this project: Darcie Furlan for her sharp design; Becky Geisler-Johnson and Roger Collier for their terrific illustrations; Peggy Herman for her pasteup; Brianna Morgan, Shawn Peck, Alice Copp Smith, Ward Webber, and Peter Weismiller for their proofreading and insightful queries; Debbie Kem and Cathy Thompson for their word processing; Ruth Pettis, Katherine Erickson, and Rodney Cook for their typesetting; and Patty Stonesifer, Jim Brown, Suzanne Viescas, Theresa Mannix, and Dean Holmes for their vision and encouragement. Special thanks also to Ray Kanemori and Tom Button for getting us started and helping with the QuickBASIC software.

In addition, a great team of testers participated in this project—this book is better for their comments and suggestions. Thanks to Craig Bartholomew, Diana Bray, Brianna Morgan, Erin O'Connor, Marjorie Schlaikjer, Mark Souder, Russell Steele, Cathy Thompson, Michael Viescas, Deb Vogel, and Jean Zimmer.

To project editor Megan Sheppard and technical editor Dail Magee, Jr., we extend a special acknowledgment and thank-you: You are truly the heroes of this book. Megan always looked out for the reader's interests, and she drove the project to completion with skill and humor. Dail brought to the project his impressive knowledge of QuickBASIC and a wealth of great trivia.

Michael Halvorson
David Rygmyr
September 1989

Introduction

The first step in learning something new is pulling together your resources. *Learn BASIC Now* makes that easy. Everything you need to learn how to program in BASIC is right here:

- The Microsoft QuickBASIC Interpreter—A state-of-the-art programming package that makes BASIC programming fast and easy

- The Microsoft QBI Express—A hands-on electronic tutorial that teaches you how to use the QuickBASIC Interpreter

- The Microsoft QBI Advisor—An electronic reference that provides documentation for each BASIC statement and function

- Sample programs—Dozens of useful and interesting programs that reinforce BASIC programming concepts

- Companion book—A hands-on, step-by-step guide to BASIC programming

- Questions and exercises—Review questions and programming exercises (with answers in the back of the book)

Whether you're a total beginner with no programming experience or a confident user with some knowledge of BASIC, this book contains what you need to become a proficient BASIC programmer. You might be most interested in the powerful QuickBASIC Interpreter, containing all but a few of the features of its big brother, the Microsoft QuickBASIC Compiler. Or perhaps you're interested in the step-by-step programming instruction starting from the *beginning* (a place few introductory books seem to start). However you use *Learn BASIC Now,* rest assured that your investment in learning to program will be of value for years to come. BASIC, along with personal computers, is here to stay.

HOW THIS BOOK IS ORGANIZED

True to the nature of programming, this book has been designed to be read sequentially. Read Chapters 1 through 6 carefully—they introduce the fundamentals of programming and cover the most important BASIC language elements. Chapters 7 though 12 build on these introductory chapters and introduce more general programming topics. If you have some previous programming experience with BASIC (such as BASICA or GW-BASIC) these chapters will be of special interest to you. The following is a summary of each chapter and appendix:

Chapter 1, "Introduction to Programming and BASIC," describes the purpose of programming languages and how programs are designed, and introduces the Microsoft QuickBASIC Interpreter.

Chapter 2, "Getting Started with the QuickBASIC Interpreter," describes how you start the QuickBASIC Interpreter and use it to load, edit, and run programs.

Chapter 3, "Introduction to the BASIC Language," discusses the anatomy of a BASIC instruction and describes the operation of the PRINT statement.

Chapter 4, "BASIC Variables and Operators," introduces the concepts of variables, data types, user input, and mathematical operators. Includes a program that calculates the price of an item including sales tax.

Chapter 5, "Controlling Program Flow," introduces decision making and structured programming with the IF and SELECT CASE statements. Includes a golden-age television trivia program.

Chapter 6, "Working with BASIC Loops," introduces the FOR, WHILE, and DO statements, which let you perform a task over and over again. Includes a simple monthly budgeting program.

Chapter 7, "Creating Your Own Subprograms and Functions," describes how to organize your program with easy-to-use modules called subprograms and functions. Includes a ready-to-play bowling program.

Chapter 8, "Working with Large Amounts of Data," teaches you how to manage large amounts of data in your programs with DATA statements and arrays. Includes a program that tracks sales information for a soda-pop distributor.

Chapter 9, "Working with Strings," describes how to work with characters and presents the many string-related statements and functions supplied in the QuickBASIC Interpreter. Includes a program that sorts a list of names in alphabetic order.

Chapter 10, "Working with Files," describes how to store information on disk. Includes a music database program that can be modified to track any type of database information.

Chapter 11, "Working with Graphics and Sound," describes how to include color, animation, graphic shapes, and sound in your programs. Includes a program that plays a song.

Chapter 12, "Debugging QuickBASIC Programs," describes the menu commands and techniques used to find bugs and fix your programs. Includes a program that you debug step by step using the debugging tools.

Chapter 13, "Learning More About BASIC," concludes the *Learn BASIC Now* programming course and describes how to get more information about BASIC programming.

Appendix A, "The QuickBASIC Interpreter Reference," is a topical quick reference that describes how to use the QuickBASIC Interpreter.

Appendix B, "ASCII and IBM Extended Character Sets," lists the 256 characters that you can display in BASIC programs.

Appendix C, "QuickBASIC Statements and Functions," lists the statements and functions available in the QuickBASIC Interpreter.

Appendix D, "Answers to Questions and Exercises," is a complete set of answers for the questions at the ends of the chapters.

Contacting Microsoft for Help

If you have a question or comment about the text or programs in *Learn BASIC Now,* or if one of the disks in your package is defective, write to Microsoft Press at the following address:

Microsoft Press
Attn: Learn BASIC Now Editor
16011 NE 36th Way
Box 97017
Redmond, WA 98073-9717

If you have a general question about the Microsoft QuickBASIC Interpreter product, call Microsoft Product Support Services in Redmond, Washington, at (206) 454-2030. Support engineers familiar with the Microsoft QuickBASIC Interpreter are standing by to answer your calls between 8:00 A.M. and 5:00 P.M. (Pacific time).

Introduction to Programming and BASIC

WHY DO PEOPLE USE COMPUTERS?

A computer is simply a tool. And, like any tool, its purpose is to serve you—to help you perform a task quickly and efficiently. But you don't need to be convinced of that. The very fact that you bought this book means you've recognized that a computer can be of use to you. But what you might wonder is why you would want to write computer programs of your own.

Why Should *I* Learn to Program?

After all, today you can choose from literally thousands of ready-made software programs—programs that lead you through the maze of tax preparation as easily as they challenge you with the maze of an adventure game. Confronted by such a wide variety of products, you might believe that the market is tapped out—that there's a program to suit your every need.

But you'd be wrong.

Programming as a problem solver

Stereotyped appearances to the contrary, professional programmers are business people. For the most part, they design programs that fulfill the broadest needs of the market: It's just not economically feasible to write a program that only a few people will buy. Translation: The more specialized your needs, the less likely you are to find an appropriate ready-made software program.

By learning to program, you can custom-design programs to meet your specific needs.

Programming as a learning tool

Another reason for learning to program a computer is that the process teaches you how computers work on the inside: You come to appreciate the step-by-step logic that results in the flashy displays and the slick printouts. Like an architect who can look at the outside of a building and see the organization of the steel beams, pipes, and support structures underneath it, a person who learns the basics of computer programming begins to get a feel for what a computer program does behind the scenes. Such familiarity also gives you a feel for what a computer can and can't do. For this reason an introductory course in computer programming is often the first class required in the study of computers in high school or college. (Plus, by learning the groundwork, you're learning to speak like the "pros." Familiarity with programming terminology and concepts helps you express yourself clearly.)

Programming as recreation

The final (and perhaps most important) reason for writing your own programs is that it can be downright *fun*. Computer programming, for beginners and experienced programmers alike, can be an enjoyable and rewarding experience.

Custom-designed Programming

But what if your needs are pretty straightforward? Perhaps you just need some organizational programs to simplify your life. BASIC lets you create programs that are as simple or detailed as you need. For example, here are a few people who could benefit by writing their own BASIC programs:

- A baseball enthusiast who wants to record team and player statistics and instantly recall items of interest

- A video-game devotee who wants to build a better adventure game

- A manager or small-business owner who wants to track appointments and important dates and be notified automatically about pending events

- A student or scientist who needs to perform specialized mathematical calculations

- A homeowner who wants to track household finances

- A doctor who wants to track patient records, prescriptions, and billing but is tired of using traditional bookkeeping methods

So as you can see, there are several good reasons for you to learn to program. But let's take a moment to talk terminology. Just what *is* a computer program, anyway?

WHAT IS A COMPUTER PROGRAM?

To perform useful work, a computer must consist of two things: *hardware* and *software*.

- Hardware is the physical part of the computer that you can see and touch, such as the keyboard and the screen.

- Software is a bit more elusive: It's the intelligence that controls the hardware and allows you to actually use the computer.

You can't use one without the other: Hardware without software is like a record player without records.

A *computer program* is software. It's simply a set of instructions that collectively cause a computer to perform a useful task, such as calculation or word processing. A program can be as short as a single instruction, or it can contain hundreds or even thousands of individual instructions.

Computers: Heroes or Villains?

Hollywood and television have done a fine job of showing us how computers can take away jobs, make life more difficult, and take over the world. Not exactly the kind of tool you'd want to take into your home or business, much less use or program!

Despite this bad press, personal computers have entered the workplaces and homes of millions, allowing people to perform useful work that makes their lives easier and more productive. People are starting to change their minds about these strange electronic devices—what once churned out reams of inscrutable punch cards and often took up more than its share of office space now sits on a desktop and displays images that are familiar, helpful, and amusing. Computers have become an integral part of business, communication, entertainment, and scientific research. Because of their ease of use and increased power, people can use today's personal computers as the tools they were designed to be.

HOW DO I WRITE A COMPUTER PROGRAM?

Preparation and organization are the important first steps in the programming process. Two questions help you get organized:

1. What do I want this program to do?

2. What steps must the program take to do this?

The set of general steps you come up with is called an *algorithm*. An algorithm isn't a computer program itself; it's just a collection of ordered notes describing what your program will do each step of the way. In fact, if you've ever used a recipe you've used an algorithm. Baking a cake, for example, involves following a step-by-step process that produces a useful (and tasty!) result.

Because an algorithm is a problem-solving tool designed to help you get the program written, there's no one right way of putting one together. Some programmers write algorithms as a list of ordered steps on a piece of paper, some draw them graphically in a diagram called a flowchart, and others (who have been working at it for some time) just organize the programming steps in their heads.

A list   A flowchart   An experienced programmer

Algorithms: There's more than one way to create them.

Whichever method you choose, it's important that you begin thinking about your program in general terms well before you sit down in front of the computer.

The BASIC Programming Language

Part of the reason for the emphasis on up-front problem solving and design is that the computer doesn't know very many words: You must spell things out for it in a language it understands.

BASIC (an acronym for Beginner's All-purpose Symbolic Instruction Code) is one of several programming languages available for personal computers. As with spoken languages, each computer language has its own "vocabulary" and its own set of rules. In addition, each language has its own strong points and weak points. Some languages are more efficient at doing certain tasks than others; some are easier to work with than others. All things considered, BASIC is an excellent language for computer programming because it's powerful, flexible, and—above all—English-like and easy to use.

Learning to "speak" BASIC, or any other computer programming language, is very much like learning to speak a foreign language. BASIC has its own vocabulary and a set of rules you must follow when using that vocabulary. Fortunately, BASIC's entire vocabulary consists of fewer than 200 words (called *keywords*), and the rules (called *syntax rules*) for using those keywords are relatively simple.

The Microsoft QuickBASIC Interpreter

But before you can start typing in BASIC instructions, your computer must have a piece of software that understands them. The Microsoft QuickBASIC Interpreter (QuickBASIC), included with this book, serves this purpose—it actually reads your BASIC instructions and translates them into a form that the computer can use. The name "interpreter" is particularly appropriate: The QuickBASIC Interpreter literally interprets each statement as you type it, checking to see if you made a typing mistake, misused a keyword, or broke a syntax rule.

The Origins of QuickBASIC

QuickBASIC is a superset of both the original BASIC language, created by John G. Kemeny and Thomas E. Kurtz in 1963 and 1964 at Dartmouth College, and of other versions of BASIC for the IBM Personal Computer and compatibles (such as BASICA and GW-BASIC). Not only is QuickBASIC a complete superset of these older versions of BASIC—that is, it understands all of the older versions' keywords and syntax—but it also provides some additional keywords and features popular in other computer languages, making it a complete system for writing your own programs.

The QuickBASIC Interpreter also provides a complete programming environment for you to work in. QuickBASIC is a single package that allows you to write and run programs immediately. With it, you can save your programs on disk, print them on your printer, and get help when you need it. It even contains many word-processor-like features that make writing and changing your programs easy.

HOW DOES THIS BOOK
HELP ME LEARN BASIC?

Besides introducing you to the BASIC computer programming language, *Learn BASIC Now* lets you put your new skills to work. As you learn, you'll be writing programs that display characters on the screen, read characters you type from the keyboard, work with words and numbers, and store information on a disk and retrieve it again. You'll even create programs that use graphics and sound. After you've worked through this book, you'll be able to create useful BASIC programs that put your computer—your tool—to work for you.

 NOTE: Starting with Chapter 2, each chapter ends with review questions and exercises. Take the time to work through them—it's a good opportunity to review material and to be sure you understand it before you go on to the next chapter. Answers to the questions and exercises can be found in Appendix D.

HOW DO I GET STARTED?

This book/disk package is a complete, step-by-step, hands-on approach to learning BASIC programming. In fact, it's time to take the first step. Follow the instructions in the rest of this chapter to

■ Make copies of the *Learn BASIC Now* disks.

■ Install the *Learn BASIC Now* programs on your computer.

■ Run the Microsoft QuickBASIC Express tutorial.

Before you know it you'll be typing in and running your own programs!

 NOTE: We assume that you have some elementary experience with the DOS operating sytem (formatting disks, changing directories, setting paths, and so on). If you need to brush up on the basics, see the documentation that came with your computer, or consult Running MS-DOS *by Van Wolverton (Microsoft Press, 1989).*

SETTING UP THE QUICKBASIC INTERPRETER

The following set of instructions guides you through the process of making backup copies of the disks included with this book and installing the files on the hard disk of your computer (if you have a hard disk). Operating instructions are also provided for systems with no hard disk.

Making an Extra Set of Disks

To protect your investment in the *Learn BASIC Now* disks, make an extra set to be used as your work copies and put the originals away in a safe place. (You should always create an extra set of disks, even if you plan to work from your hard disk.) To make an extra set you'll need three blank formatted 5¼-inch double-sided double-density (360 KB) floppy disks. The following instructions are divided into two sections, one for computers with one 5¼-inch disk drive and one for computers with two 5¼-inch disk drives.

 NOTE: If your computer uses only 3½-inch disks, turn to Appendix A for instructions on how to create an extra set of disks.

A Word About System Requirements

- To run the QuickBASIC Interpreter, you need an IBM PC, IBM PS/2, or compatible personal computer with at least 512 KB of total system memory. The QuickBASIC Interpreter also supports a printer; if you have one, be sure it is correctly configured and attached to your computer with the proper cable.

- To take full advantage of the color and graphics programs provided near the end of this book, you need an IBM Color Graphics Adapter (CGA), an IBM Enhanced Graphics Adapter (EGA), or an IBM Video Graphics Array (VGA), and a compatible monitor. If you have an IBM Monochrome Adapter (MDA), the QuickBASIC Interpreter will run in black-and-white mode on your display, but you'll still be able to run all programs in this book (with the exception of a few in Chapter 11).

- A Hercules Graphics Card will also run the QuickBASIC Interpreter in black-and-white mode, but it *can* display the graphics images in Chapter 11. If you have this adapter, run the special Hercules device driver MSHERC.COM provided on Disk 2 before you run the QuickBASIC Interpreter.

- The QuickBASIC Interpreter also supports the Microsoft Mouse. If your version of the mouse driver is earlier than 6.0 (check the mouse driver version number that appears when you first start the system), replace it with the MOUSE.COM device driver provided on Disk 3 before you run the QuickBASIC Interpreter. Both the MSHERC.COM and MOUSE.COM device drivers should be put in your AUTOEXEC.BAT file if you use them often.

If you have one floppy-disk drive

If your computer has one floppy-disk drive, enter the following command at the system prompt:

```
diskcopy a: a:
```

The DISKCOPY program will prompt you to put the source disk in drive A. Place Disk 1 (the first *Learn BASIC Now* disk supplied with this book) in the drive and press Enter. DISKCOPY will copy the first part of Disk 1 and prompt you for the target disk (the disk that will receive the copy). Remove Disk 1, insert one of the blank disks in the drive, and press Enter. DISKCOPY will continue the copy operation. During the process you'll be prompted to swap the disks one or more times. Repeat the process for Disk 2 and Disk 3 and label each of the new disks when you're finished.

If you have two floppy-disk drives

If your computer has two floppy-disk drives, enter the following command at the system prompt:

```
diskcopy a: b:
```

The DISKCOPY program will prompt you to put the source disk in drive A and the target disk in drive B. Place Disk 1 (the first *Learn BASIC Now* disk supplied with this book) in drive A, put one of the blank disks in drive B, and press Enter. DISKCOPY will copy the disk in drive A to the disk in drive B. Repeat this process for Disk 2 and Disk 3 and label each of the new disks when you're finished.

Installing the QuickBASIC Interpreter on a Hard Disk

If your computer has a hard disk, you should copy the contents of the three QuickBASIC Interpreter disks to it. An installation program named INSTALL.BAT on Disk 1 will handle this process for you. To run the installation program, put Disk 1 in drive A and enter the following command at the system prompt:

```
a:install
```

After you run the INSTALL program the QuickBASIC Interpreter is ready to run.

Operating Instructions for Systems with
Two Floppy-Disk Drives and No Hard Disk

If you have an IBM PC or compatible computer with two floppy-disk drives and no hard disk, you'll run the QuickBASIC Interpreter and its support programs directly from the working copies of the QuickBASIC Interpreter disks you made earlier. Put Disk 1 in drive A and use drive B for Disks 2 and 3. (You'll have to switch disks now and then to use the on-line help system and to load the sample programs listed in the book, but you'll be able to get along pretty well.) Before you begin working with the QuickBASIC Interpreter, enter the following PATH command at the system prompt:

```
path a:\;b:\
```

 NOTE: As your software programs increase in size, you'll find it increasingly difficult to run programs from a system with no hard disk. If you spend lots of time working with your computer, you should consider purchasing a hard disk or upgrading to a computer that has one.

THE MICROSOFT QUICKBASIC EXPRESS

Now that you know a bit about what a computer program is, and now that you've installed the QuickBASIC Interpreter on your computer, you're ready to learn about programming in BASIC. To help familiarize you with how to operate the QuickBASIC Interpreter, Disk 2 contains an introductory tutorial program called Microsoft QuickBASIC Express.

The QuickBASIC Express tutorial gives you hands-on, step-by-step experience in using the QuickBASIC Interpreter. QuickBASIC Express is completely self-contained, so you'll be putting this book aside for about 15 minutes while you go through it.

Take your time and work through all the exercises. Don't worry if you encounter a topic or two you don't understand. You'll put what you learn into actual practice when you start making your own programs.

Running the QuickBASIC Express Tutorial

You start the QuickBASIC Express tutorial in one of two ways, depending on how you installed the QuickBASIC Interpreter.

Running QuickBASIC Express from a hard disk

If you installed the QuickBASIC Interpreter on your hard disk, you must first change to the directory containing the QuickBASIC Interpreter files. To do this, type the following command and press Enter:

```
cd \qbi
```

To start QuickBASIC Express, type the following command and press Enter:

```
learn
```

Running QuickBASIC Express from a floppy disk

If you have no hard disk, insert Disk 2 into drive A and close the drive door. Make drive A the active drive by typing the following command and pressing Enter:

```
a:
```

To start QuickBASIC Express, type the following command and press Enter:

```
learn
```

After You're Through

When you're done, feel free to run QuickBASIC Express again if you'd like more practice. Or if you think you've got the hang of it, come back to this book to put what you learned to work!

Getting Started with the QuickBASIC Interpreter

Now that you've run QuickBASIC Express, you can get right down to business and start learning how to program.

STARTING THE QUICKBASIC INTERPRETER

To start programming, you must first start the QuickBASIC Interpreter. You do this in one of two ways, depending on how you installed the QuickBASIC Interpreter.

Starting the QuickBASIC Interpreter from a Hard Disk

If you installed the QuickBASIC Interpreter on a hard disk, type the following commands, pressing the Enter key after each one:

```
cd \qbi
qbi
```

Starting the QuickBASIC Interpreter from a Floppy Disk

If you're running the QuickBASIC Interpreter from floppy disks, insert Disk 1 into drive A and Disk 2 into drive B and close both drive doors. To start the QuickBASIC Interpreter, type the following command and press Enter:

```
qbi
```

You will see the drive A light go on, and the QuickBASIC Interpreter program will appear on the screen. If this does not happen, the PATH command (described in Chapter 1) is probably not set. To set it, enter the following command:

```
path a:\;b:\
```

Then type *qbi* again.

 NOTE: Throughout this book, text that you (or your users) must enter from the keyboard appears in color.

14

THE QUICKBASIC INTERPRETER SCREEN

After the QuickBASIC Interpreter is loaded, your screen looks like this:

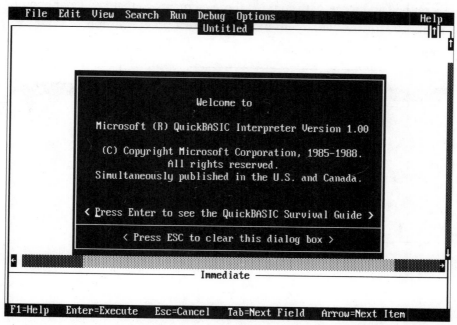

This "Welcome" message appears each time you start the QuickBASIC Interpreter. The screen offers you two options:

■ You can press Enter to enter the QuickBASIC Interpreter's built-in help system (the same help system you reached through the Help menu in the QuickBASIC Express program).

■ You can press the Esc key to clear the message from the screen and start programming.

Practice: Clearing the screen to begin programming

Because you will be programming in this chapter, press Esc to clear the message from the screen.

15

Reviewing the Screen

QuickBASIC Express introduced the various elements of the screen. Now let's review and work with some of these elements so that you can become even more familiar with them before you start programming.

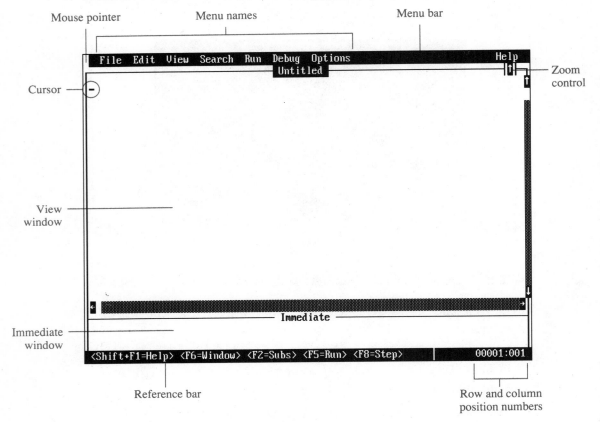

The cursor

The blinking underscore in the upper-left corner of the screen will probably catch your eye first. This is the *cursor*. The cursor indicates where the next character you type will appear on the screen.

The mouse pointer

If your computer has a mouse installed, a rectangular *mouse pointer* appears in the upper-left corner of the screen. The mouse pointer lets you move around your program quickly and choose menu items easily.

The row and column position numbers

In the lower-right corner of the screen are two numbers separated by a colon. These numbers indicate the current location of the cursor. The first number tells you which row the cursor is in; the second number (following the colon) tells you which column the cursor is in. As shown in Figure 2-1, the numbers indicate that the cursor is in row 1, column 1.

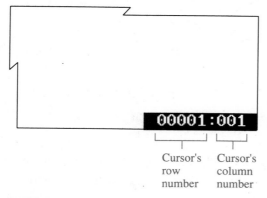

FIGURE 2-1.
Row and column position numbers.

Practice: Changing column numbers

1. Press the right-arrow key on the numeric keypad a few times and watch what happens to the column number.

2. Now press the left-arrow key until the cursor returns to column 1. (Later, when you begin typing in programs, you can practice changing row numbers with the up-arrow and down-arrow keys.)

The menu bar and the menu names

Across the top of the screen is the *menu bar*. The menu bar contains the *menu names* of all the QuickBASIC Interpreter's drop-down menus.

The View window and the Immediate window

The QuickBASIC Interpreter initially gives you two windows to work in, each with a specific purpose:

■ The upper window—where you type in and work with your own programs—is called the *View window*.

■ The lower window—where you can test out a programming instruction before you actually type it into your program—is called the *Immediate window*.

You can work in only one window at a time, although it's easy to switch between the two. The window you're currently working in is called the *active window*. Identifying the active window is easy:

■ Look for the blinking cursor; it's always in the active window.

■ Look at the window title at the top of the window; if the title is highlighted, the window is active.

Note that the title of the View window remains *Untitled* until you name the program you write and save it on disk.

The reference bar

At the bottom of the screen is the *reference bar*. The reference bar contains a list of keys, called *control keys*, that you can use in the active window. This list of control keys changes whenever you select a new active window.

Practice: Switching windows with a reference bar command

Notice that the F6 function key is the Window key. You use F6 to switch between windows. (To switch between windows with the mouse, simply move the mouse pointer anywhere within the desired window and click.) Press F6 now and see what happens.

As shown in Figure 2-2, the blinking cursor is now in the Immediate window. The shaded horizontal and vertical scroll bars have disappeared from the View window, and the highlight that was on the word *Untitled* in the View window has moved to the word *Immediate* at the top of the Immediate window. These changes tell you that the Immediate window is now the active window. If you were to type characters on the keyboard, they would now appear in the Immediate window instead of in the View

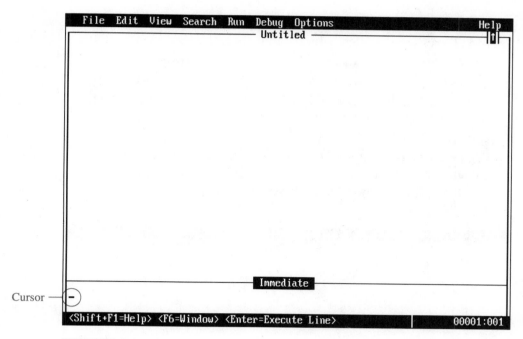

FIGURE 2-2.
Making the Immediate window the active window.

window. Note that, unlike the View window title, the Immediate window title never changes.

Also notice that a different set of control keys now appears in the reference bar at the bottom of the screen. These are the Immediate window's control keys. For now, you won't be using the Immediate window, so press F6 to make the View window active again.

The zoom control

You can make the Immediate window disappear from view. In the upper-right corner of the screen, just under the Help menu name, is a vertical rectangle with an up-arrow character. This is the *zoom control,* which causes the View window to expand and cover the Immediate window.

After you use the zoom control, the up-arrow character changes to a double-headed arrow, meaning that the View window is ''zoomed'' as far as it can go.

- To use the zoom control with the mouse, click on the zoom control. To restore the View window to its original size, click on the zoom control again.

- To use the zoom control with the keyboard, hold down the Ctrl key and press F10. To restore the View window to its original size, press Ctrl-F10 again.

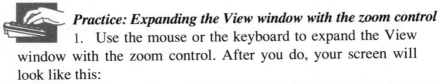

Practice: Expanding the View window with the zoom control

1. Use the mouse or the keyboard to expand the View window with the zoom control. After you do, your screen will look like this:

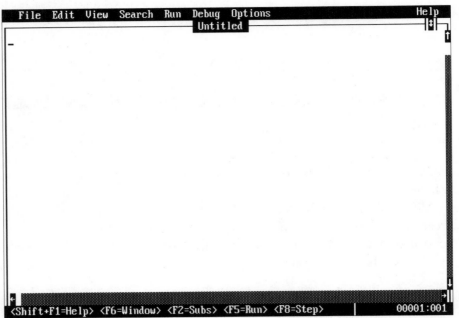

2. Now restore the View window to its regular size to make the Immediate window visible.

OPENING AN EXISTING PROGRAM

Now that you've had a little hands-on experience with the QuickBASIC Interpreter environment, you can open and run a sample program to see what the QuickBASIC Interpreter can do.

 NOTE: The following practices assume that you're some-what familiar with a menu-based environment. If you need a review on the basics of using a mouse or moving around the screen, see Appendix A, "The QuickBASIC Interpreter Reference."

To work with a program stored on disk you must first open it, just as you must open a book before you can read it. Opening a program loads it into the View window. To open a program, select the Open command from the File menu.

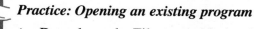 ***Practice: Opening an existing program***

1. Drop down the File menu. Notice that the Open command is followed by an ellipsis (...).

2. Select the Open command to display the Open dialog box:

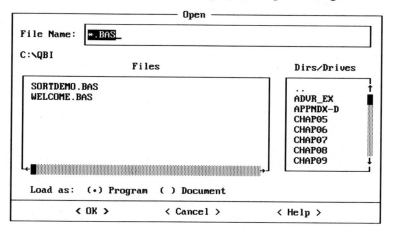

3. Move the cursor to the Files list box.

4. Highlight WELCOME.BAS.

5. Select OK. This causes the QuickBASIC Interpreter to open the program and load it into the View window.

Running a Program

To run a program, select the Start command from the Run menu. Doing this tells the QuickBASIC Interpreter to execute the instructions currently in the View window.

 Practice: Running a program
Select Start from the Run menu.

Your screen should go momentarily blank. Then words will begin "falling" from the top of the screen, accompanied by a series of tones. When the program stops, you'll see the following:

```
                        Welcome to Learn BASIC Now!




Press any key to continue
```

The Output Screen

This screen is the *output screen,* where the QuickBASIC Interpreter displays the output of the program. (Output is the end result of the instructions in your program.) When you run a program, the QuickBASIC Interpreter switches immediately to the output screen. This prevents your output from writing over the program in the View window.

The message at the bottom of the output screen, *Press any key to continue*, appears every time a program finishes running.

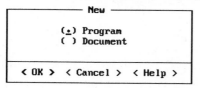

Practice: Returning to the View window

Press any key now. The QuickBASIC Interpreter returns you to the View window. Next, you'll remove the WELCOME.BAS program from the View window so that you can type in your own program.

WRITING A NEW PROGRAM

Before you can write your own program from scratch, you must clear the View window. You can have only one program in the View window at a time, whether it's a program you load from disk or a program you type in yourself. You tell the QuickBASIC Interpreter that you want to clear the View window and start with a clean slate by choosing the New command from the File menu.

Practice: Using the New command

1. Select the New command from the File menu. The QuickBASIC Interpreter displays the following dialog box:

```
┌─────────── New ───────────┐
│                           │
│      (.) Program          │
│      ( ) Document         │
│                           │
├───────────────────────────┤
│  < OK >   < Cancel >   < Help >  │
└───────────────────────────┘
```

You have two options. The Program option, currently selected, tells the QuickBASIC Interpreter that you want to type in a program you can run; the Document option tells the QuickBASIC Interpreter that you only want to type in a document, such as a memo or a letter.

> ## Editing a Document
>
> You can use the QuickBASIC Interpreter to edit simple documents (such as memos or letters) when QuickBASIC is running in *document* mode. To open an existing file in document mode, select the *Document* option button in the Open dialog box. To open a new file in document mode, select the *Document* option button in the New dialog box.

2. Because you do want to type in a program and the Program option is already selected, press Enter. The QuickBASIC Interpreter clears the WELCOME.BAS program from the View window, and you're ready to start typing your own program.

    NOTE: If you accidentally pressed any letter or number keys while the WELCOME.BAS program was in the View window, the QuickBASIC Interpreter assumes that you modified the program. When you press Enter, the QuickBASIC Interpreter displays another dialog box:

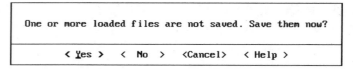

```
One or more loaded files are not saved. Save them now?

       < Yes >    < No >    <Cancel>    < Help >
```

   This box gives you the opportunity to save the modified *version of the program instead of the original (unmodified) version on the disk. You do not want to do that, so press Tab once to highlight the angle brackets around the No option, and then press Enter.*

Your First Program

Now you're ready to type in your first program! Typing in a program is very straightforward. All you need to do is type in the lines exactly as shown in this book and press Enter when you're done with each line.

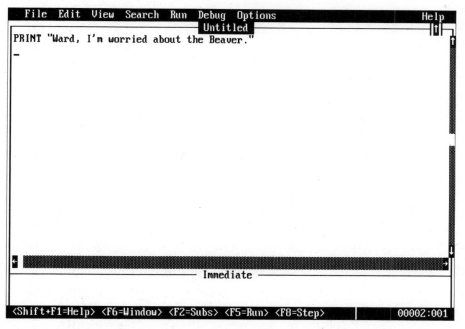

Practice: Typing in your first program

1. Type the following line exactly as shown—spaces, double quotation marks, and so on:

```
print "Ward, I'm worried about the Beaver."
```

2. Check the line carefully to be sure you didn't misspell anything. If you did, use the Backspace key to return to the mistake. Fix it, and then type in the rest of the line.

3. When you're satisfied that you didn't make any mistakes, press Enter. After you press Enter, your screen looks like this:

```
 File  Edit  View  Search  Run  Debug  Options                    Help
                         Untitled
PRINT "Ward, I'm worried about the Beaver."



                              Immediate
<Shift+F1=Help> <F6=Window> <F2=Subs> <F5=Run> <F8=Step>        00002:001
```

Notice that the word *print* is in capital letters now. The QuickBASIC Interpreter did this after you pressed Enter because the word *print* is a BASIC *keyword*—that is, it's a part of BASIC's "vocabulary." The QuickBASIC Interpreter always converts BASIC keywords to all uppercase so that you can easily distinguish them from everything else on a line.

What you just typed in, although it's only one line long, is a complete BASIC program.

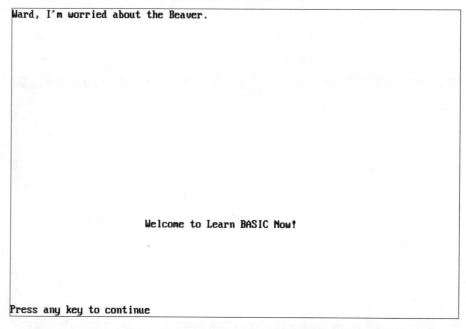

Practice: Running your first program

1. Run your program now: Select Start from the Run menu. When you do, your screen looks like this:

```
Ward, I'm worried about the Beaver.




                        Welcome to Learn BASIC Now!


Press any key to continue
```

Congratulations! You wrote and ran your first BASIC program!

Before you press a key to return to the View window, notice that the screen still contains the message *Welcome to Learn BASIC Now!* Remember, this is the output screen—the screen the QuickBASIC Interpreter uses to display any information your program instructs it to display. You can see that the output screen isn't automatically "cleaned off" each time you run a program: The message *Welcome to Learn BASIC Now!* demonstrates that.

2. Press any key to return to the View window.

Changing Your Program

You learned about one BASIC keyword, PRINT, that lets your program put information on the screen. Now you'll learn another BASIC keyword, CLS (for CLear Screen), which allows your program to completely erase the output screen. You'll be adding CLS to the program you wrote, so in the process you'll also learn how to change a program.

Putting BASIC instructions in proper order

Before you add CLS to this program, think about the order in which you want your program to carry out its instructions. In most of the programs you'll create in this book, each instruction is on a separate line. When you run your program, the QuickBASIC Interpreter executes the instructions one at a time in the order in which you list them—that is, the QuickBASIC Interpreter starts at the top of the program and executes your instructions one by one until it gets to the bottom of the list.

Your first step, then, is to decide where to put the CLS instruction in your program.

Practice: Adding another instruction to your program

Right now the cursor is one line below the letter P of your PRINT instruction.

1. Add the CLS instruction by typing the following and pressing Enter:

```
CLS
```

Your screen should now look like this:

```
 File  Edit  View  Search  Run  Debug  Options              Help
                        Untitled
PRINT "Ward, I'm worried about the Beaver."
CLS
_
```

(As before, if you typed in the CLS instruction in lowercase letters, the QuickBASIC Interpreter converts them to uppercase after you press Enter because CLS is a BASIC keyword.)

2. Run the program again: Select Start from the Run menu. If you're watching carefully, you might see the message *Ward, I'm worried about the Beaver* flash briefly on the screen, but a moment later the output screen looks like this:

```
Press any key to continue
```

There's little point in using a PRINT instruction if you're going to follow it immediately with a CLS instruction. Now you see why the order of the instructions is so important. You need to put the CLS instruction *before* the PRINT instruction to make the program behave the way you expect it to.

3. Press any key to return to the View window.

Editing a Program

When you change a program, you perform a process known as *editing*. Editing includes adding characters, deleting characters, and moving lines of instructions to other parts of your program.

The QuickBASIC Interpreter gives you several editing tools. Some of these tools are on the aptly named Edit menu; others are keys on your keyboard. Use the following Practices as an overview. If you find that you need more information, turn to Appendix A, "The QuickBASIC Interpreter Reference," which contains detailed instructions on how to use these tools.

The Cut, Copy, and Paste commands

The Cut, Copy, and Paste commands let you edit your programs efficiently. Not only do they save you time and lots of typing, they also eliminate the chance of your making typing errors.

 Practice: Editing a program with the Cut and Paste commands

Because the PRINT instruction needs to go after the CLS instruction, you need to move the entire PRINT instruction. You do this by using the Cut and Paste commands on the Edit menu.

1. Select the PRINT instruction. Your screen should look like this:

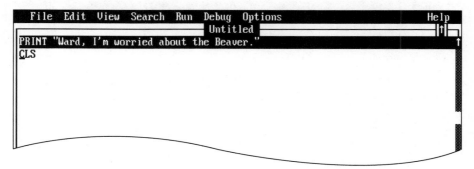

2. Drop down the Edit menu:

3. Select the Cut command from the Edit menu. The PRINT instruction should disappear from the View window, leaving you with only the CLS instruction:

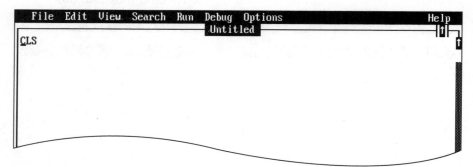

Although it's no longer on the screen, the PRINT instruction isn't really gone. It's now in the QuickBASIC Interpreter's *Clipboard*. Your next step is to paste the contents of the Clipboard back into your program.

The Clipboard

The QuickBASIC Interpreter's Clipboard stores the text most recently deleted or copied from the program. This text remains in the Clipboard until you copy or delete again (completely erasing the previous contents) or until you quit the QuickBASIC Interpreter. You cannot erase the contents of the QuickBASIC Interpreter's Clipboard.

4. Move the cursor to the location where you want the pasted text to go. Because you want to put the PRINT instruction after the CLS instruction, press the down-arrow key to put the cursor one line beneath the C in the CLS instruction.

5. Drop down the Edit menu again.

6. Select the Paste command. Your screen should now look like this:

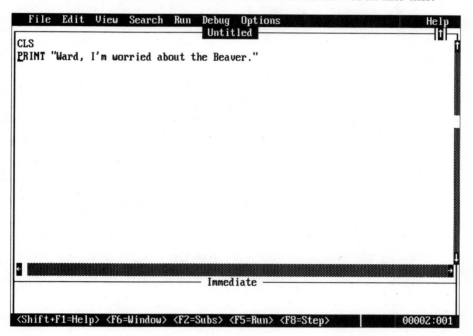

NOTE: If, after the Paste operation, the PRINT instruction appears before the CLS instruction, you probably misplaced the cursor before you chose Paste. Remember: If you want to paste the contents of the Clipboard after a particular instruction, you must ensure that the cursor is one entire line below that instruction before you choose Paste. Repeat the Cut and Paste operations if necessary so that the PRINT instruction is below the CLS instruction.

7. Run the program now to see what it does.

    With the CLS instruction before the PRINT instruction, your program should produce the following on the output screen:

```
Ward, I'm worried about the Beaver.

















Press any key to continue
```

8. Press any key to return to the View window.

Practice: Editing a program with the Copy and Paste commands

Now that you have the CLS instruction properly positioned, it's time to lengthen your program. That's easy to do with the Copy and Paste commands.

1. Select the entire PRINT instruction again.

2. Select the Copy command from the Edit menu. Notice that the line you selected remains in your program.

3. Move the cursor so that it's one line below the PRINT instruction and the highlighting disappears.

4. Select Paste from the Edit menu.

5. Select Paste again—until you have five Print instructions on your screen. Your program should now look like this:

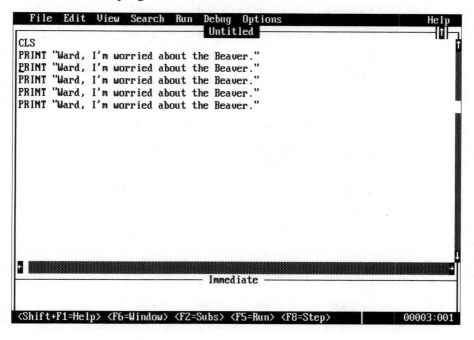

Run the program again if you want, although by now you're probably getting a little tired of seeing that same message over and over. In fact, now would be a good time to practice deleting some of these messages.

Practice: Deleting text with the Del key

1. Move the cursor to the P in the last PRINT instruction and press the Del key several times. Notice how Del erases the character the cursor is under.

2. Keep pressing Del until the entire line has been deleted.

3. Press Del a few more times; eventually, you'll hear a beep each time you press Del. This beep is the QuickBASIC Interpreter's way of telling you that there are no more characters to delete on that line. (Anytime you hear that sound, you're probably trying to do something the QuickBASIC Interpreter won't allow.)

Practice: Deleting text with the Backspace key

1. Move the cursor up one line.

2. Press End to move the cursor to the end of the line.

3. Press Backspace repeatedly until the entire instruction is gone. Note that if you continue to press Backspace after the line is deleted, the cursor moves to the end of the previous line and starts deleting characters from that line.

Practice: Deleting selected text with the Del key

1. Select part or all of the bottom PRINT instruction.

2. Press Del, and the selected text is gone forever. (If you selected only part of the line, go back now and highlight the remaining part of the line and delete it too.)

    By pressing Del instead of choosing Cut, you tell the QuickBASIC Interpreter that you do *not* want the selected text stored in the Clipboard—you want to delete it.

Practice: Deleting an entire line using Ctrl-Y

1. Move the cursor up to anyplace within the next PRINT instruction.

2. Hold down Ctrl and press Y. This has exactly the same effect as highlighting the entire line and choosing Cut from the Edit menu.

So much for the excess PRINT instructions! If you followed the instructions exactly, you're down to the CLS instruction and one PRINT instruction. If you have more instructions than that left, delete them now.

Changing Text

At times you might want to change a part of an instruction. You could simply delete the entire instruction and then retype it, but you'll find that changing only part of an instruction will save you time and reduce the chance of making a typing error.

Let's consider a PRINT instruction. A PRINT instruction prints whatever is between the two double quotation marks. If you've used a PRINT instruction in your program but decide to change the message, all you have to do is change the message between the double quotation marks. You can do this in several ways.

For example, you could delete the existing text (using one of the methods of deletion that you just practiced) and type new text in its place. Or you could simply type in new text using one of two cursors: the *insert cursor* or the *overstrike cursor*.

The insert cursor

The cursor you've been working with, the blinking underscore, is called the *insert cursor*. It's called the insert cursor because you can use it to insert text in the middle of a line without destroying any existing text. To insert text with the insert cursor, follow these steps:

1. Move the cursor to the location where you want to insert text.

2. Type in the text you want to insert.

Practice: Inserting text with the insert cursor

1. Move the cursor to the first letter after the first double quotation mark of your PRINT message.

2. Type a few letters and watch what happens. The letters currently in the message, including the letter the cursor is under, move to the right as you type, making room for the new letters to appear.

3. When you're done, use Backspace to delete the new characters you typed and restore your original message.

The overstrike cursor

The other cursor is called the *overstrike cursor*. It's called the overstrike cursor because it replaces existing characters with the new characters you type. Using the overstrike cursor can sometimes save you time because you don't have to delete characters as you would if you had only the insert cursor to work with. To use the overstrike cursor, follow these steps:

1. Move the cursor to the beginning of the characters you want to overwrite.

2. Press the Ins key. The cursor will change to a flashing rectangle.

3. Type the characters you want.

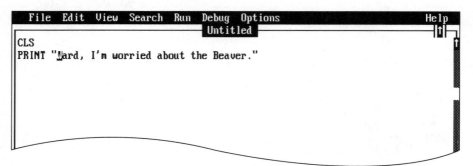

Practice: Using the overstrike cursor

1. Move the cursor to the first letter after the first double quotation mark of your PRINT message.

2. Press the Ins key. The cursor changes from a blinking underline to a blinking vertical rectangle:

```
 File  Edit  View  Search  Run  Debug  Options                    Help
                          ══════ Untitled ══════
CLS
PRINT "Ward, I'm worried about the Beaver."
```

3. Start typing a new message and watch what happens. As you type, the new characters replace the old ones.

4. If your new message is shorter than the old message, use Del to delete the remaining characters (except for the closing double quotation mark). If your new message is longer than the old message, you will have overwritten the closing double quotation mark, so be sure to type a new one.

5. Run the program again to display your new message, and then press any key to return to the View window.

6. Press Ins to change the cursor from overstrike mode back to insert mode. You'll probably want to leave the cursor in insert mode as you work through this book.

Saving Your Program on Disk

After you've typed in a program, especially one you want to keep, you should save it on disk. If you don't, and you turn off your computer, the program will be lost, and you'll have to type it in again from scratch.

The program you just typed in isn't long and would require little effort to retype. But when your programs become longer, you'll definitely want to save them on disk because retyping would be unnecessary extra work.

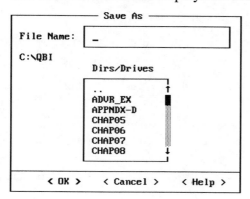

Practice: Saving a program on disk

1. Select the Save As command from the File menu. The Save As command displays the following dialog box:

```
┌──────────────── Save As ────────────────┐
│                                          │
│ File Name: ┌──────────────────────────┐  │
│            │ _                        │  │
│            └──────────────────────────┘  │
│ C:\QBI                                   │
│                                          │
│            Dirs/Drives                   │
│                                          │
│          ┌─────────────────┐ ↑           │
│          │ . .             │▓│           │
│          │ ADVR_EX         │▓│           │
│          │ APPNDX-D        │▓│           │
│          │ CHAP05          │░│           │
│          │ CHAP06          │░│           │
│          │ CHAP07          │░│           │
│          │ CHAP08          │ ↓           │
│          └─────────────────┘             │
│                                          │
├──────────────────────────────────────────┤
│  < OK >    < Cancel >    < Help >        │
└──────────────────────────────────────────┘
```

2. Type the following into the File Name text box:

    `my-first.bas`

     NOTE: Because the QuickBASIC Interpreter assumes that the file you are saving is a program that warrants a .BAS extension, it will put the .BAS extension on your program filename if you don't do it yourself.

3. Press Enter to carry out the Save As command. The QuickBASIC Interpreter will save your program on disk under the filename MY-FIRST.BAS.

After you've saved the program on disk, the QuickBASIC Interpreter returns you to the View window, which now displays the filename at the top of the window. This lets you know at all times what program you're currently working with—if it says *Untitled*, you know that you haven't saved the program on disk yet.

A program doesn't have to be complete before you save it. So how do you know when to save it for the first time, and how often after that do you need to save it again? Simply ask yourself how much work you'd lose and how upset you'd be if the power went off *right now*, and you should be able to answer that question.

Naming Files

The following hints will help you name your files effectively:

■ Filenames can be no more than eight characters in length.

■ The more descriptive the filename, the better.

■ Filenames can be a combination of letters, numbers, and some punctuation marks; you can't use spaces or the following characters:

   `* = + [ ] ; : " ? < > / \ ¦`

■ The extension of your program filenames always should be `.BAS`. This tells the QuickBASIC Interpreter that the file is a legitimate BASIC program file.

Changing a Saved File

If, after using Save As to save a program on disk, you make any changes to the program, the QuickBASIC Interpreter will treat the program in the View window as a separate program from the one you just stored on disk. The QuickBASIC Interpreter will not let you choose New or let you quit until after it asks you what you want to do about the changed version of the program: Do you want to overwrite the *saved* version of the file with the *changed* version of the file? Or do you just want to discard the changes altogether?

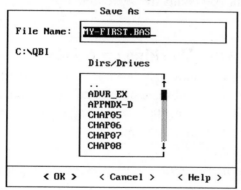 ***Practice: Working with changes to a saved file***

1. Make some changes to the program in the View window. The changes are up to you—maybe change the PRINT message a little or add a second PRINT instruction.

2. After making the changes, select Save As from the File menu.

```
┌──────────────── Save As ─────────────────┐
│                                           │
│ File Name: │MY-FIRST.BAS│                 │
│                                           │
│ C:\QBI                                    │
│               Dirs/Drives                 │
│           ┌─────────────────┐↑            │
│           │ ..              │▓            │
│           │ ADVR_EX         │▓            │
│           │ APPNDX-D        │▓            │
│           │ CHAP05          │▓            │
│           │ CHAP06          │▓            │
│           │ CHAP07          │▓            │
│           │ CHAP08          │↓            │
│           └─────────────────┘             │
│                                           │
├───────────────────────────────────────────┤
│   < OK >     < Cancel >    < Help >       │
└───────────────────────────────────────────┘
```

Note that the File Name text box already contains the name you gave the program. You have several options at this point:

☐ Choose OK to save the changed version of the program on disk, replacing the original version.

☐ Type a new name for the changed program and choose OK. This saves the changed version of the program under a different name and leaves the original version intact.

☐ Choose Cancel to cancel the Save As operation and return to the View window.

☐ Choose Help to display another dialog box that explains the Save As dialog box.

3. Press Enter to choose OK and save the changed program under the same name on disk.

Save Often

Until you save a program on disk, anything you type into the View window is held in the computer's temporary memory. Save your programs on disk regularly to avoid losing work. If your computer lost power as the result of a blackout or the accidental unplugging of the power cord, everything in the computer's memory—including your program—would be lost forever. If you had stored that program on disk, though, you could simply load it again.

Starting a New Program After Working on Another

If you have a program in the View window that has not yet been saved to disk, or a program that you did save but subsequently made changes to, the QuickBASIC Interpreter will not let you start a new program until it finds out what you want to do with the existing program.

Practice: Starting a new program after working on another

1. Make another change to the program in the View window, such as changing the message PRINT displays.

2. After you've made the changes, select New from the File menu.

3. Press Enter to tell the QuickBASIC Interpreter that you want to start a new program. The following dialog box appears.

```
┌─────────────────────────────────────────────────────────┐
│                                                         │
│  One or more loaded files are not saved. Save them now? │
│                                                         │
├─────────────────────────────────────────────────────────┤
│      < Yes >    < No >    <Cancel>    < Help >          │
└─────────────────────────────────────────────────────────┘
```

If you press Enter to select the default response Yes, the QuickBASIC Interpreter saves the changed version of the program on disk using the name currently displayed at the top of the View window. This overwrites the older version already on the disk. You are not given the option of typing in another filename—to do that, you must first press Esc to exit from this dialog box, and then select Save As from the Edit menu to give the changed program another name.

If you select No, the QuickBASIC Interpreter doesn't save the changes you made since the last time you saved the file. Don't be too hasty about selecting No—be sure you're not discarding something you meant to save!

4. If you want to save your changed program, press Enter. Otherwise, press Tab once to highlight the No command button and then press Enter.

QUITTING THE QUICKBASIC INTERPRETER

When you've finished programming, you should always exit the QuickBASIC Interpreter before you turn off your computer. If you don't, the instant your screen goes dark you may realize that you forgot to save your program.

To quit the QuickBASIC Interpreter, select Exit from the File menu. Remember, if you have a program in the View window that you have not saved, or a program that you saved earlier but then changed, QuickBASIC will ask if you intend to save the program.

Working with the QuickBASIC Interpreter

You can find out more about working in the QuickBASIC editing environment by reviewing the material in Appendix A, "The QuickBASIC Interpreter Reference." Use the Appendix A material to supplement the skills you've learned here and in the QuickBASIC Express tutorial. The following topics are discussed:

- Working with menu commands and dialog boxes
- Working with keyboard commands
- Editing programs
- Getting help
- Getting a printout
- Changing display colors
- Using startup options
- Converting 5¼-inch disks to 3½-inch disks

SUMMARY

You're well on your way to learning to program in BASIC. You know how to start, use, and quit the QuickBASIC Interpreter, and how to write and run your own programs. In the next chapter, you'll learn more BASIC instructions, and you'll be looking at BASIC instructions in a little greater detail.

QUESTIONS AND EXERCISES

1. How do you start the QuickBASIC Interpreter?

2. True or False: Opening a program file stored on a disk erases that file from the disk.

3. What is the difference between the View window and the Immediate window?

4. On the File menu, what is the difference between the New command and the Open command?

5. What is the difference between the View window and the output screen?

6. On the Edit menu, what is the difference between the Cut command and the Copy command?

7. What are the four ways to delete text from a program, and how do they differ?

8. What is the difference between the insert cursor and the overstrike cursor? How can you tell the difference between the two? How do you change back and forth between the two?

9. Not including the .BAS extension, what is the maximum number of characters you can use to name your file?

10. Which of the following names *can't* you use to name your programs? Why not?

PRINTNAME.BAS	HI-AND-LO.BAS	50%DONE.BAS
HELLO!.BAS	BUSINESS.BAS	1ST*PROG.BAS
BIG+BAD.BAS	BALLOON.BAS	MY_WAY.BAS
BIG RED.BAS	PROG[1].BAS	IT'S-OK.BAS

11. How do you quit the QuickBASIC Interpreter program? What happens if you try to quit before you save your work, and what are your options?

Introduction to the BASIC Language

In the last chapter you became familiar with the Microsoft QuickBASIC Interpreter, and you used a couple of BASIC instructions to write a short program. In this chapter you'll take a closer look at the BASIC language and expand upon what you've already learned.

ANATOMY OF A BASIC INSTRUCTION

So far, we've referred to the BASIC lines you've been typing in as *instructions*. As you learned in Chapter 1, each line in a BASIC program is simply an instruction that the computer carries out when you run the BASIC program. BASIC recognizes two types of instructions: *statements* and *functions*.

Statements and Functions

Statements and functions look very much alike and are equally easy to use. They differ primarily in purpose:

- A statement simply does what you tell it to when you run the program. When your program executes a statement, the result is usually obvious or tangible. (For example, the PRINT statement puts characters on the output screen, and the CLS statement clears the output screen.)

- A function returns information that you can use in your program—often doing its work in a not-so-obvious way. A function appears within a statement and performs its work when the statement is executed.

Each statement and function has a *syntax,* which dictates how the statement or function must be used in your program.

BASIC Syntax

The syntax of a BASIC instruction, whether statement or function, is simply a keyword followed by the information that the instruction needs to do its work.

The syntax of some BASIC instructions, such as BEEP, consists of only the name of the statement or function. Start the QuickBASIC Interpreter (if you haven't already done so), and type in the following single-line program:

```
BEEP
```

Run the program and see what happens. The BEEP statement causes the speaker inside your computer to emit a brief tone.

Now let's take a look at some instructions of greater substance. Throughout this chapter we'll use the PRINT statement as our example.

PRINT statement syntax

The PRINT statement has the following syntax:

```
PRINT [expressionlist][,!;]
```

Looks a bit different than the PRINT statement in Chapter 2, doesn't it? The PRINT statement is quite versatile; in the previous chapter, you used only one of the PRINT statement's many features.

Let's take a moment to become familiar with the structure of a syntax line (Figure 3-1):

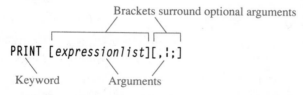

FIGURE 3-1.
Structure of a syntax line.

Each item in a syntax line except for the keyword is called an *argument*. Arguments provide the instruction with the additional information it needs in order to do its work. Some arguments are optional; they appear within square brackets both in this book and in the QuickBASIC Interpreter's built-in help system. If you decide to use one of these optional arguments in your instruction, do not type in the square brackets. (Along the same lines, do not type in the ¦ symbol—it simply indicates that you are to choose one of the arguments surrounding the ¦. In the case of Figure 3-1, you would choose either the comma or the semicolon.)

In a PRINT statement, both arguments are optional: You can use the PRINT keyword by itself.

Practice: Using a PRINT statement without arguments

1. Select the New command from the File menu.

2. Type in the following program and run it:

```
CLS
PRINT "This statement uses an argument."
PRINT
PRINT "So does this one."
```

Your screen will look like this:

```
This statement uses an argument.

So does this one.
```

As you can see, a PRINT statement without any arguments prints a blank line. (Simply pressing Enter to create blank lines won't work.) Let's look at three types of arguments you can use with a PRINT statement: text, numeric expressions, and functions.

Using text as an argument

In the last chapter, you used text surrounded by quotation marks (''Ward, I'm worried about the Beaver.'') as an *expressionlist* argument to the PRINT statement. Such text is called a *string*. You can use any numbers, letters, spaces, and punctuation marks—except double quotation marks—in a string. (BASIC perceives a double quotation mark within a string as the end of the string.)

Using numeric expressions as arguments

Another valid *expressionlist* argument is a *numeric expression*. A numeric expression is a number, a mathematical equation, or, as you'll learn in the next chapter, a special kind of word called a numeric *variable*. Numeric expressions are not enclosed in double quotation marks.

Practice: Using numeric expressions as arguments

1. Modify your program so that it contains only the following PRINT statement:

```
CLS
PRINT 42
```

2. Now run the program. Your output screen will look like this:

```
42
```

Using functions as arguments

A third valid *expressionlist* argument is a BASIC function. Functions generally perform a background task and return information that you can use in your program. They are not enclosed in double quotation marks.

Practice: Using functions as arguments

BASIC has two functions, named DATE$ and TIME$, that obtain the current date and time from the clock that is built into your computer. You cannot use these functions by themselves. (In other words, you can't just put DATE$ or TIME$ on a line and expect anything to happen.) You can, however, use them as arguments for a PRINT statement.

1. Select the New command from the File menu.

2. Type in the following program and run it:

```
CLS
PRINT DATE$
PRINT TIME$
```

Your output screen will look similar to this:

```
03-25-1990
21:13:09
```

Although the date and time displayed here don't match what you see on your output screen, the underlying principle remains sound: DATE$ and TIME$ performed a task and returned a value in an unobtrusive manner. That's the beauty of BASIC functions: You simply use them, and they perform useful work without your having to worry about the details.

Printing More than One Item with PRINT

So far, you've used a single argument, such as a single string or a single function, as an argument for each of your PRINT statements. You can use multiple arguments in a single PRINT statement, but only if you use a special character called a *separator* between them. The PRINT statement recognizes two separator characters: a comma and a semicolon.

The comma separator

You can think of the comma separator as the programming equivalent of the Tab key. When PRINT encounters a comma, it prints the next argument at the beginning of the next print zone. (Print zones are the programming equivalent of tab stops; they are 14 characters long.) This ability to print arguments at specific locations makes comma separators a natural choice when you want to print information in columns.

 Practice: Using comma separators

    1.   Select the New command from the File menu.

2.   Type in and run the following program to see how comma separators work:

```
CLS
PRINT "Comma", "separators", "separate", "arguments"
PRINT "They", "also", "align", "arguments"
```

Your output screen will look like this:

```
Comma         separators    separate      arguments
They          also          align         arguments
```

 NOTE: If you did not put a space after each comma, the QuickBASIC Interpreter put them in for you when you pressed Enter to end the line. The QuickBASIC Interpreter always adds a space after a separator if you forget, giving your programs a neat, consistent appearance.

You can even use commas by themselves without having an argument between them, as shown in the following practice session.

Practice: Positioning arguments with comma separators

1. Select the New command from the File menu.

2. Type in and run the following program, which uses commas to position arguments near the center of the screen:

```
CLS
PRINT , , "Use comma separators"
PRINT , , "to position arguments"
```

Your output screen will look like this:

```
                    Use comma separators
                    to position arguments
```

The semicolon separator

When PRINT encounters a semicolon separator, it prints the next argument immediately after the argument it just printed. PRINT places no spaces between these arguments: You must supply them if you want them.

Practice: Using semicolon separators

1. Select the New command from the File menu.

2. Type in and run the following program, which uses semicolon separators with and without added spaces:

```
CLS
PRINT "This"; "is"; "what"; "semicolons"; "do"
PRINT "If "; "you "; "want "; "spaces, "; "add "; "them"
```

Your output screen will look like this:

```
Thisiswhatsemicolonsdo
If you want spaces, add them
```

Using both commas and semicolons

Just as you can use more than one kind of argument on a line, you can use more than one kind of separator on a line. You can mix commas and semicolons however you like, and they always work as advertised.

Practice: Using both commas and semicolons

1. Select the New command from the File menu.

2. Type in and run the following program, which uses commas and semicolons on the same line:

```
CLS
PRINT "These"; "words"; "run"; "together", "These", "are", "apart"
```

Your output screen will look like this:

```
Thesewordsruntogether      These           are          apart
```

Using a separator at the end of a PRINT statement

When you place a comma or semicolon separator at the end of a PRINT statement, you dictate where the result of the *subsequent* PRINT statement appears on the output screen:

- A comma prints the next PRINT statement's output at the beginning of the next print zone.

- A semicolon prints the next PRINT statement's output immediately following the output from the current PRINT statement.

Practice: Using separators at the end of a PRINT statement

1. Select the New command from the File menu.

2. Type in and run the following program, which uses a semicolon at the end of a PRINT statement:

```
CLS
PRINT "This is the first line ";
PRINT "and this is the second"
```

Your output screen will look like this:

```
This is the first line and this is the second
```

3. Now change the semicolon to a comma and run the program again.

NOTE: If you use the semicolon at the end of a PRINT statement and there are no more PRINT statements in your program, it has no effect.

SUMMARY

In this chapter you learned more about BASIC program instructions and learned how various syntax options make a BASIC statement more versatile. In the next chapter, you'll learn about two very important topics that will add even more flexibility to your programs: BASIC variables and operators.

QUESTIONS AND EXERCISES

1. Briefly describe the difference between a statement and a function.

2. Which of the following BASIC keywords are statements and which are functions?

BEEP	DATE$	TIME$
CLS	PRINT	

3. In a BASIC syntax line, what is the significance of an item in square brackets? What does the ¦ character signify?

4. What is an argument?

5. What is the difference between a string and a numeric expression?

6. How will the output from the following two PRINT statements differ?

   ```
   PRINT "Hello", ; "there"
   PRINT "Hello"; , "there"
   ```

7. What happens when you put a semicolon or a comma at the end of a PRINT statement?

BASIC Variables and Operators

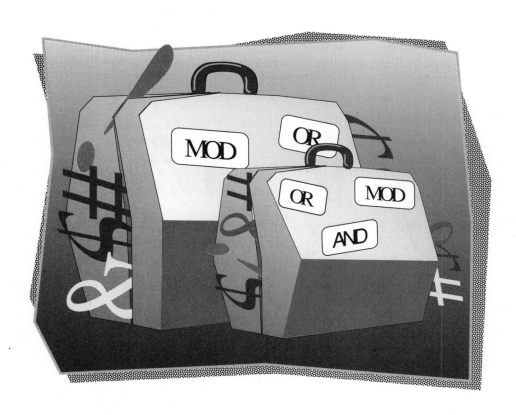

As you program, you may need to print certain numbers or strings of characters more than once. BASIC provides you with a handy method of doing just that—a method that doesn't require a lot of retyping on your part. In BASIC, you can store data and use it whenever and as often as you like, simply by using the name of the storage location in your program. You name these storage locations, which are known as *variables,* according to the type and size of data they contain.

WHAT DO YOU WANT TO STORE?

Variables are of two types: *string* and *numeric*. A string variable is a name representing a storage location for a string. A numeric variable is a name representing a storage location for a number. In addition, numeric variables have several subtypes. Figure 4-1 shows the valid variable types in BASIC.

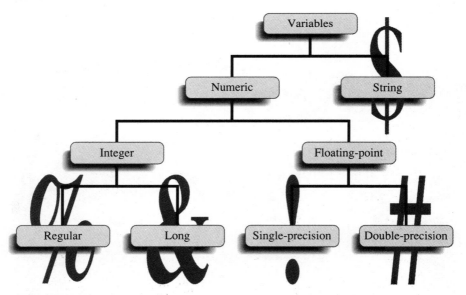

FIGURE 4-1.
An overview of variable types used in BASIC.

As you read through this chapter, keep the following questions in mind. As you'll see, the answers to these questions help you determine which type of variable is most suited to your purposes.

■ **Is your data text or a number?** Text is stored in a string variable; a number is stored in a numeric variable.

■ **If you are storing a number, does it have a decimal point?** An integer—that is, a number without a decimal point—is stored in an *integer variable*. A number with a decimal point is stored in a *floating-point variable*.

■ **How large is the number you want to store?** The size of the number plays a part when you determine which variable to use.

USING VARIABLES—AN OVERVIEW

When you decide to use a variable, you must first *declare* it in your program; that is, you must inform BASIC of three things:

■ The variable's name

■ The variable's type

■ The variable's value

You can see the elements of a declaration in Figure 4-2, which uses a string variable declaration as an example.

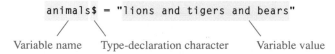

```
animals$ = "lions and tigers and bears"
```
Variable name   Type-declaration character   Variable value

FIGURE 4-2.
The elements of a variable declaration.

The following sections describe how to use each of these elements.

Naming Variables

These rules and suggestions will help you choose appropriate names for your BASIC variables:

■ Variable names can be up to 40 characters in length.

- Names can be any combination of uppercase and lowercase letters. (Keep in mind, however, that all-uppercase names might be hard to distinguish from BASIC keywords.)
- BASIC keywords, such as PRINT or BEEP, can't be used as variable names.
- The appropriate type-declaration character must be the last character of the variable name. (See ''Declaring the Variable Type.'')
- The most effective variable names are usually the most descriptive. For example, the string variable names *firstName$* and *lastName$* leave little doubt in your mind as to what these variable names represent.

 NOTE: The QuickBASIC Interpreter is sensitive to how you use uppercase and lowercase letters. So sensitive, in fact, that if you type in a variable name you've already used with different capitalization, QuickBASIC adjusts the previously typed names to reflect the new capitalization.

Declaring the Variable Type

If you look again at Figure 4-2, you'll notice that the final character of the variable name is the *type-declaration character*. The type-declaration character tells BASIC what type of variable you are declaring. Each type has its own symbol:

If the variable is	Use this as the type-declaration character:
String	$
Integer	
Regular	%
Long	&
Floating-point	
Single-precision	!
Double-precision	#

When BASIC encounters the type-declaration character in the variable name, it knows what kind of data is stored in that variable.

Declaring the Value of a Variable

When you declare the value of a variable, be sure that the value type matches the type-declaration character. For example, a string variable can't hold an integer value.

What Next?

Now that you've been introduced to the overall structure of a variable declaration, you can begin to learn about the different types of variables themselves. First you'll learn about string variables and numeric variables. Then you'll learn about getting information from the keyboard and storing it in variables. The final part of this chapter describes how BASIC works with mathematics in general.

STRING VARIABLES IN BASIC

A string variable is a storage location for a string of text that you want to use throughout a program.

To declare a string variable, use the dollar sign type-declaration character ($) at the end of the variable name. Enclose the string in double quotation marks exactly as you would in a PRINT statement. For example,

```
beatAuthors$ = "Kerouac, Ginsberg, Ferlinghetti"
```

The size and content of string variables can change within a program, as you'll learn in Chapter 9.

Practice: Declaring and using a string variable

1. Select the New command from the File menu.

2. Type in and run the following program, which assigns a value to a string variable and then prints the string:

```
CLS
tvDocs$ = "Welby, Casey, Kildare, McCoy"
PRINT tvDocs$
```

Your output screen should look like this:

```
Welby, Casey, Kildare, McCoy
```

NUMERIC VARIABLES IN BASIC

BASIC uses two types of numeric variables: *integer numeric variables* and *floating-point numeric variables*. Each type has subtypes designed for numbers of different sizes. (Remember, we told you earlier that the size of the number helps you determine which type of variable to use.) Figure 4-3 shows the relationship of numeric variables in BASIC.

First you'll learn about the two types of integer variables and when to use them; then you'll be introduced to the two types of floating-point variables.

Integer Variables

BASIC uses two types of integer variables: *regular integer variables* and *long integer variables*. The difference between the two is the size of the integer number they can represent.

How BASIC Looks at Numbers

Whether you're balancing your checkbook or preparing reports and proposals, you're likely to spend a little time each day working with numbers. What you probably don't realize is that you are actually working with different *types* of numbers. For a lot of people, the "proper" names for these numbers—whole numbers, integers, and so on—are only a dim memory from a grade-school math class. But to BASIC, the differences between two particular types of numbers are crucial:

- An integer is a number with no decimal point.

- A floating-point number is a number with a decimal point.

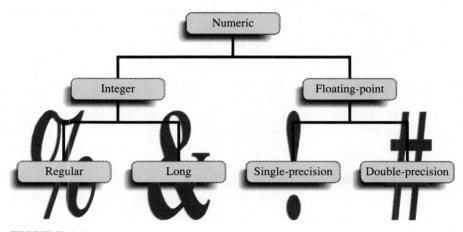

FIGURE 4-3.
Numeric variables in BASIC.

Regular integer variables

A regular integer variable can store any whole number from −32,768 through 32,767.

To declare a regular integer variable, use the percentage sign type-declaration character (%) at the end of the variable name. For example,

```
henrysWives% = 6
```

Practice: Declaring and using a regular integer variable

1. Select the New command from the File menu.

2. Type in and run the following program, which declares a regular integer variable and prints its value:

```
CLS
daysofXmas% = 12
PRINT daysofXmas%
```

Your output screen should look like this:

```
12
```

An Extra Space for Numbers

When you use the PRINT statement in your BASIC program to display numbers, you'll notice that all numbers are preceded by an extra space. If a number is negative, the QuickBASIC Interpreter uses this space to display a minus sign. If a number is positive, the QuickBASIC Interpreter prints a space.

Long integer variables

To work with an integer that is outside the range of a regular integer variable, use a long integer variable. A long integer variable can represent a whole number from −2,147,483,648 through 2,147,483,647.

To declare a long integer variable, use the ampersand type-declaration character (&) at the end of the variable name. For example,

```
cityPopulation& = 175000
```

You Can't Use Commas in Numbers

In everyday life, you use commas to break large numbers into recognizable segments. (For example, the number 1,653,892,000 is certainly easier to comprehend than 1653892000.) But because commas have a special use as separator characters in BASIC, you must learn to get along without them when you enter numbers.

If you forget and try to use a comma as part of a number within your program, the QuickBASIC Interpreter displays an error message:

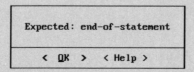

```
Expected: end-of-statement

   < OK >    < Help >
```

Likewise, if the person running your program types in a number with commas, the QuickBASIC Interpreter asks the user to type the number in again.

Practice: Declaring and using a long integer variable

1. Select the New command from the File menu.

2. Type in and run the following program, which declares a long integer variable and prints its value:

```
CLS
freefall& = 84700
PRINT "The longest free fall, in feet, was"; freefall&
```

Your output screen should look like this:

```
The longest free fall, in feet, was 84700
```

Floating-Point Numbers

So far you've worked only with integers. In real life, however, you often deal with numbers that have a fractional part—that is, a number followed by a decimal point and some other numbers.

BASIC provides two variable types to represent floating-point numbers: *single-precision floating-point variables* and *double-precision floating-point variables*. The difference between the two variables is the size of the floating-point numbers they can represent.

Using the Wrong-Sized Variable

As you've seen, working with numbers in BASIC requires a lot of attention to the size of the number. If you accidentally assign an out-of-range number to a variable, the QuickBASIC Interpreter displays a dialog box that indicates that the number is invalid for that variable type:

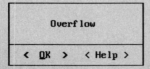

You can help prevent such mistakes by choosing variables of the correct size and displaying the range of valid values for the user.

- A single-precision floating-point variable can represent a number up to seven digits in length. The decimal point can be anywhere within those digits.

- A double-precision floating-point variable can represent a number up to 15 digits in length. The decimal point can be anywhere within those digits.

The following table shows some sample floating-point values:

Single-precision	Double-precision
412.002	1.000032478
19246.34	4280000.0055
.00025	7160.0000000005
657926.3	.10000000001

Single-precision floating-point variables

To declare a single-precision floating-point variable, use the exclamation point type-declaration character (!) at the end of the variable name. For example,

```
1pSpeed! = 33.3333
```

 Practice: Declaring and using a single-precision floating-point variable

1. Select the New command from the File menu.

2. Type in and run the following program, which declares a single-precision floating-point variable and displays its value.

```
CLS
carPrice! = 12999.99
PRINT "This sporty new car costs"; carPrice!
```

Your output screen should look like this:

```
This sporty new car costs 12999.99
```

Double-precision floating-point variables

Double-precision floating-point variables, which can be up to 15 digits in length, are useful for scientific work that requires large and precise numbers.

To declare a double-precision floating-point variable, use the pound sign type-declaration character (#) at the end of the variable name. For example,

```
bigFloat# = 5.0000000127
```

 Practice: Declaring and using double-precision floating-point variables

1. Select the New command from the File menu.

2. Type in and run the following program, which declares a double-precision floating-point variable and displays its value:

    ```
    CLS
    pi# = 3.141592654
    PRINT "The value of pi is"; pi#
    ```

    Your output screen should look like this:

    ```
    The value of pi is 3.141592654
    ```

Which Numeric Variable Should You Use?

You've learned that BASIC provides four types of numeric variables for you to use in your programs: regular integer, long integer, single-precision floating-point, and double-precision floating-point. When you want to assign a variable name to a numeric value in your program, you have to choose the type of variable you want to use. Ask yourself the following questions:

■   Is the number an integer? Will the number remain an integer throughout the program? If so, use an integer variable.

■   Does the number have a decimal point? Or, more important, *might* the number have a fractional part later on in the program? If so, use a floating-point variable.

Once you've determined the type of variable—integer or floating-point—you have to determine what size variable to use.

Choosing the proper variable size

At first glance you might think that because they can hold large numbers, long integer variables and double-precision floating-point variables would be the obvious choice to use at all times. After all, using these larger-sized variables would certainly reduce your chances of receiving *Overflow* error messages.

However (you knew there had to be a catch, right?), these larger variables have a disadvantage that you need to be aware of. Their size does provide you with greater storage space for your values, but they also take up a lot of memory in your computer. When you use the large variables unnecessarily, it's like using a grain silo to store a 5-pound bag of flour. Computer memory, like acreage, is limited. If you build a silo every time you buy a bag of flour, you eventually use up your acreage. Take the time to make wise use of your resources; determine the smallest possible variable type you can use—then use it.

Don't use a larger variable than you need.

Changing the contents of a variable

The word "variable" itself gives one clue as to why variables are so useful: Their contents can vary depending on the needs of the program or the needs of the user. You can change the contents of a variable simply by assigning a new value to the variable. Remember, however, that the *current value* of a variable is the value it was last assigned.

 Practice: Changing the value of a variable

1. Select the New command from the File menu.

2. Type in and run the following program, which declares and then changes the value of a variable:

```
CLS
fruit$ = "apple"
PRINT fruit$
fruit$ = "orange"
PRINT fruit$
fruit$ = "pear"
PRINT fruit$
```

Your output screen will display the following result:

```
apple
orange
pear
```

USING USER-SUPPLIED INFORMATION IN A VARIABLE

Now that you've become acquainted with variables, let's look at an area of BASIC programming that relies heavily on the use of variables, namely, getting characters from the person using a program. This process is sometimes called "reading characters from the keyboard."

Reading Characters with the INPUT Statement

The most commonly used BASIC statement for reading characters from the keyboard is the INPUT statement. You can't use an INPUT statement by itself, however. It must be followed by the variable name (including the variable type) you want to assign to the characters typed by the user.

Practice: Using the INPUT statement

1. Select the New command from the File menu.

2. Type in and run the following program:

```
CLS
PRINT "Type in a word and press Enter"
INPUT word$
PRINT "The word you typed in was "; word$
```

Your output screen will display the result of the operation:

```
Type in a word and press Enter
? Buckaroo
The word you typed in was Buckaroo
```

Take a look at what happened:

■ First your program cleared the screen, and then it used a PRINT statement to tell the user what to do.

■ Following the instructions of the PRINT statement, you typed in a word and pressed Enter. The word you typed in was assigned by the INPUT statement to the *word$* variable.

■ The final PRINT statement used both a string and the *word$* variable to show what you typed in.

Asking the user for input

The preceding program used a PRINT statement to ask the user to supply information. You can, however, make the message requesting input a part of your INPUT statement. This forces the INPUT statement to do double duty: It both asks the user for input *and* reads in what the user types.

Practice: Placing a message within INPUT

Change the program you just typed in to this:

```
CLS
INPUT "Type in a word and press Enter"; word$
PRINT "The word you typed in was "; word$
```

After you run the program, your output screen will look like this:

```
Type in a word and press Enter? Buckaroo
The word you typed in was Buckaroo
```

Note the differences between this program and the one you typed in earlier:

■ Because the user-friendly message is part of the INPUT statement, the cursor waits for your input on the same line as the message instead of on a line by itself.

■ The INPUT statement displays the question mark at the end of the message. (To eliminate the question mark, simply change the semicolon at the end of the INPUT message to a comma and rerun the program.)

Practice: Getting creative with INPUT

Now that you know a little about variables and how to get information from the keyboard using INPUT, you can add a little spice to your programs.

1. Select the New command from the File menu.

2. Type in and run the following program:

```
CLS
INPUT "Type in your first name and press Enter:  ", firstName$
PRINT
INPUT "How old are you (I promise not to tell anyone)?  ", age%
PRINT
INPUT "How much change do you have in your pocket?  $", money!
PRINT
PRINT "Thank you, "; firstName$; ".  You said that you are"; age%
PRINT "years old and have $"; money!; "worth of change."
```

After you run the program, your output screen will look similar to this:

```
Type in your first name and press Enter:  Pat

How old are you (I promise not to tell anyone)?  45

How much change do you have in your pocket?  $1.16

Thank you, Pat.  You said that you are 45
years old and have $ 1.16 worth of change.
```

BASIC MATHEMATICAL OPERATORS

BASIC provides several symbols you can use to perform mathematical calculations in your programs. These symbols, called *operators,* let you perform tasks such as addition, subtraction, multiplication, and division.

Several BASIC operators are the same as those you use in everyday life. For example, in BASIC you use + for addition and − for subtraction. Other BASIC operators are represented by some special symbols. The following table shows the operators you can use in BASIC:

Operator	*Mathematical operation*
+	Addition
−	Subtraction
*	Multiplication
/	Division
\	Integer division
MOD	Remainder division
^	Exponentiation (raising to a power)

The last three operators, \, MOD, and ^, are special-purpose operators that will be described shortly.

Commenting Your Programs

To help you keep track of what your program does, BASIC lets you place comments within your programs. Comments are preceded by the REM statement or the ' symbol and are for the programmer's use only. Comments do not appear in output produced by the program. Type in and run the following program to see how the REM statement works:

```
REM SAMPLE.BAS
REM A sample program demonstrating the use of comments.
REM
REM Programmers:  Mike and Dave
REM Date:  November 1, 1990

CLS

PRINT "This is a program with comments!"
```

The program produces the following output:

```
This is a program with comments!
```

The ' symbol can also be used as a less obtrusive equivalent of the REM statement, as shown in the following program:

```
' SAMPLE.BAS
' A sample program demonstrating the use of comments.
'
' Programmers:  Mike and Dave
' Date:  November 1, 1990

CLS

PRINT "This is a program with comments!"
```

When you run the above program it produces the same result:

```
This is a program with comments!
```

We'll be using the second commenting style in the programs in this book. As you write your own programs, be sure to include comments not only for yourself but also for others who might need to make sense of your program someday.

Working with BASIC Operators

To perform calculations in BASIC, simply use the operators as you would in "real life." For example, to add the numbers 12 and 16, you would type

```
12 + 16
```

You can't just put a mathematical operation like this on a line by itself, however. You can do two things:

- Assign the mathematical operation to a numeric variable:

```
total% = 12 + 16    'Assign the result to a variable
```

- Use the mathematical operation as the argument for a BASIC statement:

```
PRINT 12 + 16       'Print the result directly
```

When you assign a mathematical operation to a variable, you're assigning the *result* of the operation to the variable, as shown here:

The result is assigned to the variable.

```
total% = 12 + 16
```

When you use a mathematical operation as a statement argument, you're using the *result* of the operation as the statement argument, as shown here:

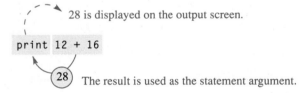

28 is displayed on the output screen.

```
print 12 + 16
```

The result is used as the statement argument.

Practice: Working with BASIC operators

In Chapter 2 you learned that the Immediate window is a convenient place to try out a program line before you put it in your program. We'll use the Immediate window to experiment with BASIC operators.

Using the Immediate Window

The Immediate window lets you test individual program lines before you type them into the View window. The following hints will help you use the Immediate window effectively:

- You can execute only one line at a time in the Immediate window.

- To run a line in the Immediate window, simply press Enter. You needn't choose Run.

- You can't save any lines you enter in the Immediate window unless you use the editing commands to move the lines to the View window.

1. Press F6 to make the Immediate window the active window, and then enter the following line:

   ```
   CLS
   ```

2. Press any key to return to the Immediate window, and then enter the following line:

   ```
   PRINT 7 * 7
   ```

   Your output screen will display the result of the PRINT statement:

   ```
   49
   ```

3. Press any key to return to the Immediate window, and then enter the following line:

   ```
   PRINT 75 / 6
   ```

   The output screen will display the result of the PRINT statement:

   ```
   12.5
   ```

The \, MOD, and ^ Operators

BASIC has three special-purpose operators: \, MOD, and ^. These operators provide a useful complement to the more familiar addition, subtraction, multiplication, and division operators.

The \ (integer division) operator

The integer division operator (\) works just like the standard division operator (/), except that when it divides two numbers it discards any remainder and returns only the integer portion of the result.

 Practice: Using the \ operator

Enter the following line in the Immediate window:

```
PRINT 5 \ 2
```

Your output screen will display the result of the operation:

```
 2
```

Whereas standard division would provide a result of 2 with a remainder of 1, integer division discards the remainder and gives you a result of 2.

The MOD operator

Although MOD doesn't look like a typical single-symbol operator, it is in fact a legitimate BASIC operator.

The MOD operator is also called the *remainder* operator. Its result is the opposite of the integer division (\) operator's: When you divide two numbers with the MOD operator, the QuickBASIC Interpreter discards the integer portion of the result and returns only the remainder.

 Practice: Using the MOD operator

Enter the following line in the Immediate window:

```
PRINT 5 MOD 2
```

Your output screen will display the result of the operation:

```
 1
```

Again, with standard division the result of this operation would be 2 with a remainder of 1. Because you used the MOD operator, the QuickBASIC Interpreter discarded the integer portion of the result and used only the remainder.

Different Rules for Division

The standard division operator (/) literally divides one number by another. For example, the following statement displays a result of 2.5—the same result a calculator provides:

```
PRINT 5 / 2
```

The \ and MOD operators, however, use the more traditional, or "long," method of division. That is, the results given by these two operators take into account a whole-number portion and a remainder portion.

The ^ (exponentiation) operator

The exponentiation operator (^) lets you raise a number to another power. For example, the BASIC equivalent of 10^3 (ten to the third power) looks like this:

```
10 ^ 3
```

Practice: Using the ^ operator

Enter the following line in the Immediate window:

```
PRINT 10 ^ 3
```

Your output window will display the result of the operation:

```
 1000
```

Numeric Expressions

A *numeric expression,* commonly called a formula, is simply a combination of numbers, numeric variables, numeric operators, and numeric functions that collectively yield a result. The multiplication, division, and exponentiation exercises you just did were all simple examples of numeric expressions.

The QuickBASIC Interpreter allows you to create a wide range of numeric expressions, from the simple ones you just practiced to elaborate ones. Best of all, creating numeric expressions isn't complicated at all. All you need do is learn a few basic rules and you'll be able to calculate almost anything.

Using more than one operator

The examples you just worked with all used a single operator. The QuickBASIC Interpreter will let you use more than one operator in the same numeric expression, allowing you to do several calculations at once.

 Practice: Using more than one operator

Enter the following statement in the Immediate window:

```
PRINT 14 + 26 + 15.75 - 33.2
```

The output screen should display the result of the operation:

```
 22.55
```

As you can see, the Immediate window can come in very handy as a calculator!

Order of calculation

The QuickBASIC Interpreter follows a strict set of rules when it calculates a numeric expression that contains more than one operator. Consider the following numeric expression:

$3 + 4 * 5$

What's the result of this expression? Actually, there are two different results, depending on how you calculate it. If you perform addition first, the answer is 35. If you perform multiplication first, the answer is 23.

To avoid such confusion, the QuickBASIC Interpreter calculates operations in the following order:

- Exponentiation (^) is performed first.

- Multiplication and division (*, /, \, and MOD) are performed next.

- Addition and subtraction (+ and −) are performed last.

These rules don't cover all circumstances, however. What about expressions in which operators are all of the same type or "level of importance"? For example,

*3 * 5 * 7*

or

*100 / 4 * 3*

When the QuickBASIC Interpreter encounters such expressions, it calculates them from left to right.

 Practice: Working with operator precedence
Enter the following statement in the Immediate window:

```
PRINT 3 + 4 * 5
```

Your output screen will display the result of the operation:

```
 23
```

Because the QuickBASIC Interpreter does the multiplication before the addition, the result is 23. Press any key to return to the Immediate window, then enter the following statement:

```
PRINT 100 / 4 * 3
```

Your output screen will display the result of the operation:

```
 75
```

Because the division (/) and multiplication (*) operators have the same weight—that is, the same priority in the list of operator precedence—the QuickBASIC Interpreter calculates the expression from left to right.

Using parentheses to control the order of calculation

Consider the numeric expression you looked at earlier:

*3 + 4 * 5*

As you just learned, the QuickBASIC Interpreter performs the multiplication before it performs the addition, resulting in the value 23. But what if you *want* the addition to be performed before the multiplication?

BASIC lets you control how a numeric expression is calculated. If you put part of a numeric expression inside *parentheses,* the QuickBASIC Interpreter performs that part of the calculation before any other. For example, the following numeric expression produces a result of 35 because the QuickBASIC Interpreter calculates the contents of the parentheses before it calculates the remainder of the expression:

*(3 + 4) * 5*

If you use two or more operators within the same set of parentheses, the QuickBASIC Interpreter calculates the contents of the parentheses using the standard rules. For example, the following numeric expression produces a result of 23:

*(3 + 4 * 5)*

 Practice: Using parentheses to control how a numeric expression is calculated

1. Enter the following statement in the Immediate window:

```
PRINT 3 + 4 * 5
```

Your output screen will display the result of the operation:

23

2. Press any key to return to the Immediate window, and then enter the following statement:

```
PRINT (3 + 4) * 5
```

Your output screen will display the result of the operation:

35

Using parentheses within parentheses

If you need to use a numeric expression that requires more control than separate sets of parentheses can provide, you can use *nested* parentheses — that is, one set of parentheses within another.

Consider the following numeric expression:

*2 + 3 * 4 ^ 2*

The QuickBASIC Interpreter would calculate the exponentiation first, then the multiplication, and finally the addition. But what if you wanted QuickBASIC to perform the addition first, then the multiplication, and then the exponentiation? If you used

$(2 + 3 * 4)^2$

the QuickBASIC Interpreter would calculate the contents of the parentheses first and do the exponentiation last, but it would still perform the multiplication before the addition. The answer would be to use a set of nested parentheses, like this:

$((2 + 3) * 4)^2$

When the QuickBASIC Interpreter encounters nested parentheses, it always calculates the contents of the innermost parentheses before calculating the contents of the outermost parentheses. In the example above, the QuickBASIC Interpreter would perform the addition first because it's in the innermost parentheses, then the multiplication, and finally the exponentiation.

BASIC's Mathematical Functions

As you learned in Chapter 3, a function returns a value to a program. BASIC provides you with several mathematical functions. (As with any other BASIC function, you must use these functions within a BASIC statement.)

The symbol n in the table on the next page represents the number, numeric variable, or expression upon which you want the function to operate. Notice that n is enclosed in parentheses. You must use these parentheses when you provide a value.

Practice: Working with BASIC's numeric functions
Enter the following statement in the Immediate window:

```
PRINT SQR(36)
```

Your output screen should display the result of the operation, in this case the square root of 36:

6

Function	Purpose
ABS(n)	Returns the absolute value of n
ATN(n)	Returns the arctangent, in radians, of n
COS(n)	Returns the cosine of angle n expressed in radians
EXP(n)	Returns the logarithm of n
SGN(n)	Returns −1 if n is less than zero, returns 0 if n is zero, and returns +1 if n is greater than zero
SIN(n)	Returns the sine of angle n expressed in radians
SQR(n)	Returns the square root of n
TAN(n)	Returns the tangent of angle n expressed in radians

Using mathematical functions in numeric expressions

You can use mathematical functions in a numeric expression along with other BASIC operators. In the following example, the SQR function solves a problem involving a right triangle.

Practice: Using the SQR function

Suppose you have a pole 12½ feet high and a metal stake in the ground 15 feet from the base of the pole (Figure 4-4). You plan to string a cable from the top of the pole to the stake, but you aren't sure how much cable to buy.

You can write a BASIC program that uses the SQR function to calculate the length for you. The formula for this calculation is

$$\sqrt{length^2 + height^2}$$

1. Press the F6 function key to make the View window the active window.

2. Select the New command from File menu, and then type in the following program.

```
CLS

PRINT "This program calculates how much cable you need to"
PRINT "run from the top of a pole to a stake in the ground."
PRINT
INPUT "Enter the height, in feet, of the pole:  ", height!
PRINT
PRINT "Enter the length, in feet, from the base"
INPUT "of the pole to the stake in the ground:  ", length!

cable! = SQR((height! ^ 2) + (length! ^ 2))

PRINT
PRINT "You need to buy"; cable!; "feet of cable."
```

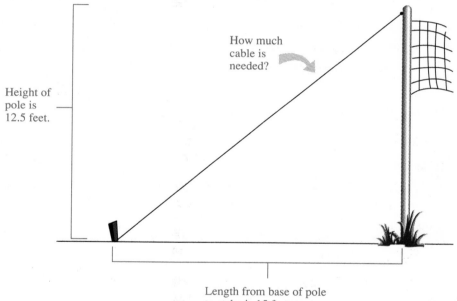

FIGURE 4-4.
Finding the length of a cable.

3. Run the program, and enter the height and length measurements given in Figure 4-4—12.5 and 15, respectively. Your output will look like this:

```
This program calculates how much cable you need to
run from the top of a pole to a stake in the ground.

Enter the height, in feet, of the pole:  12.5

Enter the length, in feet, from the base
of the pole to the stake in the ground:  15

You need to buy 19.52562 feet of cable.
```

Notice that the program uses single-precision floating-point variables throughout. By using this type of variable, you're not limiting the user to using whole numbers.

   Also, notice that the line

```
cable! = SQR((height! ^ 2) + (length! ^ 2))
```

uses nested parentheses. In this case, because of BASIC's rules of precedence, the nested parentheses aren't actually needed. You would get the same result if you didn't use them. However, you'll sometimes find your formulas are easier to read if you use extra sets of parentheses like this.

4. Run the program again, this time using height and length measurements of your own choosing. (If you actually used a program like this, you'd need to allow for some slack in the line, as well as for additional length to tie off the cable.)

 NOTE: If you had included the measurements as part of your program, such as

```
height! = 12.5
length! = 15
```

you would have had to change the program itself if you wanted to use another set of measurements. By allowing the measurements to be entered by the user, however, you can run the program again and again without having to change anything.

THE CONST STATEMENT

When you have a value that will never change throughout a program, such as a local or state sales tax or a discount rate, declare it as a constant with the CONST statement.

To use the CONST statement, simply place the keyword before the constant declaration. For example, the following statement tells the QuickBASIC Interpreter that you want the single-precision floating-point constant named *TAXRATE!* to always represent a value of 0.081:

```
CONST TAXRATE! = .081
```

If your program tries to assign another value to *TAXRATE!* later in the program, the QuickBASIC Interpreter will display the following dialog box when you try to run the program:

```
┌─────────────────────────────┐
│  Duplicate definition       │
│                             │
├─────────────────────────────┤
│  <  OK  >    < Help >       │
└─────────────────────────────┘
```

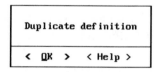

Practice: Declaring constants with the CONST statement

Suppose you want to calculate the *real* price of one or more items—that is, the price of the item plus the sales tax. You can write a BASIC program to help you do this quickly and efficiently.

1. Select the New command from the File menu.

2. Type in and run the following program:

```
CLS

CONST TAXRATE! = .081           ' Sales tax rate in Seattle

PRINT "Enter the price of the item.  Please do"
INPUT "not use a dollar sign or any commas:  ", price!

tax! = price! * TAXRATE!        ' Calculate the tax amount
total! = price! + tax!          ' Calculate the total cost
```

(continued)

83

continued

```
PRINT
PRINT "Cost of the item is"; price!
PRINT "Sales tax would be"; tax!
PRINT "----------------------------"
PRINT "Total cost would be"; total!
```

Your output screen should look something like this:

```
Enter the price of the item.  Please do
not use a dollar sign or any commas:  2500

Cost of the item is 2500
Sales tax would be 202.5
----------------------------
Total cost would be 2702.5
```

You can run this program as often as you like. If you have a lot of items to calculate, you'll find this program to be much faster and more accurate than a calculator.

This program also demonstrates that you can use variables and constants to create new variables. Notice the lines

```
tax! = price! * TAXRATE!        ' Calculate the tax amount
total! = price! + tax!          ' Calculate the total cost
```

There are no numbers involved here, only numeric variables and a constant. Because BASIC treats numeric variables and constants just as it would numbers, you can use them anywhere you would normally use a number.

SUMMARY

Congratulations! You have just taken a major step forward in your journey toward becoming a BASIC programmer. Variables (both string and numeric) and operators are important topics—topics that find their way into the very heart of most BASIC programs. In the next chapter, you'll add some intelligence to your programs by allowing them to make decisions on their own based on a set of rules you give them.

QUESTIONS AND EXERCISES

1. What are the four types of BASIC numeric variables and how do they differ?

2. Why does BASIC put a space in front of a positive number?

3. What does it mean when the QuickBASIC Interpreter displays an *Expected: end-of-statement* dialog box?

4. What does it mean when the QuickBASIC Interpreter displays an *Overflow* dialog box or error message?

5. What type of variable would you use for each of the following numbers?

   a. −32679   d. 14.000001   g. 268110

   b. 12.3774   e. −1286.0   h. −10.222222

   c. 142286.9   f. −268.0005   i. −.0000001

6. What is the difference between regular division with the / operator, integer division with the \ operator, and remainder division with the MOD operator?

7. From highest priority to lowest priority, what is the order of precedence that BASIC applies to mathematical operators?

8. What is the result of this calculation?

   ```
   (((5 + 8) - (1 + 3) / 4) * ((7 - 2) ^ 2))
   ```

9. Write a program (complete with comments) that calculates and prints the following values:

   ☐ ABS(−10) + 5

   ☐ SQR(36)

   ☐ SQR(4) ^ 2

   ☐ COS(3.141592654)

10. The value of the mathematical constant π can be approximated as 3.141592654. The formula for the circumference of a circle is

    $2 \times \pi \times radius$

    (*radius* is the distance from the center of the circle to the edge of the circle.) Write a program that asks the user for the radius of the circle and then displays a message telling the user the circumference of the circle.

11. (BONUS) You're setting up a volleyball net. The top of the pole is 8 feet off the ground, and the string tied to the top of the pole is 14 feet long:

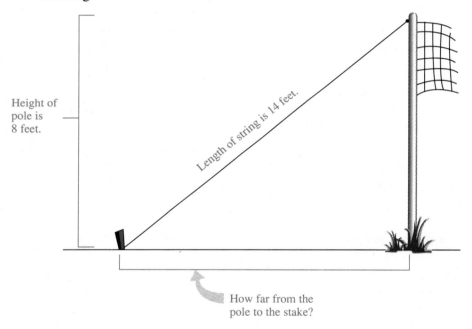

Height of pole is 8 feet.

Length of string is 14 feet.

How far from the pole to the stake?

The formula for calculating the distance from the bottom of the pole to where the stake should go is

$$\sqrt{string\_length^2 - height^2}$$

Write a BASIC program that asks the user for the height of the pole and the length of the string and then prints out how many feet away from the bottom of the pole the stake should be driven.

Controlling
Program Flow

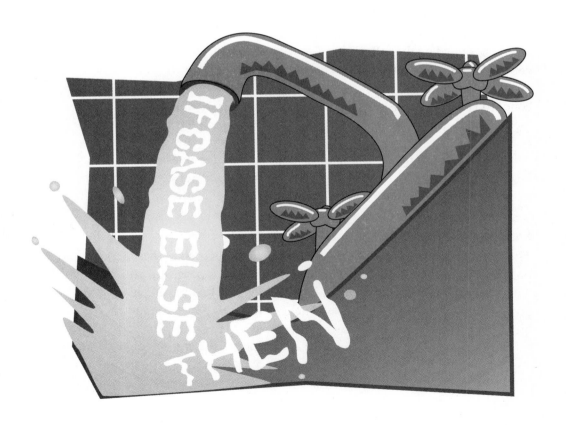

The programs you've written thus far have all run in a very straight-forward way: The Microsoft QuickBASIC Interpreter runs the first instruction and then works progressively toward the final instruction. At times, however, you might want the QuickBASIC Interpreter to run certain parts of your program under a certain set of circumstances. This chapter teaches you how to program in this way.

INTRODUCTION TO DECISION MAKING

You make thousands of decisions every day. Some decisions require that you weigh your options; others require little or no thought. For example, the decision whether to breakfast on a fruit cup or a jelly doughnut might give you pause, while the decision to reach up and scratch your ear would likely be spontaneous.

Other decisions can lead to separate sets of actions. For example, if you're on a long driving trip, you need to be sure you don't run low on gas. Let's examine a typical decision-making process you would go through each time you checked your gas gauge.

As depicted on the following page, you would check the status of your gas tank. If it were full, you'd continue driving. If it were near empty, you'd pull into a gas station and fill the tank. You might then check the condition of your windshield. If it were clean, you'd pay the attendant and then drive down the road. If it were dirty, however, you would wash it before paying the attendant and continuing down the road.

It's easy to see how a single decision, based on the question *Am I low on gas?*, caused you to do one of two things, based entirely on the answer to the question.

Decision Making in BASIC

The BASIC language lets you include decision points such as these in your program. You place a questionlike statement in your program, and along with it you write instructions that tell the QuickBASIC Interpreter what to do based on the answer. When the QuickBASIC Interpreter encounters the question, it determines the answer. If the answer is yes, the QuickBASIC Interpreter takes a particular course of action. If the answer is no, the

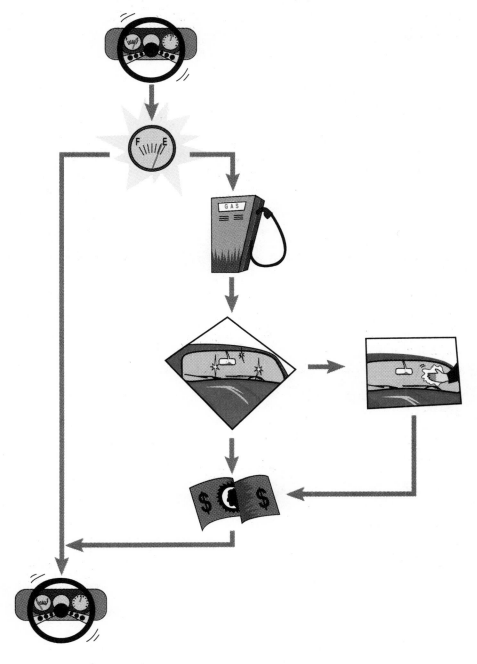

Decision making at work: Checking your gas gauge.

QuickBASIC Interpreter takes a different course of action, based on the instructions you've written. Note that the answer "maybe" never occurs in BASIC or in any other programming language. The answer to a question is always yes or no.

True and False Conditions

You don't actually place yes-or-no questions in a BASIC program. Instead, you establish "questions" by placing *conditional expressions* in your programs. QuickBASIC evaluates these conditional expressions—not to determine a yes-or-no answer, but to determine whether the conditional expressions are *true* or *false*.

IF the Expression's Conditional THEN it's Boolean

In BASIC, conditional expressions are actually *Boolean expressions*. Boolean expressions, named after nineteenth-century English mathematician George Boole, are expressions that can be evaluated as true or false. Here are some examples of Boolean expressions:

Boolean expression	Evaluation
A pint is larger than a gallon.	False
Twelve is greater than ten.	True
Five is less than or equal to six.	True
Eleven inches is equal to one foot.	False

Creating conditional expressions

To create conditional (Boolean) expressions in your program, you must use a *relational operator,* a *logical operator,* or a combination of both. QuickBASIC provides the following relational operators (you'll learn about logical operators in the next section).

Relational operator	Meaning
=	Equal to
<>	Not equal to
>	Greater than
<	Less than
>=	Greater than or equal to
<=	Less than or equal to

For example, the following list shows some sample conditional expressions and their results:

Condition	Result
3 < 7	True (3 is less than 7)
14 >= 22	False (14 is not greater than or equal to 22)
11 <> 16	True (11 is not equal to 16)
5 = −5	False (positive 5 is not equal to negative 5)
12 > 14	False (12 is not greater than 14)
11 >= 11	True (11 is greater than or equal to 11)
total% < 5	True if the value of *total%* is less than 5; otherwise false
num1% = num2%	True if the value of *num1%* is equal to the value of *num2%*; otherwise false

You'll get a chance to work with relational operators and conditional expressions shortly. Right now, let's take a look at some of the BASIC statements that allow you to use these conditional expressions in your programs.

> ### Numeric and Conditional Expressions
>
> In the last chapter, you learned about *numeric* expressions. Numeric expressions and conditional expressions look similar: Both consist of an operator and data. The difference between a numeric expression and a conditional expression is that a numeric expression uses a numeric operator (such as +, −, /, or MOD) and a conditional expression uses a conditional operator (such as >=, <, <>, or <=). Also, a numeric expression yields a numeric result, but a conditional expression yields a true-or-false result.

THE IF STATEMENT

The IF statement lets you evaluate a condition and works together with the THEN clause to take a course of action based on the evaluation.

In their simplest form, IF and THEN form a single statement. The syntax of a single-line conditional statement using IF and THEN is as follows:

```
IF condition THEN statement
```

The *condition* portion of the statement is one of the conditional expressions you just learned about. The *statement* portion is another BASIC statement that is executed only if *condition* is true. If *condition* is false, the QuickBASIC Interpreter ignores *statement* and moves on to the next line in your program. Here's an example:

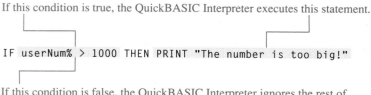

If this condition is true, the QuickBASIC Interpreter executes this statement.

```
IF userNum% > 1000 THEN PRINT "The number is too big!"
```

If this condition is false, the QuickBASIC Interpreter ignores the rest of the line and executes the next statement.

The statement following THEN can be any legal BASIC statement. But remember that the QuickBASIC Interpreter executes the statement following THEN *only* if the condition following IF is true.

Loading Programs from Disk

By now, you've had plenty of practice typing in and running your own programs—one of the best ways to learn to program in BASIC. From this point on, however, because the programs become long, feel free to load the example programs from your hard disk or from *Learn BASIC Now* Disk 2.

Programs that appear in shaded boxes in the book are available on disk and are listed by name.

- If you have a hard disk and used the INSTALL.BAT program to install QuickBASIC, the example programs are located in chapter subdirectories in the \QBI directory on drive C (CHAP05 through CHAP12).

- If you're using a two-floppy system, the example programs are located in chapter subdirectories on Disk 2 (CHAP05 through CHAP12).

Use these instructions to load example programs from disk:

1. Select the Open command from the File menu.

2. Select the file you want to open by typing the complete pathname in the text box or by selecting the file with the Files and Dirs/Drives list boxes. To see the chapter subdirectories in the \QBI directory on your hard disk, type *C:\QBI* in the text box and press Enter. To see the chapter subdirectories on Disk 2, put Disk 2 in drive B and type *B:* in the list box.

3. Press Enter to open the file and load it into the View window.

Practice: Using the IF statement

1. Load the IF-1.BAS program (Figure 5-1) from the CHAP05 subdirectory on disk and run it.

```
' IF-1.BAS
' This program demonstrates the IF statement.

CLS

INPUT "How many Rockettes dance at Radio City Music Hall?  ", guess%
IF guess% = 36 THEN PRINT "That's right!!"
IF guess% <> 36 THEN PRINT "Sorry!  The correct answer is 36!"
PRINT "Radio City Music Hall opened on December 27, 1932."
```

FIGURE 5-1.
IF-1.BAS: A program demonstrating the IF statement.

2. Enter the number *36*. Your output screen will look like this:

```
How many Rockettes dance at Radio City Music Hall?  36
That's right!!
Radio City Music Hall opened on December 27, 1932.
```

Because you entered a value of 36, the condition in the first IF statement of the program was true, so the QuickBASIC Interpreter executed the PRINT statement at the end of the line. Also, because the condition in the second IF statement was *not* true, the QuickBASIC Interpreter did not execute the PRINT statement at the end of the second IF statement.

3. Run the program again, entering a value other than 36. Your output screen should look something like this:

```
How many Rockettes dance at Radio City Music Hall?  4
Sorry!  The correct answer is 36!
Radio City Music Hall opened on December 27, 1932.
```

This time, the value you entered caused a different set of actions to occur. Because the value 4 is not equal to the value 36, the condition in the first IF statement was false, so the QuickBASIC Interpreter ignored the rest of that statement. However, this time the condition in the second IF statement was true, so the QuickBASIC Interpreter did execute the remainder of that statement.

Notice that in both cases the final PRINT statement of the program printed the message *Radio City Music Hall opened on December 27, 1932*. This demonstrates that even if the condition in an IF statement is false, the QuickBASIC Interpreter executes the rest of the program as it normally would. Only the statement that follows the THEN portion of an IF statement is ignored if the condition is not true.

Using More Than One Condition with IF

In the preceding program, QuickBASIC evaluated a single condition in each IF statement. You can, however, specify multiple conditions in an IF statement by using the *logical operators* AND and OR. You use logical operators in conditional expressions much as you use math operators in numeric expressions.

The AND logical operator

The AND operator lets you specify multiple conditions that must be true before an action can be taken. Here's the syntax line of an IF statement that uses the AND operator:

```
IF condition1 AND condition2 THEN statement
```

Both *condition1* and *condition2* must be true before the QuickBASIC Interpreter can execute *statement*. Here's an example:

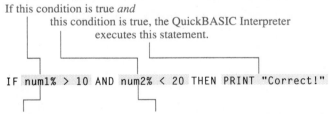

If this condition is true *and*
   this condition is true, the QuickBASIC Interpreter
    executes this statement.

```
IF num1% > 10 AND num2% < 20 THEN PRINT "Correct!"
```

If this condition is false *or* if this condition is false, or if *both* are false, the QuickBASIC Interpreter ignores the rest of the line and executes the next statement.

Note that the IF statement contains two conditions. Because AND is used, both *num1% > 10* and *num2% < 20* must be true before the QuickBASIC Interpreter can execute the PRINT statement following THEN.

Practice: Working with the AND operator

1. Load the IF-2.BAS program (Figure 5-2) from disk and run it.

```
' IF-2.BAS
' This program demonstrates the AND logical operator.

CLS

INPUT "How many teenagers can fit in a phone booth?  ", guess%
PRINT
IF guess% > 9 AND guess% < 13 THEN PRINT "That's right!!"
PRINT "Depending on their size, approximately 10 to 12"
PRINT "teenagers can fit in a phone booth."
```

FIGURE 5-2.
IF-2.BAS: A program demonstrating the AND logical operator.

2. Enter the number *10*. Your output screen will look like this:

```
How many teenagers can fit in a phone booth?  10

That's right!!
Depending on their size, approximately 10 to 12
teenagers can fit in a phone booth.
```

Because you entered a value of 10, both conditions in the IF statement were true. If you run the program again and enter a value less than 10 or more than 12, one of the conditions will be false and the QuickBASIC Interpreter will not execute the PRINT statement at the end of the IF statement.

The OR logical operator

The OR operator lets you create a more flexible set of conditions that must be met before an action can take place. The syntax line for an IF statement using the OR operator is as follows:

```
IF condition1 OR condition2 THEN statement
```

Note that the IF statement contains two conditions. Only *one* of these conditions need be true before the QuickBASIC Interpreter can execute the statement following THEN. The QuickBASIC Interpreter also executes the statement following THEN if both conditions are true. Here's an example:

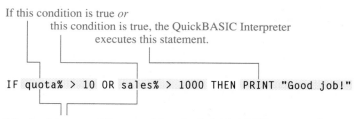

If this condition is true *or*
        this condition is true, the QuickBASIC Interpreter
            executes this statement.

```
IF quota% > 10 OR sales% > 1000 THEN PRINT "Good job!"
```

If both of these conditions are false, the QuickBASIC Interpreter ignores the rest of the line and executes the next statement.

Practice: Working with the OR operator

1. Load the IF-3.BAS program (Figure 5-3) from disk.

```
' IF-3.BAS
' This program demonstrates the OR logical operator.

CLS

PRINT "I'm thinking of a number between 1 and 100."
PRINT "Can you guess what it is?"
INPUT "Please enter a number between 1 and 100:  ", guess%
PRINT
IF guess% = 63 THEN PRINT "That's right!!"
IF guess% < 53 OR guess% > 73 THEN PRINT "You're way off!"
PRINT "Thanks for playing!"
```

FIGURE 5-3.
IF-3.BAS: A program demonstrating the OR logical operator.

2. Run the program. Enter a value of *63*, the number the program is "thinking of." Your output screen will look like this:

```
I'm thinking of a number between 1 and 100.
Can you guess what it is?
Please enter a number between 1 and 100:  63

That's right!!
Thanks for playing!
```

3. Run the program again, and use a number that is less than 53 or greater than 73. Your output screen will look something like this:

```
I'm thinking of a number between 1 and 100.
Can you guess what it is?
Please enter a number between 1 and 100:  76

You're way off!
Thanks for playing!
```

Look at the second IF statement. By entering a value that was 11 or more less than or greater than the number the program was "thinking of," you caused the QuickBASIC Interpreter to print the message *You're way off!*

The NOT logical operator

The NOT operator lets you *negate* a condition. In other words, if a condition is false, the NOT operator makes the condition true; if a condition is true, NOT makes it false. The syntax line for an IF statement using the NOT operator is as follows:

```
IF NOT condition THEN statement
```

NOT is useful when you want to execute a statement when a condition is *not* true. Here's an example:

If this condition is false, the QuickBASIC Interpreter executes this statement.

```
IF NOT age% >= 18 THEN PRINT "You can't vote."
```

If this condition is true, the QuickBASIC Interpreter ignores the rest of the line and executes the next statement.

Using ELSE with IF and THEN

Now you know how to make the QuickBASIC Interpreter evaluate a condition and take an action if the condition is true or if the condition is false. But what if you want the QuickBASIC Interpreter to choose between *two* actions based on the condition?

When paired with IF and THEN, the ELSE clause lets you specify two separate actions for the QuickBASIC Interpreter to follow: one action (following THEN) if the condition is true, and a different action (following ELSE) if the condition is false.

Here's the syntax of an IF statement using THEN and ELSE:

IF *condition* THEN *statement1* ELSE *statement2*

where *condition* is the logical condition you want the QuickBASIC Interpreter to evaluate, *statement1* is the BASIC statement the QuickBASIC Interpreter executes if *condition* is true, and *statement2* is the BASIC statement the QuickBASIC Interpreter executes if *condition* is false. IF, THEN, and ELSE must all appear on the same line. Here's an example:

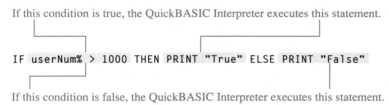

If this condition is true, the QuickBASIC Interpreter executes this statement.

IF userNum% > 1000 THEN PRINT "True" ELSE PRINT "False"

If this condition is false, the QuickBASIC Interpreter executes this statement.

 Practice: Working with IF, THEN, and ELSE

    1. Load the IF-4.BAS program (Figure 5-4) from disk.

```
' IF-4.BAS
' This program demonstrates the ELSE statement.

CLS

INPUT "Enter a number between 1 and 5:  ", guess%
PRINT
IF guess% = 3 THEN PRINT "That's right!!" ELSE PRINT "Sorry!"
PRINT "Thanks for playing!"
```

FIGURE 5-4.
IF-4.BAS: A program demonstrating the ELSE clause.

2. Run the program and enter the number *3*. Your output screen will look like this:

```
Enter a number between 1 and 5:  3

That's right!!
Thanks for playing!
```

Because you entered a value of 3, the condition is true, so the QuickBASIC Interpreter executed the PRINT statement following THEN.

3. Run the program again, entering a value other than 3. Your output screen will look something like this:

```
Enter a number between 1 and 5:  4

Sorry!
Thanks for playing!
```

This time the condition was not true, so the QuickBASIC Interpreter executed the PRINT statement following ELSE.

Making Longer Conditional Statements with END IF

Using ELSE with IF and THEN is a handy way to give the QuickBASIC Interpreter two options to take depending on the evaluation of a particular condition. However, as you just saw, packing all that information on a single line doesn't allow much room for creativity.

That's where END IF comes in. By using END IF, you can create longer programs by placing each possible course of action on a separate line. The syntax line for an IF statement that uses THEN, ELSE, and END IF is as follows:

```
IF condition THEN
    statements executed if condition is true
ELSE
    statements executed if condition is false
END IF
```

An IF statement of this type actually consists of several individual lines, which are collectively known as a *block*. The *condition* portion of the statement is the conditional expression you want the QuickBASIC Interpreter to evaluate. The THEN keyword ends the line. It must always appear in the same line as IF.

If *condition* is true, the QuickBASIC Interpreter

■ Executes the statements between THEN and ELSE

■ Bypasses the statements between ELSE and END IF

■ Continues executing the program

You can include any number of statements between THEN and ELSE.

If *condition* is false, the QuickBASIC Interpreter

■ Bypasses the statements between THEN and ELSE

■ Executes the statements between ELSE and END IF

■ Continues executing the program

You can include any number of statements between ELSE and END IF. Here's an example:

If this condition is true, the QuickBASIC Interpreter executes these statements.

```
IF choice$ = "YES" THEN
    PRINT "Yes sir!  The 1958 Edsel is the car for you!"
    PRINT "Power this, power that, and just plain fun!"
ELSE
    PRINT "Perhaps you'd care to look at some of the other"
    PRINT "sleek, modern cars from the 1958 model year."
END IF
```

If this condition is false, the QuickBASIC Interpreter executes these statements.

Notice how the indentation of related statements keeps the program easy to read. You should develop the habit of using indentation in your own programs.

Practice: Working with IF, THEN, ELSE, and END IF

1. Load the IF-5.BAS program (Figure 5-5) from disk.

```
' IF-5.BAS
' This program demonstrates the block IF statement.

CLS

PRINT "Welcome to Automobile Trivia!"
PRINT
PRINT "In what year did Karl-Friedrich Benz test-drive"
INPUT "the first successful gasoline-driven automobile?  ", guess%
PRINT
IF guess% = 1885 THEN
    PRINT "That's right!  You're quite a car buff!"
ELSE
    PRINT "No, he first drove it at Mannheim, Germany,"
    PRINT "in 1885.  (It was patented on January 29, 1886.)"
END IF
PRINT "Thanks for guessing!"
```

FIGURE 5-5.
IF-5.BAS: A program demonstrating the block IF statement.

2. Run the program. Enter the value *1885*, which is the value that causes the condition following IF to be true. Your output screen will look like this:

```
Welcome to Automobile Trivia!

In what year did Karl-Friedrich Benz test-drive
the first successful gasoline-driven automobile?  1885

That's right!  You're quite a car buff!
Thanks for guessing!
```

3. Run the program again, but this time enter a value other than 1885. Your output screen will look something like this:

```
Welcome to Automobile Trivia!

In what year did Karl-Friedrich Benz test-drive
the first successful gasoline-driven automobile?  1776

No, he first drove it at Mannheim, Germany,
in 1885.  (It was patented on January 29, 1886.)
Thanks for guessing!
```

As you can see, using END IF with IF, THEN, and ELSE allows you to use entire blocks of statements.

The ELSEIF Keyword

ELSEIF is similar to ELSE in that it provides an alternate course of action if *condition* is false. With ELSEIF, however, you supply another condition for the QuickBASIC Interpreter to evaluate. Here's the syntax of an IF statement that uses ELSEIF:

```
IF condition1 THEN
      statements executed if condition1 is true
ELSEIF condition2 THEN
      statements executed if condition2 is true
ELSEIF condition3 THEN
      statements executed if condition3 is true
:
ELSE
      statements executed if all conditions are false
END IF
```

The column of dots between ELSEIF and ELSE in the preceding syntax indicates that you can have more ELSEIF statements followed by other conditions if you want to. There is no limit to the number of ELSEIF statements and associated conditions you can use.

 NOTE: You must use THEN at the end of an ELSEIF statement. The use of ELSE is optional. We've included it in the preceding syntax to show where it goes if you decide to include it.

If *condition1* is true, the QuickBASIC Interpreter

■ Executes the statements on the following lines until it encounters the first ELSEIF

■ Jumps down to END IF

■ Continues executing the program

If *condition1* is false, the QuickBASIC Interpreter jumps down to the first ELSEIF and evaluates *condition2*. If *condition2* is true, the QuickBASIC Interpreter

■ Executes the statements on the following lines until it encounters the next ELSEIF or, if you included one, the ELSE clause

■ Jumps down to END IF and continues executing the program

If the condition associated with an ELSEIF statement is false, the QuickBASIC Interpreter jumps down to the next ELSEIF statement and evaluates its condition. The QuickBASIC Interpreter continues this process until an ELSEIF statement evaluates to true or until it encounters an ELSE statement.

Here's an example:

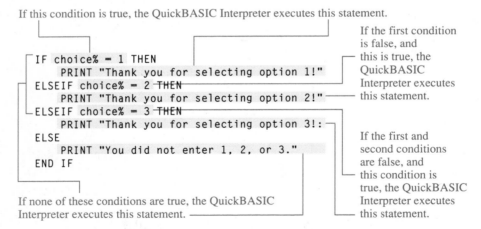

If this condition is true, the QuickBASIC Interpreter executes this statement.

If the first condition is false, and this is true, the QuickBASIC Interpreter executes this statement.

```
IF choice% = 1 THEN
    PRINT "Thank you for selecting option 1!"
ELSEIF choice% = 2 THEN
    PRINT "Thank you for selecting option 2!"
ELSEIF choice% = 3 THEN
    PRINT "Thank you for selecting option 3!:
ELSE
    PRINT "You did not enter 1, 2, or 3."
END IF
```

If the first and second conditions are false, and this condition is true, the QuickBASIC Interpreter executes this statement.

If none of these conditions are true, the QuickBASIC Interpreter executes this statement.

Notice how using the ELSEIF keyword allows you to specify different conditions and different courses of action for the QuickBASIC Interpreter to take.

Practice: Working with ELSEIF

1. Load the ELSEIF.BAS program (Figure 5-6) from disk.

```
' ELSEIF.BAS
' This program demonstrates the use of ELSEIF.

CLS

PRINT "Welcome to Motion Picture Trivia!"
PRINT "In what year did the film Ben Hur win"
PRINT "the Academy Award for Best Picture?"
PRINT
INPUT "Please enter a year from 1950 to 1959:  ", year%
PRINT

IF year% = 1950 THEN
    PRINT "Incorrect.  In 1950, the Academy Award for"
    PRINT "Best Picture went to All About Eve."
ELSEIF year% = 1951 THEN
    PRINT "Incorrect.  In 1951, the Academy Award for"
    PRINT "Best Picture went to An American in Paris."
ELSEIF year% = 1952 THEN
    PRINT "Incorrect.  In 1952, the Academy Award for"
    PRINT "Best Picture went to The Greatest Show on Earth."
ELSEIF year% = 1953 THEN
    PRINT "Incorrect.  In 1953, the Academy Award for"
    PRINT "Best Picture went to From Here to Eternity."
ELSEIF year% = 1954 THEN
    PRINT "Incorrect.  In 1954, the Academy Award for"
    PRINT "Best Picture went to On the Waterfront."
ELSEIF year% = 1955 THEN
    PRINT "Incorrect.  In 1955, the Academy Award for"
    PRINT "Best Picture went to Marty."
ELSEIF year% = 1956 THEN
    PRINT "Incorrect.  In 1956, the Academy Award for"
    PRINT "Best Picture went to Around the World in 80 Days."
```

FIGURE 5-6.

(continued)

ELSEIF.BAS. A motion-picture trivia game that uses ELSEIF.

FIGURE 5-6. *continued*

```
ELSEIF year% = 1957 THEN
    PRINT "Incorrect.  In 1957, the Academy Award for"
    PRINT "Best Picture went to The Bridge on the River Kwai."
ELSEIF year% = 1958 THEN
    PRINT "Incorrect.  In 1958, the Academy Award for"
    PRINT "Best Picture went to Gigi."
ELSEIF year% = 1959 THEN
    PRINT "Correct!  Ben Hur, directed by William Wyler,"
    PRINT "won 11 Academy Awards in 1959, including"
    PRINT "Best Picture."
ELSE
    PRINT "You did not enter a number between 1950 and 1959."
    PRINT "Please run the program again and enter an"
    PRINT "appropriate value."
END IF
```

2. Run the program and enter a value of *1959*, which is the correct answer to the question. Your output screen will look like this:

```
Welcome to Motion Picture Trivia!
In what year did the film Ben Hur win
the Academy Award for Best Picture?

Please enter a year from 1950 to 1959:  1959

Correct!  Ben Hur, directed by William Wyler,
won 11 Academy Awards in 1959, including
Best Picture.
```

3. Run the program again, this time entering a value other than 1959. Your output screen will look something like this:

```
Welcome to Motion Picture Trivia!
In what year did the film Ben Hur win
the Academy Award for Best Picture?

Please enter a year from 1950 to 1959:  1950

Incorrect.  In 1950, the Academy Award for
Best Picture went to All About Eve.
```

4. Run the program one more time, this time entering a value that is not in the range 1950 through 1959. Your output screen will look something like this:

```
Welcome to Motion Picture Trivia!
In what year did the film Ben Hur win
the Academy Award for Best Picture?

Please enter a year from 1950 to 1959:  1596

You did not enter a number between 1950 and 1959.
Please run the program again and enter an
appropriate value.
```

THE SELECT CASE STATEMENT

Another tool that allows you to work with conditional statements is the SELECT CASE statement. The SELECT CASE statement is similar in function to the IF statement. In fact, in many cases you can use either an IF statement or a SELECT CASE statement to perform the same job. However, the differences between the two make each better suited to a particular set of circumstances.

The CASE and END SELECT Keywords

Just as the IF statement needs other keywords in order to do its job properly, the SELECT CASE statement needs to be used with other BASIC keywords—namely CASE and END SELECT—to do its work.

Here is the syntax for a SELECT CASE statement (related statements are indented for clarity):

```
SELECT CASE variable
    CASE value1
        statements to be executed if value1 matches variable
    CASE value2
        statements to be executed if value2 matches variable
    CASE value3
        statements to be executed if value3 matches variable
    ⋮
END SELECT
```

Unlike the IF statement, a complete SELECT CASE statement can't be specified on a single line. You must use the block syntax shown.

variable can be a numeric or string variable. You can think of the variable following SELECT CASE as the "gateway" to the individual CASE clauses below it—the QuickBASIC Interpreter uses the value of *variable* to determine which CASE clause to use.

The CASE clauses are separate conditional statements. The *value* of each is related to *variable*. There is no limit to the number of individual CASE clauses you can put between SELECT CASE and END SELECT.

Each CASE clause is followed by one or more BASIC statements that the QuickBASIC Interpreter executes if the value in the preceding CASE clause matches the value of the variable following SELECT CASE. Here's an example.

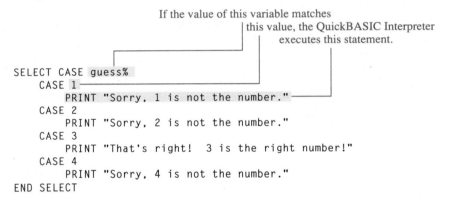

When the QuickBASIC Interpreter encounters a SELECT CASE statement, it takes note of the value of the variable (in this example, the value of *guess%*) and then examines the value specified in the first CASE clause. If that value matches the value of the variable, the QuickBASIC Interpreter

- Executes the statements following that CASE until it encounters the next CASE or the END SELECT statement

- Jumps down to the statement following END SELECT and continues executing the program

If the value in the first CASE clause does not match the value of the variable, the QuickBASIC Interpreter checks the value of each CASE clause until it finds a match.

If none of the CASE clauses contain a value matching the value of the variable following SELECT CASE, the QuickBASIC Interpreter jumps down to the statement following END SELECT and continues executing the program.

*Practice: **Working with the SELECT CASE statement***

1. Load the SELECT-1.BAS program (Figure 5-7) from disk.

```
' SELECT-1.BAS
' This program asks the user for his or her name, prints a menu,
'    and asks the user to choose a menu item.  The program then
'    displays a message based on which menu item the user chose.

CLS

INPUT "Please enter your name:  ", userName$
PRINT
PRINT "Congratulations, "; userName$; "!  You've won the final"
PRINT "round of Go Ahead--Make My Deal!!  Please choose"
PRINT "which prize you want:"
PRINT
PRINT , "1.  Door #1"
PRINT , "2.  What's behind the curtain"
PRINT , "3.  The Big Pink Box"
PRINT
INPUT "Please enter 1, 2, or 3:  ", menuNum%
PRINT

SELECT CASE menuNum%
    CASE 1
        PRINT "** It's a new car!!! **"
        PRINT "Yes, it's the new Land Yacht 2000,"
        PRINT "complete with Guzzle-O-Matic!"
```

FIGURE 5-7.   *(continued)*
SELECT-1.BAS: A program demonstrating the SELECT CASE statement.

109

FIGURE 5-7. *continued*

```
   CASE 2
        PRINT "** 500 pogo sticks!!! **"
        PRINT "Yes, you and your entire family can hop till you"
        PRINT "drop with the latest in pogoing fun!"
   CASE 3
        PRINT "** A lifetime supply of pickled herring!!! **"
        PRINT "Yes, twelve thousand jars of Smelz-Good"
        PRINT "pickled herring delivered to your front door!"
END SELECT

PRINT
PRINT "Thanks for playing!"
```

2. Run the program. Your output screen will look something like this:

```
Please enter your name:  Torvald

Congratulations, Torvald!  You've won the final
round of Go Ahead--Make My Deal!!  Please choose
which prize you want:

               1.  Door #1
               2.  What's behind the curtain
               3.  The Big Pink Box

Please enter 1, 2, or 3:  2

** 500 pogo sticks!!! **
Yes, you and your entire family can hop till you
drop with the latest in pogoing fun!

Thanks for playing!
```

After you entered a value for *menuNum%*, the QuickBASIC Interpreter used it to check the value in each CASE clause. Because a value of 2 was entered here, the QuickBASIC Interpreter found a match in the second CASE clause and executed the statements associated with that CASE clause. Then, because it had found a match, the QuickBASIC Interpreter jumped over the remaining CASE clause and executed the remainder of the program.

3. Run the program again, but this time use a value other than 1, 2, or 3. Your output screen will look something like this:

```
Please enter your name:  Dexter

Congratulations, Dexter!  You've won the final
round of Go Ahead--Make My Deal!!  Please choose
which prize you want:

              1.  Door #1
              2.  What's behind the curtain
              3.  The Big Pink Box

Please enter 1, 2, or 3:  5


Thanks for playing!
```

This time the QuickBASIC Interpreter didn't display a prize-winning message because it couldn't find a matching value in any of the CASE clauses.

Using CASE ELSE

Recall from earlier in the chapter that, when used in an IF statement, the ELSE clause lets you specify one or more actions to be executed when conditional expressions evaluate to false. You use CASE ELSE to do the same job with a SELECT CASE statement.

The syntax of a SELECT CASE statement using CASE ELSE is

```
SELECT CASE variable
    CASE value
        statements to be executed if value matches variable
    ⋮
    CASE ELSE
        statements to be executed if no values match variable
END SELECT
```

Practice: Using a CASE ELSE statement

1. Load the SELECT-2.BAS program (Figure 5-8) from disk.

```
' SELECT-2.BAS
' This program demonstrates the use of CASE ELSE.

CLS

PRINT "Welcome to Golden-Age Television Trivia!"
PRINT "In what year did the top-rated show"
PRINT "I Love Lucy first appear on television?"
PRINT
INPUT "Please enter a year from 1950 to 1959:  ", year%
PRINT

SELECT CASE year%
    CASE 1950
        PRINT "Incorrect.  In 1950, the popular show"
        PRINT "Your Show of Shows made its television debut."
    CASE 1951
        PRINT "Correct!  I Love Lucy first aired in October 1951."
        PRINT "From 1952 through 1954 it was the most popular"
        PRINT "television show in the United States."
    CASE 1952
        PRINT "Incorrect.  In 1952, the popular show"
        PRINT "Dragnet made its television debut."
    CASE 1953
        PRINT "Incorrect.  In 1953, the popular show"
        PRINT "Name That Tune made its television debut."
    CASE 1954
        PRINT "Incorrect.  In 1954, the popular show"
        PRINT "Lassie made its television debut."
    CASE 1955
        PRINT "Incorrect.  In 1955, the popular show"
        PRINT "Gunsmoke made its television debut."
```

FIGURE 5-8. *(continued)*

SELECT-2.BAS: A television trivia game that uses CASE ELSE.

FIGURE 5-8. *continued*

```
    CASE 1956
        PRINT "Incorrect.  In 1956, the popular show"
        PRINT "Playhouse 90 made its television debut."
    CASE 1957
        PRINT "Incorrect.  In 1957, the popular show"
        PRINT "Leave It to Beaver made its television debut."
    CASE 1958
        PRINT "Incorrect.  In 1958, the popular show"
        PRINT "Peter Gunn made its television debut."
    CASE 1959
        PRINT "Incorrect.  In 1959, the popular show"
        PRINT "The Twilight Zone made its television debut."
    CASE ELSE
        PRINT "You did not enter a number between 1950 and 1959."
        PRINT "Please run the program again and enter an"
        PRINT "appropriate value."
END SELECT
```

2. Run the program and enter the value *1951*—the correct answer to the trivia question. Your output screen will look like this:

```
Welcome to Golden-Age Television Trivia!
In what year did the top-rated show
I Love Lucy first appear on television?

Please enter a year from 1950 to 1959:  1951


Correct!  I Love Lucy first aired in October 1951.
From 1952 through 1954 it was the most popular
television show in the United States.
```

3. Now run the program again, but this time enter a value outside the proper range. Your output screen will look something like this:

```
Welcome to Golden-Age Television Trivia!
In what year did the top-rated show
I Love Lucy first appear on television?

Please enter a year from 1950 to 1959:  1598
```

(continued)

113

```
You did not enter a number between 1950 and 1959.
Please run the program again and enter an
appropriate value.
```

Because the QuickBASIC Interpreter couldn't find a matching CASE clause, it executed the statements following CASE ELSE. Using CASE ELSE is a convenient means of handling unforeseen difficulties in your SELECT CASE statements.

Using IS with CASE

The IS keyword lets you use a conditional expression (instead of only a single numeric or string value) in any CASE clause. The QuickBASIC Interpreter executes the statements following that CASE clause only if the condition is true. Here's the syntax for a CASE clause using IS:

```
SELECT CASE variable
    CASE IS condition
        statements to be executed if condition is true
    ⋮
END SELECT
```

This syntax is identical to the standard SELECT CASE statement, except for the addition of "IS *condition*" to the CASE clause. When it evaluates the condition, the QuickBASIC Interpreter uses the value of the SELECT CASE variable as the basis of the comparison.

Here's an example:

If the value of *userNum%* is less than or equal to 4, the QuickBASIC Interpreter executes this statement.

If the value of *userNum%* is 5, the QuickBASIC Interpreter executes this statement.

```
SELECT CASE userNum%
    CASE IS <= 4
        PRINT "The number you entered was 4 or less."
    CASE 5
        PRINT "The number you entered was 5."
    CASE IS >= 6
        PRINT "The number you entered was 6 or more."
END SELECT
```

If the value of *userNum%* is greater than or equal to 6, the QuickBASIC Interpreter executes this statement.

The QuickBASIC Interpreter compares the value entered by the user with the conditional portions of the CASE clauses. In this example, if the user entered a value of 4 or less, the condition in the first CASE clause would be true, so the QuickBASIC Interpreter would execute the associated PRINT statement. (The second CASE clause simply uses a value. You can mix values and IS conditional expressions.)

Practice: Working with SELECT CASE and IS

1. Load the SELECT-3.BAS program (Figure 5-9) from disk.

2. Run the program and enter a value. Your output screen will look something like this:

```
How many cups of coffee will you drink today?  3

A moderate level.
```

```
' SELECT-3.BAS
' This program analyzes the user's daily coffee consumption.

CLS

INPUT "How many cups of coffee will you drink today?  ", cupsCoffee%
PRINT

SELECT CASE cupsCoffee%
    CASE 0
        PRINT "Don't you LIKE my coffee??"
    CASE IS <= 3          ' 1 to 3 cups a day
        PRINT "A moderate level."
    CASE IS <= 7          ' 4 to 7 cups a day
        PRINT "I see decaf in your future..."
    CASE IS >= 8          ' 8 or more cups a day
        PRINT "Caffeine overload!"
END SELECT
```

FIGURE 5-9.
SELECT-3.BAS: A coffee-consumption "analysis" program that uses IS.

115

Press a key to return to the View window. In the program, notice how the conditions are set up. If you entered a value of 3 when you ran the program, as we did, you'll see that it caused the second CASE clause to be true. Notice also, however, that technically a value of 3 would cause the third CASE clause to be true as well, and you might be wondering why the QuickBASIC Interpreter didn't execute the associated PRINT statement as well. Remember: Once the QuickBASIC Interpreter finds a CASE clause with a true condition, it jumps over the remaining CASE clauses without even considering them and continues executing your program.

Using TO with SELECT CASE

To specify a range of valid values in a CASE clause, use the TO keyword. The syntax for using TO in a CASE clause is as follows:

```
SELECT CASE variable
    CASE value1 TO value2
        statements to be executed if CASE is true
    ⋮
END SELECT
```

The two values in the CASE clause can be two numeric values or two text strings in double quotation marks.

Using numeric values with the TO keyword

Here's an example of using two numeric values with the TO keyword in a CASE clause:

If the value of *userNum%* is 1 through 5, inclusive, the QuickBASIC Interpreter executes this statement.

```
SELECT CASE userNum%
    CASE IS 1 TO 5
        PRINT "The number you entered was between 1 and 5."
    CASE IS 6 TO 10
        PRINT "The number you entered was between 6 and 10."
END SELECT
```

If the value of *userNum%* is 6 through 10, inclusive, the QuickBASIC Interpreter executes this statement.

Note that the lesser of the two values is to the left of the TO keyword. You must list the values in this order; if you don't, the QuickBASIC Interpreter will misinterpret the condition and will always evaluate the expression as false.

This is also true for negative values. Here's an example using a negative number in the correct position:

```
CASE -12 TO 3
```

Because negative 12 is less than positive 3, you must put the negative 12 to the left of the TO keyword.

Using text strings with the TO keyword

You can also use a range of text strings in a CASE clause if you use the TO keyword. Here's an example:

```
SELECT CASE word$
    CASE IS "a" TO "m"
        PRINT "The word you entered was in the range a to m."
    CASE IS "m" TO "z"
        PRINT "The word you entered was in the range m to z."
END SELECT
```

At first glance, a range of text strings might not seem as obvious as a range of numbers, but both work in a similar way.

Recall from a previous example that the QuickBASIC Interpreter treats each character separately. For example, as far as the QuickBASIC Interpreter is concerned, the letters *a* and *A* are different.

The reason for this lies in how your computer deals with information. Although you type uppercase and lowercase letters on your keyboard, and although your computer can display uppercase and lowercase letters on your screen, your computer cannot work with letters directly. The microchips inside your computer can work only with numbers. (And you thought computers were smart....) When you press a character key on your keyboard, your computer temporarily translates that character into a number it can work with. Then, when it needs to do something with that number, such as display it on your screen, the QuickBASIC Interpreter changes it back to the character you originally typed in.

Relax—you don't need to learn how this numbering business works, but you do need to know that it happens if you intend to understand how the QuickBASIC Interpreter works with individual characters or strings of characters. Even though you deal with the characters or strings of characters themselves, you must understand that your computer and the QuickBASIC Interpreter simply consider them numbers.

In the preceding example, notice the overlap between the two CASE clauses. In the first CASE clause the range is from *a* to *m*, and in the second CASE clause the range is from *m* to *z*. Why the overlap? The following practice session will demonstrate.

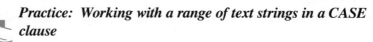

Practice: *Working with a range of text strings in a CASE clause*

1. Load the TO-1.BAS program (Figure 5-10) from disk.

```
' TO-1.BAS
' This program demonstrates the TO keyword in a CASE clause.

CLS

INPUT "Please enter a name:  ", name$
PRINT

SELECT CASE name$
    CASE "a" TO "m"
        PRINT "The name is in the range a to m."
    CASE "m" TO "z"
        PRINT "The name is in the range m to z."
    CASE "A" TO "M"
        PRINT "The name is in the range A to M."
    CASE "M" TO "Z"
        PRINT "The name is in the range M to Z."
END SELECT
```

FIGURE 5-10.
TO-1.BAS: A text-comparison program that uses TO.

118

2. Run the program and enter the name *billy*. Your output screen will look like this:

```
Please enter a name:  billy
```

```
The name is in the range a to m.
```

Because the first letter of *billy* is a lowercase *b*, it caused the first CASE statement to be true because a lowercase *b* falls within the range of *a* to *m*.

3. Run the program again, and enter only the letter *m*. Your output screen will look like this:

```
Please enter a name:  m
```

```
The name is in the range a to m.
```

Again, because the lowercase letter *m* caused the first CASE to be true, the QuickBASIC Interpreter executed the statement following the first CASE.

4. Run the program again, and enter the name *mildred*. Your output screen will look like this:

```
Please enter a name:  mildred
```

```
The name is in the range m to z.
```

Notice that entering the word *mildred* caused the second CASE to be true, but that in the previous example entering only the letter *m* caused the first CASE to be true. Why did this happen?

Recall that inside a computer, all letters are treated as numbers. In a sense, then, you can think of a string of characters as a series of numbers. In the preceding example, the word *mildred* had a higher "value" than the letter *m*, just as the number 15 has a higher value than the number 1. Even though both numbers—1 and 15—begin with a 1, the rules of numbers and mathematics tell you that 15 has a greater value than 1.

This rule loosely applies to strings of characters, but there is a difference. In the example above, the QuickBASIC Interpreter didn't consider the entire word *mildred* when it examined the CASE clauses. It needed merely to examine the first two letters—*mi*. Because the letter combination *mi* has a higher "value" than simply the letter *m*, and because the single letter *m* is at the top of the range of *a* to *m*, the QuickBASIC Interpreter needed to look no further—it knew the first condition was not true.

The QuickBASIC Interpreter did, however, find a match in the second condition. Although the string *mildred* is longer than the single-letter match the QuickBASIC Interpreter was looking for, the first letter of *mildred* does fall within the range of *m* to *z*, so the QuickBASIC Interpreter determined that the second condition was true.

Practice: More work with a range of text strings

1. Load the TO-2.BAS program (Figure 5-11) from disk.

```
' TO-2.BAS
' This program demonstrates the TO keyword in a CASE clause.

CLS

INPUT "Please enter a name:  ", name$
PRINT

SELECT CASE name$
    CASE "a" TO "mz"
        PRINT "The name is in the range a to m."
    CASE "n" TO "z"
        PRINT "The name is in the range n to z."
    CASE "A" TO "Mz"
        PRINT "The name is in the range A to M."
    CASE "N" TO "Z"
        PRINT "The name is in the range N to Z."
END SELECT
```

FIGURE 5-11.
TO-2.BAS: A modified version of TO-1.BAS.

TO-2.BAS is identical to TO-1.BAS except for some changes to the conditions—note especially the first and third CASE clauses.

120

2. Run the program, and enter a capital *M*. (We'll use capital letters this time for a little variety.) Your output screen will look like this:

```
Please enter a name:  M

The name is in the range A to M.
```

3. Now run the program again, and enter the name *Mildred*. Your output screen will look like this:

```
Please enter a name:  Mildred

The name is in the range A to M.
```

This time, because the condition in the third CASE clause has a range of *A* to *Mz*, the third condition is true because *Mz* has a greater "value" than the first two letters of *Mildred*, the name you typed in.

Using Multiple Conditions with CASE

So far, the conditions you've used in each CASE clause have been a single value, condition, or range of values. To specify multiple conditions within a single CASE clause, simply separate the conditions with commas. Here's an example:

If any of these values matches the value of *number%*, the QuickBASIC Interpreter executes this statement.

```
SELECT CASE number%
    CASE 1, 3, 5, 7, 9
        PRINT "The number you entered was odd."
    CASE 2, 4, 6, 8, 10
        PRINT "The number you entered was even."
END SELECT
```

If any of these values matches the value of *number%*, the QuickBASIC Interpreter executes this statement.

Using a comma within a CASE clause is similar to using the OR operator in an IF statement: If one of the items causes that CASE to be true, the QuickBASIC Interpreter executes the associated statements.

Items needn't be of the same type: You can mix values, conditions, and ranges of values. For example, the following CASE clause is valid:

```
CASE 5, IS <> 6, 20 TO 30
```

121

Practice: Working with commas and CASE

Load the TO-3.BAS program (Figure 5-12) from disk and run it. As you can see, using commas to specify multiple items allows you greater flexibility in your SELECT CASE statements.

```
' TO-3.BAS
' This program demonstrates the use of commas with CASE.

CLS

PRINT "Enter a month, and I will tell you how many"
PRINT "U.S. holidays there are in that month."
INPUT "Please enter a number from 1 to 12:  ", month%
PRINT

SELECT CASE month%
    CASE 8
        PRINT "There are no U.S. holidays in that month."
    CASE 3, 4, 7
        PRINT "There is 1 U.S. holiday in that month."
    CASE 6
        PRINT "There are 2 U.S. holidays in that month."
    CASE 1, 2, 9 TO 11
        PRINT "There are 3 U.S. holidays in that month."
    CASE 12
        PRINT "There are 4 U.S. holidays in that month."
    CASE 5
        PRINT "There are 5 U.S. holidays in that month."
END SELECT
```

FIGURE 5-12.
TO-3.BAS: A program demonstrating the use of multiple conditions within a CASE clause.

WHAT KIND OF CONDITIONAL STATEMENT SHOULD YOU USE?

Both the IF and the SELECT CASE statements have plenty of options and many different configurations. When you want to include a conditional statement in your program, answers to the following questions should help you choose the most appropriate statement for your needs.

■ **Which statement are you most comfortable using?** Through the help of associated keywords such as ELSE and ELSEIF with an IF statement, and CASE and CASE ELSE with a SELECT CASE statement, you can get the same result using either statement. Therefore, consider using the statement you're most comfortable with.

■ **How many conditions does your statement have?** SELECT CASE requires a minimum of three separate instructions to set up even a single condition! So, if you have only one condition, a simple IF statement is your best bet. If your statement has two or more conditions, IF and SELECT CASE are equally easy to use.

If you have many conditions, SELECT CASE is a good choice. It is visually less cluttered and therefore easier to read and comprehend than an IF statement. A SELECT CASE statement is also a good candidate for situations where you're looking for a number of specific values that don't fit neatly into a range.

SUMMARY

Conditional statements allow your programs to be much more flexible and "smarter." By using conditional statements in your program, you can control how your program runs, based on information typed in by the user or on information changed by the program as it runs. You've just taken another major step on your journey toward becoming a BASIC programmer, because you'll be using conditional statements as an integral part of most programs you write.

QUESTIONS AND EXERCISES

1. What are the differences between a numeric expression and a conditional expression?

2. Which of the following are *not* conditional operators?

a. <=	d. <	g. <>	j. /
b. ><	e. >=	h. >	k. <<
c. ==	f. ^	i. =<	l. =

3. True or False: You must always use the THEN keyword on the same line as the IF keyword.

4. What is the difference between the AND operator and the OR operator?

5. What does the ELSE keyword allow you to do? How does it differ from the THEN keyword?

6. How does the ELSEIF keyword work? What other BASIC keyword must you use with ELSEIF?

7. Write a program that asks the user a yes-or-no question. Instruct the user to enter a *Y* for yes or an *N* for no. Include a set of statements that will be executed if the user enters *Y* and a separate set of statements that will be executed if the user enters *N*. Also include a third set of statements that will be executed if the user does not enter a proper response. (Hint: Remember to check for uppercase and lowercase letters.)

8. How does the SELECT CASE statement work?

9. What does the CASE ELSE clause do?

10. In a CASE statement, what do the IS and TO keywords do?

11. Write a program that offers to describe three items to the user. Have the program display a numbered list of the items, and then have it ask the user to enter the number corresponding to the item to be described. Use a SELECT CASE statement to display appropriate information, and also include statements that will be executed if the user does not enter an appropriate response.

Working with
BASIC Loops

You've now learned most of the fundamentals of the BASIC language. In this chapter, you'll learn how to use one of BASIC's most powerful tools: the loop. By using loops in BASIC, you can have the computer perform certain repetitive tasks in a fraction of the time it would take to do the job yourself.

INTRODUCTION TO BASIC LOOPS

A *loop* is simply one or more BASIC statements that you direct the QuickBASIC Interpreter to repeat. Loops can repeat in two ways:

- A specific number of times
- Until a certain condition is met

The BASIC language includes three statements—FOR, WHILE, and DO—that allow you to add loops to your program. In the FOR statement you specify the number of times you want a loop executed; in the WHILE and DO statements you specify a condition, and the QuickBASIC Interpreter is responsible for evaluating the condition and executing the loop as long as the condition is met. Although the FOR, WHILE, and DO statements perform a similar function, each performs its task in a slightly different manner. As you'll see, this makes each of these statements suited for a particular type of work.

THE FOR STATEMENT

To create a loop that executes a specific number of times (the most common type of loop in BASIC), use the FOR statement. The FOR statement always ends with the NEXT statement, as shown in the following syntax:

```
FOR variable = start TO end
     statements to be repeated
NEXT variable
```

variable is a numeric variable that reflects how many times the QuickBASIC Interpreter has executed the loop. It's a counter of sorts. The QuickBASIC Interpreter increments *variable* each time it executes the loop. (Note that *variable* follows both the FOR statement and the NEXT statement. These variable names must be exactly the same.)

start is the numeric value—either a number or a numeric expression—at which you want the QuickBASIC Interpreter to start counting. *end* is also a numeric value, either a number or a numeric expression, that tells the QuickBASIC Interpreter how high it should count, that is, how many times it should repeat the loop. When you assign values to *start* and *end*, keep the following hints in mind:

- You can use positive or negative values for *start* and for *end*.

- The value of *start* must be less than or equal to the value of *end*.

- The value of *start* needn't be 1.

The statements between the FOR statement and the NEXT statement are the BASIC statements that the QuickBASIC Interpreter executes the specified number of times. There is no limit to the number of statements you can use, and the statements needn't be of the same type.

The QuickBASIC Interpreter uses the NEXT statement to count how many times it has executed the statements between the FOR statement and the NEXT statement. Here's an example of a FOR statement that prints a message five times, incrementing the variable *i%* each time it does so:

```
FOR i% = 1 TO 5
    PRINT "I am in a loop."
NEXT i%
```

Each time it completes the loop, the QuickBASIC Interpreter jumps back up to the FOR statement to compare the value of *i%* with the value of *end* (which is 5). As soon as *i%* exceeds *end*, the QuickBASIC Interpreter jumps to the statement following NEXT and continues executing the program.

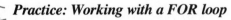

Practice: Working with a FOR loop

1. Load the FOR-1.BAS program (Figure 6-1) from the CHAP06 subdirectory on disk.

```
' FOR-1.BAS
' This program demonstrates the FOR loop.

CLS

INPUT "Please enter a number between 2 and 5:  ", times%
PRINT

FOR i% = 1 TO times%
    PRINT "These lines will print"; times%; "times."
    PRINT "This is time"; i%
    PRINT
NEXT i%
```

FIGURE 6-1.
FOR-1.BAS: A simple FOR loop.

2. Run the program. Your output screen will look something like this:

```
Please enter a number between 2 and 5:  4

These lines will print 4 times.
This is time 1

These lines will print 4 times.
This is time 2

These lines will print 4 times.
This is time 3

These lines will print 4 times.
This is time 4
```

 ***Practice: When* start *is greater than* end**

1. Load the FOR-2.BAS program (Figure 6-2) from disk. Note that *start* is greater than *end*.

```
' FOR-2.BAS
' This program demonstrates the FOR loop.

CLS

FOR i% = 6 TO 5
    PRINT "The current value of i% is"; i%
NEXT i%
```

FIGURE 6-2.
FOR-2.BAS: A FOR loop that never loops.

2. Run the program. Except for the message *Press any key to continue*, your output screen will be blank. (The QuickBASIC Interpreter saw the counter at 6, a value greater than *end*, and therefore considered its task complete.)

Why Use *i%*?

In most of the FOR loops in this book, you'll notice that *i%* is the loop variable. Why is this?

Before BASIC was invented, many programmers used a language called FORTRAN. In FORTRAN, the first letter of a variable name specified its type. For instance, any variable name that started with a letter from *I* through *N* denoted an integer variable, much as a percent sign (%) appended to a BASIC variable name denotes an integer variable.

Most FOR loop counters are integers. Thus, to save typing time, a FORTRAN programmer usually used the variable *i* as the loop counter. Programmers needing to nest two or more loops (see "Nesting FOR Loops" later in this chapter) would use *j*, then *k*, and so on. This tradition has been adopted by many BASIC programmers.

Must you use *i%*, *j%*, and *k%*? No—you can use any valid BASIC variable name, for example, *count%*, *numLines%*, or *dayOfMonth%*.

Practice: Using equal* start *and* end *values

1. Change the FOR statement in the FOR-2.BAS program so that *start* and *end* have the same value:

```
FOR i% = 5 TO 5
```

2. Run the program. Your output screen will look like this:

```
The current value of i% is 5
```

This time, the QuickBASIC Interpreter executed the body of the FOR statement once. Since the *start* and *end* values are the same, the QuickBASIC Interpreter assumed that this was its last "lap" so it executed the PRINT statement one time before moving on.

Looping and the COLOR Statement

You'll learn more about the COLOR statement in Chapter 11, but for now just sit back and enjoy this demonstration, which uses both the COLOR statement and a FOR loop within a program.

Practice: Changing foreground colors with a FOR loop

1. Load the FOR-3.BAS program (Figure 6-3) from disk.

```
' FOR-3.BAS
' This program uses a FOR loop and the COLOR statement
'    to demonstrate the various foreground colors.

CLS

FOR i% = 1 TO 15          ' use colors 1 through 15
    COLOR i%              ' use value of i% for color
    PRINT "This line is printed using color"; i%
NEXT i%
```

FIGURE 6-3.
FOR-3.BAS: Using the COLOR statement in a FOR loop.

NOTE: You can run this program even if you don't have a color monitor attached to your computer. Your experience won't be as colorful, but it will be enlightening all the same.

The COLOR Statement

The COLOR statement lets you specify the foreground (text) and background colors for your output screen. Here's the syntax of the COLOR statement:

```
COLOR [foreground][, background]
```

Both *foreground* and *background* are numbers that represent colors:

Value	Resulting color
0	Black (default background)
1	Blue
2	Green
3	Cyan
4	Red
5	Magenta
6	Brown
7	White (default foreground)
8	Gray
9	Light blue
10	Light green
11	Light cyan
12	Light red
13	Light magenta
14	Yellow
15	Bright white

For example, the statement

```
COLOR 14, 1
```

causes the QuickBASIC Interpreter to display yellow text on a blue background.

2. Run the program. Your output screen will look like this, except that each line will be a different color:

```
This line is printed using color 1
This line is printed using color 2
This line is printed using color 3
This line is printed using color 4
This line is printed using color 5
This line is printed using color 6
This line is printed using color 7
This line is printed using color 8
This line is printed using color 9
This line is printed using color 10
This line is printed using color 11
This line is printed using color 12
This line is printed using color 13
This line is printed using color 14
This line is printed using color 15
```

 Practice: Changing foreground and background colors with a FOR loop

1. Load the FOR-4.BAS program (Figure 6-4) from disk.

```
' FOR-4.BAS
' This program uses a FOR loop and the COLOR statement
'   to change both the foreground and background colors.

CLS

FOR i% = 1 TO 15          ' use colors 1 through 15
    COLOR i%, i% - 1
    PRINT "Current foreground color is"; i%;
    PRINT "; current background color is"; i% - 1
NEXT i%
```

FIGURE 6-4.
FOR-4.BAS: Changing both foreground and background colors with a FOR loop.

2. Run the program. Your output screen will look like this, but will be in color:

```
Current foreground color is 1; current background color is 0
Current foreground color is 2; current background color is 1
Current foreground color is 3; current background color is 2
Current foreground color is 4; current background color is 3
Current foreground color is 5; current background color is 4
Current foreground color is 6; current background color is 5
Current foreground color is 7; current background color is 6
Current foreground color is 8; current background color is 7
Current foreground color is 9; current background color is 8
Current foreground color is 10; current background color is 9
Current foreground color is 11; current background color is 10
Current foreground color is 12; current background color is 11
Current foreground color is 13; current background color is 12
Current foreground color is 14; current background color is 13
Current foreground color is 15; current background color is 14
```

3. Press a key to return to the View window and then look at the COLOR statement in the FOR loop. Notice the values used to set the foreground and background colors. The foreground color is set to the current value of *i%*, and the background color is set to the value of *i%* minus one. Using a technique such as this prevents setting the foreground color and background color to the same value—if the foreground and background values are the same, you won't be able to read the text.

Looping and the SOUND Statement

Another fun BASIC statement is SOUND. (Again, you'll be hearing more about SOUND in Chapter 11.) In the following practice, the FOR statement combined with the SOUND statement provides audible proof of the power of loops.

The SOUND Statement

The SOUND statement does exactly what the name implies—it causes your computer to create a sound. Here's the syntax of a SOUND statement:

SOUND *frequency, duration*

The *frequency* argument is an integer from 37 through 32,767 that indicates the frequency of the sound in cycles per second, or hertz. The *duration* argument is an integer or floating-point number from 0 through 65,535 that indicates how long the sound should last (the value 18.2 = one second). For example, the following BASIC statement causes the QuickBASIC Interpreter to play a sound of 500 hertz for one-half second:

SOUND 500, 9.1

Practice: Using the FOR and SOUND statements

1. Load the FOR-5.BAS program (Figure 6-5) from disk.

```
' FOR-5.BAS
' This program uses the SOUND statement inside a
'    FOR loop to generate sound effects.

CLS

PRINT , "SOUND-EFFECTS GENERATOR"
PRINT , "Please choose the sound you'd like to hear"
PRINT , "from the following menu:"
PRINT
PRINT , "1.  Ray gun"
PRINT , "2.  European siren"
PRINT , "3.  Takeoff!"
PRINT
INPUT "              Please enter 1, 2, or 3:  ", choice%
PRINT
```

FIGURE 6-5.
FOR-5.BAS: A sound-effects generator.

(continued)

FIGURE 6-5. *continued*

```
SELECT CASE choice%
    CASE 1                          ' ray gun
        FOR i% = 1 TO 50
            SOUND 850, .3
            SOUND 800, .3
            SOUND 825, .3
        NEXT i%
    CASE 2                          ' european siren
        FOR i% = 1 TO 5
            SOUND 500, 10
            SOUND 450, 10
        NEXT i%
    CASE 3                          ' takeoff!
        FOR i% = 500 TO 2500
            SOUND i%, .03           ' uses value of i% for sound
        NEXT i%
END SELECT
```

2. Run the program. Your output screen will look like this:

```
SOUND-EFFECTS GENERATOR
Please choose the sound you'd like to hear
from the following menu:

1.  Ray gun
2.  European siren
3.  Takeoff!

Please enter 1, 2, or 3:
```

3. Enter an appropriate value to hear the sound of your choice.

Run the program several times and try out each of the sounds. Next, try experimenting with this program by changing some of the values in the various SOUND statements and running the program again. Notice that most of the duration values are small. Smaller duration values work well for sound effects, whereas you'll need to use larger values to create a melody.

Controlling the Count with STEP

As you've seen, when the QuickBASIC Interpreter executes a FOR loop, it begins by assigning the *start* value to the variable following FOR and then loops through the block of statements until the value of the counter variable is greater than the value of *end*. Each time it encounters the NEXT statement, the QuickBASIC Interpreter increments the value of the counter by one.

You can tell the QuickBASIC Interpreter to increment the counter by a value other than one if you use the STEP clause. Here's an example:

```
FOR i% = 5 TO 25 STEP 5
    PRINT "This message will print 5 times."
NEXT i%
```

When the QuickBASIC Interpreter encounters the NEXT statement, it increments the counter by the number you specified after STEP.

The number in the STEP clause doesn't have to be positive. If you place a negative number after STEP, the QuickBASIC Interpreter *decrements* the value of the counter each time it encounters the NEXT statement. The STEP value also affects the values you assign to *start* and *end*:

■ If the number is positive, *start* must be less than or equal to *end*.

■ If the number is negative, *start* must be *greater* than or equal to *end*.

Think about it: If you use a negative STEP value and *end* is greater than *start*, the QuickBASIC Interpreter will assume that its work is done, jump over the block of statements without executing it, and continue executing the rest of the program.

Practice: Using STEP

1. Load the FOR-6.BAS program (Figure 6-6) from disk.

```
' FOR-6.BAS
' This program demonstrates the use of STEP.

CLS

FOR i% = 15 TO 1 STEP -1
    COLOR i%
    PRINT "Falling!"
    SOUND (50 * i%), 1
NEXT i%
```

FIGURE 6-6.
FOR-6.BAS: Using STEP in a FOR statement.

2. Run the program. The QuickBASIC Interpreter will print the word *Falling!* 15 times, each time in a different color, with accompanying sound.

Nesting FOR Loops

Nesting is the term that describes the practice of putting one loop within another. Here's an example of a nested FOR loop:

```
FOR i% = 1 TO 5
    FOR j% = 1 TO 5
        PRINT "You'll see this message 25 times."
    NEXT j%
NEXT i%
```

Here's where indentation really helps you see what's going on. In a nested FOR loop, the inner FOR loop is actually a statement for the outer loop. That is, the outer FOR loop executes the inner loop as many times as you specify. In this example, the outer loop executes the inner loop a total of 5 times. Because the inner loop executes its statements 5 times, the QuickBASIC Interpreter will end up executing the PRINT statement a total of 25 times.

Practice: Working with nested FOR loops

1. Load the FOR-7.BAS program (Figure 6-7) from disk.

```
' FOR-7.BAS
' This program demonstrates nested FOR loops.

CLS

PRINT "The inner loop will print the colored numbers:"
PRINT

FOR i% = 1 TO 5
    COLOR 7                 ' set outer loop color to white
    PRINT                   ' print a blank line
    PRINT "Outer loop lap number"; i%
    FOR j% = 1 TO 10
        COLOR j%
        PRINT j%;
        SOUND (j% * 100), 1
    NEXT j%
NEXT i%
```

FIGURE 6-7.
FOR-7.BAS: Using nested FOR loops.

2. Run the program. When the program has finished running, your
    output screen will look like this:

```
The inner loop will print the colored numbers:

Outer loop lap number 1
 1  2  3  4  5  6  7  8  9  10
Outer loop lap number 2
 1  2  3  4  5  6  7  8  9  10
Outer loop lap number 3
 1  2  3  4  5  6  7  8  9  10
Outer loop lap number 4
 1  2  3  4  5  6  7  8  9  10
Outer loop lap number 5
 1  2  3  4  5  6  7  8  9  10
```

The SOUND statement within the inner loop created a sound after each of the inner loop's numbers was printed. If you want, press a key to return to the View window and change some of the values. Try to anticipate what the program will do before you run it, and then run the program to see if you were right.

THE WHILE STATEMENT

To design a loop that repeats as long as a specific condition is true, use the WHILE statement. The WHILE statement always ends with the WEND statement, as shown in the following syntax:

```
WHILE condition
    statements to be repeatedly executed
WEND
```

condition can be any conditional expression (such as *wage! = 11.50*, *year% <= 1959*, or *temperature% < 32*).

When it encounters a WHILE statement, the QuickBASIC Interpreter evaluates *condition*:

■ If *condition* is true, QuickBASIC executes the block of statements between the WHILE and WEND statements and then checks *condition* again.

■ If *condition* is false, QuickBASIC jumps to the WEND statement and moves on to the rest of the program.

To use a WHILE loop successfully, you must make provisions *inside* the loop to alter the condition following the WHILE statement.

 NOTE: Be sure that condition *eventually becomes false; if you don't, your loop will never stop, and the rest of your program will never run. (A loop that never stops is called an* infinite *or* endless *loop. To stop an endless loop in the QuickBASIC Interpreter, hold down the Ctrl key and press Break.)*

Practice: Working with the WHILE loop

In the following program, all activity takes place within the loop. And because QuickBASIC increments the value of *userNum%* each time it executes the loop, *userNum%* eventually becomes greater than 12. This creates a false condition and causes the QuickBASIC Interpreter to stop executing the loop.

1. Load the WHILE.BAS program (Figure 6-8) from disk.

```
' WHILE.BAS
' This program demonstrates the WHILE loop.

CLS

INPUT "Please enter a number between 1 and 10:  ", userNum%
PRINT

WHILE userNum% <= 12
    COLOR userNum%
    PRINT "The current value of userNum% is"; userNum%
    SOUND ((userNum% * 30) + 300), .5
    userNum% = userNum% + 1
    PRINT
WEND
```

FIGURE 6-8.
WHILE.BAS: Using a WHILE loop with a counter.

2. Run the program. Your output screen will look something like this:

```
Please enter a number between 1 and 10:  9

The current value of userNum% is 9

The current value of userNum% is 10

The current value of userNum% is 11

The current value of userNum% is 12
```

Nesting WHILE Loops

Just as you can nest FOR statements, you can place one WHILE statement inside another. Each WHILE statement has its own *condition* and closing WEND statement; the two conditions need not be related to each other.

The syntax for a nested WHILE loop is as follows:

```
WHILE condition
    WHILE condition
        statement for inner WHILE loop
    WEND
WEND
```

The inner WHILE statement serves as the statement of the outer WHILE statement.

 NOTE: To prevent infinite loops, remember that both the inner condition and the outer condition must eventually evaluate as false.

THE DO STATEMENT

You use the DO statement together with the LOOP statement to develop two kinds of loops:

- A loop that repeats *as long as* a certain condition is true (DO WHILE)

- A loop that repeats until a certain condition *becomes* true (DO UNTIL)

DO WHILE: Looping as Long as a Condition Is True

To create a loop that repeats as long as a condition is true, use a DO loop with the following syntax:

```
DO WHILE condition
    block of statements to be executed
LOOP
```

A DO loop of this type works just like a WHILE statement. The QuickBASIC Interpreter examines *condition*:

■ If *condition* is true, the QuickBASIC Interpreter executes the statements and continues to do so as long as *condition* is true.

■ If *condition* is false, the QuickBASIC Interpreter jumps past the LOOP statement to execute the rest of the program.

The Condition-Statement Connection

As you learned in Chapter 2, BASIC executes instructions in the order in which they appear in your programs. The importance of order is particularly apparent within the DO statement, which requires you to place a condition in one of two places, based on the result you want from your program:

■ If you want the statements to execute based solely on the value of *condition*, place *condition* on the line with the DO statement:

```
DO {WHILE!UNTIL} condition
    block of statements to be executed
LOOP
```

In this form, the inner statements are executed only if *condition* is true.

■ If you want the statements to execute at least once, no matter what the value of *condition*, place *condition* on the line with the LOOP statement:

```
DO
    block of statements to be executed
LOOP {WHILE!UNTIL} condition
```

By the time *condition* is evaluated, the QuickBASIC Interpreter has already executed the statements one time.

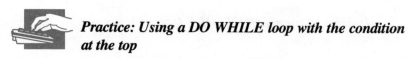

Practice: Using a DO WHILE loop with the condition at the top

1. Load the DO-1.BAS program (Figure 6-9) from disk.

```
' DO-1.BAS
' This program demonstrates a DO WHILE loop.  Notice
'   that the condition is at the top of the loop.

CLS

INPUT "Please enter a number between 10 and 15:  ", userNum%
PRINT

DO WHILE userNum% >= 10
    COLOR userNum%
    PRINT "The value of userNum% is"; userNum%
    userNum% = userNum% - 1    ' decrement userNum% by 1
LOOP
```

FIGURE 6-9.
DO-1.BAS: Using a DO WHILE loop.

2. Run the program. Your output screen will look something like this:

```
Please enter a number between 10 and 15:  13

The value of userNum% is 13
The value of userNum% is 12
The value of userNum% is 11
The value of userNum% is 10
```

3. Run the program again, but this time enter a value of 9 or less. Your output screen will look something like this:

```
Please enter a number between 10 and 15:  6
```

QuickBASIC perceived the condition was false and therefore skipped the statements within the loop.

Practice: Using a DO WHILE loop with the condition at the bottom

Program DO-2.BAS is identical to DO-1.BAS, but the condition has been moved to the bottom of the loop.

1. Load the DO-2.BAS program (Figure 6-10) from disk.

```
' DO-2.BAS
' This program demonstrates a DO WHILE loop.  Notice
'   that the condition is at the bottom of the loop.

CLS

INPUT "Please enter a number between 10 and 15:  ", userNum%
PRINT

DO
    COLOR userNum%
    PRINT "The value of userNum% is"; userNum%
    userNum% = userNum% - 1    ' decrement userNum% by 1
LOOP WHILE userNum% >= 10
```

FIGURE 6-10.
DO-2.BAS: A DO WHILE loop with the condition at the bottom.

2. Run the program. Your output screen will look something like this:

```
Please enter a number between 10 and 15:   13

The value of userNum% is 13
The value of userNum% is 12
The value of userNum% is 11
The value of userNum% is 10
```

Looks just like the output of DO-1.BAS, doesn't it? But wait.

3. Run the program again, but this time enter a value of 9 or less. Your output screen will look something like this:

```
Please enter a number between 10 and 15:   6

The value of userNum% is 6
```

Here's where you can see the difference. Even though the value of *userNum%* caused the condition in the LOOP statement to be false, the QuickBASIC Interpreter didn't encounter that condition until *after* it had executed the body of the DO loop once.

DO UNTIL: Looping Until a Condition Becomes True

To create a loop that executes until a condition *becomes* true, use a DO loop with the following syntax:

```
DO UNTIL condition
    block of statements to be executed
LOOP
```

The QuickBASIC Intepreter examines *condition*:

- If *condition* is true, the QuickBASIC Interpreter jumps past the LOOP statement to execute the rest of the program.

- If *condition* is false, the QuickBASIC Interpreter executes the statements and continues to do so until *condition* is true.

 Practice: Using a DO UNTIL loop with the condition at the top

1. Load the DO-3.BAS program (Figure 6-11) from disk.

```
' DO-3.BAS
' This program demonstrates a DO UNTIL loop.  Notice
'    that the condition is at the top of the loop.

CLS

INPUT "Please enter a number between 1 and 10:  ", userNum%
PRINT

DO UNTIL userNum% > 10
    COLOR userNum%
    PRINT "The value of userNum% is"; userNum%
    userNum% = userNum% + 1    ' increment userNum% by 1
LOOP
```

FIGURE 6-11.
DO-3.BAS: Using a DO UNTIL loop.

2. Run the program. Your output screen will look something like this:

```
Please enter a number between 1 and 10:   7

The value of userNum% is 7
The value of userNum% is 8
The value of userNum% is 9
The value of userNum% is 10
```

Because the condition *userNum% > 10* was false when the QuickBASIC Interpreter first encountered the loop, QuickBASIC continued to execute the loop until the condition became true.

3. Run the program again, this time entering a value of 11 or more. Your output screen will look something like this:

```
Please enter a number between 1 and 10:   13
```

This time, because the condition was true when the QuickBASIC Interpreter encountered the loop, the QuickBASIC Interpreter jumped over the loop and executed the rest of the program.

Practice: Using a DO UNTIL loop with the condition at the bottom

1. Load the DO-4.BAS program (Figure 6-12) from disk.

2. Run the program. Your output screen will look something like this:

```
Please enter a number between 1 and 10:   7

The value of userNum% is 7
The value of userNum% is 8
The value of userNum% is 9
The value of userNum% is 10
```

The output of this program is the same as that of the previous program.

```
' DO-4.BAS
' This program demonstrates a DO UNTIL loop.  Notice
'   that the condition is at the bottom of the loop.

CLS

INPUT "Please enter a number between 1 and 10:  ", userNum%
PRINT

DO
    COLOR userNum%
    PRINT "The value of userNum% is"; userNum%
    userNum% = userNum% + 1    ' increment userNum% by 1
LOOP UNTIL userNum% > 10
```

FIGURE 6-12.
DO-4.BAS: A DO UNTIL loop with the condition at the bottom.

3. Run the program again, but this time enter a value of 11 or more. Your output screen will look something like this:

```
Please enter a number between 1 and 10:   13

The value of userNum% is 13
```

This time, because the condition was at the bottom of the loop, the QuickBASIC Interpreter executed the contents of the loop once because it did not know what the condition was until it got to the bottom of the loop.

Nesting DO Loops

You can nest DO loops the same way you nest FOR and WHILE loops.

The loops are totally unrelated in terms of how you set them up. In other words, if you have two nested DO loops and you put the condition at the top of the outer loop, you needn't put the condition at the top of the inner loop. Of course, as with a single DO loop, you must ensure that both the outer loop and the nested loop will eventually terminate.

NESTING DIFFERENT KINDS OF LOOPS

So far we've discussed nesting loops of the same kind—a FOR loop inside another FOR loop, a WHILE loop inside another WHILE loop, and so on.

You can, however, mix whatever kinds of loops you want, especially if by doing so you can perform a job more efficiently. The following program nests a FOR loop inside a DO loop. The DO loop allows you to execute the FOR loop as many times as you want without having to start the program each time.

 Practice: Nesting different kinds of loops

1.   Load the NESTING.BAS program (Figure 6-13) from disk.

```
' NESTING.BAS
' This program demonstrates nesting different kinds of loops.

CLS

DO
    PRINT "How many tones do you want to hear?"
    INPUT "(Enter 0 to end)   ", numSounds%
    PRINT

    FOR i% = 1 TO numSounds%
        SOUND (i% * 100), 1
    NEXT i%

LOOP UNTIL numSounds% = 0
```

FIGURE 6-13.
NESTING.BAS: Nesting different kinds of loops.

2.   Run the program. Your output screen will look something like this:

```
How many tones do you want to hear?
(Enter 0 to end)  5
```

(continued)

148

continued

```
How many tones do you want to hear?
(Enter 0 to end)  20

How many tones do you want to hear?
(Enter 0 to end)  0
```

PRACTICAL USES FOR BASIC LOOPS

Now that you've been introduced to loops, it's time to see what they can really do for you. The following examples present some practical and fun applications for loops.

Using a Loop to Collect Information

Let's say you want to automate your monthly budget planning. The philosophy behind budgeting is relatively straightforward: You subtract expenses from monthly income.

And, using the tools you've learned so far, you could likely write a BASIC program to help you do this. You might use several INPUT statements: one to get the starting amount, then one for each expenditure. After

---

Which Loop Should You Choose?

Keep the following points in mind when deciding which type of loop to use in a program:

■ Use a FOR loop when you want to execute a block of statements a specific number of times.

■ Use a WHILE or DO loop to execute statements based on the value of a condition.

■ You can make a DO loop do anything a WHILE loop can. Get into the habit of using the more versatile DO loop whenever possible. (The QuickBASIC Interpreter supports the WHILE loop so that you can run programs that were written for earlier versions of BASIC.)

some calculations, you could have the QuickBASIC Interpreter print out how much money you'd have left. Figure 6-14 is an example of such a program.

```
' This program helps you figure out how much money is
'   left over after you've paid your monthly bills.

CLS

COLOR 2                    ' green foreground
PRINT "Budget Calculator"
COLOR 7                    ' restore default white color
PRINT
INPUT "Enter your total income for this month:  $", total!
PRINT

INPUT "Enter expense # 1:  $", expense1!
total! = total! - expense1!
INPUT "Enter expense # 2:  $", expense2!
total! = total! - expense2!
INPUT "Enter expense # 3:  $", expense3!
total! = total! - expense3!
INPUT "Enter expense # 4:  $", expense4!
total! = total! - expense4!

PRINT
PRINT "You have $"; total!; "left over this month."
```

FIGURE 6-14.
A sample budgeting program.

This program would work fine, but it does have limitations:

- Because your number of expenditures might change from month to month, you'd have to alter the program each time you ran it.

- Each expenditure you enter must be immediately subtracted from the running total. This isn't a problem, but it is a lot of repetitive calculation. Consider how long this program would be if you had 20 or more expenses each month!

Programs with this degree of repetition are ideal candidates for a loop. The BUDGET.BAS program in Figure 6-15 does the same job as the program in Figure 6-14 but offers some advantages:

- It's a shorter program.

- It accommodates a changing number of expenditures by asking you for the total number of bills you plan to enter.

- It uses a loop both to ask you for the bill amount and to subtract the amount from the running total.

```
' BUDGET.BAS
' This program helps you figure out how much money is
'    left over after you've paid your monthly bills.

CLS

COLOR 2                    ' green foreground
PRINT "Budget Calculator"
COLOR 7                    ' restore default white foreground
PRINT
INPUT "Enter your total income for this month:  $", total!
PRINT
INPUT "How many bills will you have this month?  ", bills%

FOR i% = 1 TO bills%
    PRINT "Enter expense #"; i%;
    INPUT ":  $", thisExpense!
    total! = total! - thisExpense!
NEXT i%

PRINT
PRINT "You have $"; total!; "left over this month."
```

FIGURE 6-15.
BUDGET.BAS: A better budgeting program.

Using Loops with Random Numbers

Dice. Roulette. Keno. Bingo. Lottery. All of these games make use of *random numbers*—numbers that occur in no predictable order. This section describes three of the tools that BASIC provides for creating random numbers: RND, RANDOMIZE TIMER, and INT.

Creating random numbers

The RND function instructs the QuickBASIC Interpreter to return a random number to your program. (The number is a single-precision floating-point number between 0 and 1.) Because RND is a function, you must use it within a BASIC statement. Here's the syntax for the simplest form of the RND function:

```
RND
```

By itself, RND returns the same series of numbers whenever you run your program. To create a *different* series of numbers each time, use RANDOMIZE TIMER as one of the first statements in your program. The syntax of the RANDOMIZE TIMER statement is as simple as that of the RND function:

```
RANDOMIZE TIMER
```

Practice: Creating random numbers

The RND-1.BAS program (Figure 6-16) uses a FOR loop to create six random numbers. (To create more random numbers, simply change the *6* in the FOR statement to a higher value.)

1. Load the RND-1.BAS program from disk.

2. Run the program. Your output screen will look something like this:

```
.2494013
.3081127
3.670245E-02
.574261
.4791026
.1495265
```

The numbers you get will undoubtedly be different from these—remember, these are just random numbers.

```
' RND-1.BAS
' This program generates random numbers between 0 and 1.

CLS

RANDOMIZE TIMER

FOR i% = 1 TO 6
    PRINT RND
NEXT i%
```

FIGURE 6-16.
RND-1.BAS: Creating random numbers.

Customizing the results of RND

Because numbers between 0 and 1 might not always meet your needs, you can use BASIC's mathematical operators to change the size of RND's results.

Practice: Creating larger random numbers

The RND-2.BAS program (Figure 6-17) is identical to RND-1.BAS, but it multiplies the result of RND by 100, creating values that range between 0 and 100.

1. Load the RND-2.BAS program from disk.

```
' RND-2.BAS
' This program generates random numbers between 0 and 100.

CLS

RANDOMIZE TIMER

FOR i% = 1 TO 6
    PRINT RND * 100
NEXT i%
```

FIGURE 6-17.
RND-2.BAS: Creating larger random numbers.

2. Run the program. Your output screen will look something like this:

```
85.67621
42.35302
87.795
48.80183
42.53306
24.83424
```

Very Small and Very Large Numbers in BASIC

The values produced by the QuickBASIC Interpreter's RND function are always greater than 0 and less than 1. Sometimes the values are very small.

When QuickBASIC tries to print a value that's too small or too large to display without using a lot of digits, it switches to BASIC's version of exponential notation. To put it simply, when you see an *E* or a *D* in a number, the decimal point was shifted from its actual location. The number after the *E* or *D* indicates in which direction and by how many places the decimal point was moved. If that number is positive, the decimal point actually resides to the *right* of its displayed location; if the number is negative, the decimal point belongs to the *left* of its displayed location.

For example, in the sample output from RND-1.BAS you can see the number *3.670245E-02*. The *E-02* means that the decimal point actually belongs two places to the left. In other words, you'd normally write the number as 0.03670245.

So why not simply display the number as it usually appears? Often the number won't fit neatly on the screen. Take the number *4.136111E28*. If printed in its entirety, it would look like this:

```
41361110000000000000000000000000
```

For those of you who are familiar with standard scientific notation, here is the same number in that format:

4.136111×10^{28}

Creating random integers

If you'd like to create random numbers that are integers (numbers without decimal points), use the INT function along with the RND function. INT rounds a floating-point number to the nearest integer and takes the following form:

INT(*number*)

number is the floating-point number you want to round. As with all functions that return integers, the integer result of INT must be assigned either to a statement that accepts integer values or to an integer variable.

The following practice session demonstrates how to use the INT function with RND to create random integer numbers.

Practice: Creating a guess-a-number game

Random numbers are ideal for guessing games. The following program uses a DO loop to demonstrate this:

1. Load the GUESS.BAS program (Figure 6-18) from disk.

2. Run the program. Your output screen will look something like this:

```
Guess-a-number game

I'm thinking of a number between 1 and 100.
Can you guess what it is?

What is your guess?  50
Brrr!  You're cold!  Try a bigger number.

What is your guess?  99
Brrr!  You're cold!  Try a smaller number.

What is your guess?  65
You're warm...

What is your guess?  71
Congratulations!!

You guessed the number in 4 tries!
```

```
' GUESS.BAS
' This program is a guess-a-number game.  The program generates a
'   random number and asks the user to guess what it is.  After the
'   user has guessed the number, the program displays the number
'   of guesses made.

CLS

PRINT "Guess-a-number game"
PRINT
PRINT "I'm thinking of a number between 1 and 100."
PRINT "Can you guess what it is?"
PRINT

RANDOMIZE TIMER

randNum% = INT(RND * 100)                    ' generate random number
numGuesses% = 0                              ' start with a clean slate

DO
    INPUT "What is your guess?  ", guess%
    SELECT CASE guess%
        CASE IS = randNum%
            PRINT "Congratulations!!"
        CASE IS < randNum% - 10
            PRINT "Brrr!  You're cold!  Try a bigger number."
        CASE IS > randNum% + 10
            PRINT "Brrr!  You're cold!  Try a smaller number."
        CASE IS <> randNum%
            PRINT "You're warm..."
    END SELECT

    numGuesses% = numGuesses% + 1            ' chalk up one guess
    PRINT                                    ' print a blank line

LOOP UNTIL guess% = randNum%

PRINT "You guessed the number in"; numGuesses%; "tries!"
```

FIGURE 6-18.
GUESS.BAS: A guessing game.

Practice: Writing a computer simulation

Let's say you want to write a program that calculates how many times, out of 100 rolls of 2 dice, the number 7 comes up. Here's where the RND function comes in handy again.

The DICE.BAS program (Figure 6-19) does just that.

```
' DICE.BAS
' This program asks the user to enter how many times the QuickBASIC
'   Interpreter should "roll" two dice, and then calculates how many
'   times the number 7 comes up.

CLS

RANDOMIZE TIMER

COLOR 4                 ' red color for title
PRINT "DICE-SIMULATION PROGRAM"
COLOR 7                 ' restore default white color
PRINT
numSeven% = 0           ' start with 7 counter equal to zero

INPUT "How many times should I roll the dice?  ", rolls%
PRINT
PRINT "Working..."  ' make sure the user knows nothing is wrong

FOR i% = 1 TO rolls%
    die1% = INT(RND * 7)        ' "roll" the first die
    die2% = INT(RND * 7)        ' "roll" the second die
    IF die1% + die2% = 7 THEN numSeven% = numSeven% + 1
NEXT i%

PRINT
PRINT "Out of"; rolls%; "rolls, the number 7 came"
PRINT "up"; numSeven%; "times."
```

FIGURE 6-19.
DICE.BAS: A dice-simulation program.

When you run DICE.BAS you receive output similar to the following:

```
DICE-SIMULATION PROGRAM

How many times should I roll the dice?  50

Working...

Out of 50 rolls, the number 7 came
up 3 times.
```

SUMMARY

Loops let you create powerful programs that repeat a task a specific number of times or until a condition is met. In this chapter you've learned about FOR, WHILE, and DO loops. Combine this knowledge with the COLOR and SOUND statements, the RND function, and the skills you've picked up in previous chapters, and you're ready to take on some impressive programming projects. The following chapters will get you started.

QUESTIONS AND EXERCISES

1. What is the purpose of the counter variable in a FOR loop?

2. What types of values can be assigned to the *start* and *end* elements of a FOR loop?

3. What number would you specify as an argument to the COLOR statement if you wanted to set the foreground color to red?

4. What does the SOUND statement do?

5. What is a nested loop?

6. What is the effect of putting the condition in a DO loop at the top of the loop? What is the effect of putting the condition at the bottom of the loop?

7. Under what circumstances might you use a FOR loop? A WHILE or DO loop?

8. Write a program that keeps track of the amount of money spent on gasoline in a week. Use a FOR loop to collect the dollars and cents spent and keep a running total with a single-precision floating-point variable.

9. Write a program that prompts the user for valid frequency and duration values and plays them back with the SOUND statement. Use a DO UNTIL loop to collect information until the user types in *−999* as the frequency.

10. Write a program that rolls one simulated die 10 times. Print the value of the die after each roll and display the message *Nice Roll!* in green if the die shows 6.

Creating Your Own Subprograms and Functions

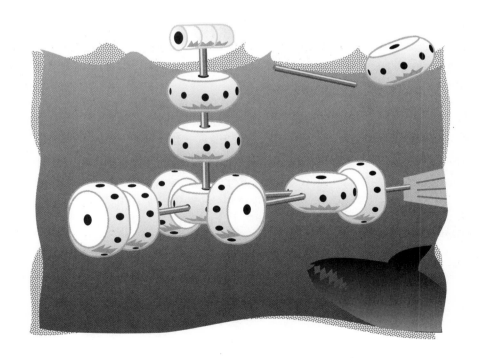

Up to now, you've written relatively short programs—none has exceeded 30 lines in length. But now that you've learned the basics of BASIC, you're ready to write longer programs. This chapter presents techniques that allow you to write longer programs with a minimum of extra time and effort.

In this chapter you'll learn about two program structures: *subprograms* and *functions*. (You'll see how these functions differ from the built-in functions you've been using.) You use these structures to separate a program into easy-to-use units called *procedures*. We'll show you how to declare subprograms and functions and how to use them in your programs. You'll also learn how the QuickBASIC environment is designed for modular programming. By the end of this chapter, you'll have all the tools you need to write compact and well-organized programs.

WHY PROCEDURES?

Suppose you want to write a program that prints lyrics of the traditional American song "Clementine." Using the skills you've already learned, you would likely write the song with PRINT statements, as shown in the SONG.BAS program.

Practice: Running the SONG.BAS program

Load the SONG.BAS program (Figure 7-1) from the CHAP07 subdirectory on disk and run it.

SONG.BAS is quite straightforward: It prints each verse and each chorus of the song, pausing when the screen is full so that you have time to read the lyrics (and sing along!) before they scroll past.

Notice that the SONG.BAS program contains a chorus that is repeated over and over without modification. Repetitive text like this not only takes time and effort to type in, but it clutters up the program listing, making it more difficult to work with. Is there an easier way to code a program that has repetitive parts?

```
' SONG.BAS
' This program displays the lyrics of the folk song "Clementine."

CLS
PRINT "----------------------- Clementine ------------------------"
PRINT

PRINT "In a cavern, in a canyon,"              ' first verse
PRINT "Excavating for a mine,"
PRINT "Lived a miner, forty-niner,"
PRINT "And his daughter, Clementine."

PRINT
PRINT "Oh my darling, oh my darling,"          ' chorus
PRINT "Oh my darling, Clementine,"
PRINT "You are lost and gone forever,"
PRINT "Dreadful sorry, Clementine."
PRINT

PRINT "Light she was and like a fairy,"        ' second verse
PRINT "And her shoes were number nine;"
PRINT "Herring boxes without topses,"
PRINT "Sandals were for Clementine."

PRINT
PRINT "Oh my darling, oh my darling,"          ' chorus
PRINT "Oh my darling, Clementine,"
PRINT "You are lost and gone forever,"
PRINT "Dreadful sorry, Clementine."
PRINT

INPUT "Press Enter for more...", dummy$        ' pause
PRINT
```

FIGURE 7-1.   *(continued)*

SONG.BAS: A program that prints the lyrics to the song "Clementine" using a series of PRINT statements.

FIGURE 7-1. *continued*

```
PRINT "Drove she ducklings to the water,"      ' third verse
PRINT "Ev'ry morning just at nine;"
PRINT "Hit her foot against a splinter,"
PRINT "Fell into the foaming brine."

PRINT
PRINT "Oh my darling, oh my darling,"          ' chorus
PRINT "Oh my darling, Clementine,"
PRINT "You are lost and gone forever,"
PRINT "Dreadful sorry, Clementine."
PRINT

PRINT "Ruby lips above the water,"             ' fourth verse
PRINT "Blowing bubbles soft and fine;"
PRINT "But alas, he was no swimmer,"
PRINT "So he lost his Clementine."

PRINT
PRINT "Oh my darling, oh my darling,"          ' chorus
PRINT "Oh my darling, Clementine,"
PRINT "You are lost and gone forever,"
PRINT "Dreadful sorry, Clementine."
PRINT

INPUT "Press Enter for more...", dummy$        ' pause
PRINT

PRINT "Then the miner, forty-niner,"           ' fifth verse
PRINT "Soon began to peak and pine;"
PRINT "Thought he oughter join his daughter,"
PRINT "Now he's with his Clementine."

PRINT
PRINT "Oh my darling, oh my darling,"          ' chorus
PRINT "Oh my darling, Clementine,"
PRINT "You are lost and gone forever,"
PRINT "Dreadful sorry, Clementine."
PRINT
```

The Procedure Advantage

The answer is *Yes!* QuickBASIC provides a programming structure called a *procedure* that lets you type a block of statements, assign a name to it, and then call it by name whenever you want it to appear in a program. Procedures provide the following advantages:

- **Procedures eliminate repeated lines.** Procedures can be defined once and executed any number of times.

- **Procedures make programs easier to read.** A program divided into a collection of smaller parts is easier to take apart and understand.

- **Procedures simplify program development.** Programs separated into logical units are easier to design, write, and debug. Plus, if you're writing a program with a friend, you can exchange procedures instead of entire programs.

- **Procedures can be reused in other programs.** General-purpose procedures can be incorporated into other programming projects.

- **Procedures extend the BASIC language.** Procedures can often perform tasks that can't be accomplished directly by built-in QuickBASIC statements and functions.

In this chapter you'll learn to create and use two QuickBASIC procedures: *subprograms* and *functions*. Subprograms let you subdivide your program into smaller units that can be called one or more times. Functions are specifically designed to return a value.

CREATING SUBPROGRAMS

Subprograms both make your code easy to read and reduce repetition. A subprogram is a block of code between SUB and END SUB statements. You can call a subprogram as often as you like in a program. When a subprogram ends, control returns to the statement that follows the subprogram call. In QuickBASIC, you create and store subprograms separately from main programs.

Syntax of a Subprogram

The syntax of a subprogram is as follows:

```
SUB SubprogramName (parameterList)
    local variable and constant declarations
    subprogram statements
END SUB
```

- SUB is the QuickBASIC statement that marks the beginning of the subprogram definition.

- *SubprogramName* is the name of the subprogram. It can be up to 40 characters long and is the name the main program uses to call the subprogram. It can't be a BASIC keyword or be the same as any variable name or procedure name in your program.

- (*parameterList*) is an optional list of variables. (See "Passing Arguments to a Subprogram," later in this chapter.) If you use *parameterList*, you must enclose it in parentheses.

- *local variable and constant declarations* is an optional list of variables and constants declared and used within—and only within—the subprogram. They have no effect on variables or constants with the same name elsewhere in the program.

- *subprogram statements* is the working part of the subprogram. You can use almost any BASIC statements in a subprogram.

- END SUB is the QuickBASIC statement that marks the end of the subprogram definition.

To see how these elements work together, examine the following subprogram named *Chorus*. Every time *Chorus* is executed, it prints a blank line, the four-line chorus to "Clementine," and another blank line.

```
SUB Chorus

' The Chorus subprogram prints the chorus of the song "Clementine."

PRINT
PRINT "Oh my darling, oh my darling,"        ' chorus
```

(continued)

continued

```
PRINT "Oh my darling, Clementine,"
PRINT "You are lost and gone forever,"
PRINT "Dreadful sorry, Clementine."
PRINT

END SUB
```

Creating a Subprogram

In the QuickBASIC Interpreter, menus help you create and work with subprograms quickly and easily. QuickBASIC provides two menu commands for working with subprograms:

- The New SUB command (on the Edit menu)
- The SUBs command (on the View menu)

The New SUB command

The New SUB command is the QuickBASIC menu command you use to add a subprogram to your program. To create a subprogram, you perform the following steps:

1. Select the New SUB command to display the New SUB dialog box.

2. Enter the name of the subprogram (if it isn't already there).

3. Type in the parameters and body of the subprogram.

The SUBs command

You can examine and edit your subprograms by using the SUBs command. Selecting the SUBs command brings up a dialog box from which you select the part of the program you want to work with: the main program, a subprogram, or a function.

 NOTE: The shortcut key for the SUBs command is F2— pressing this key is the fastest way to get to the SUBs dialog box.

Dividing Up a Program

This chapter describes how to organize a program into three self-contained blocks of code: the *main program,* the *subprograms,* and the *functions.* You can have any number of subprograms and functions (collectively called *procedures*) in your program or none at all. Every program, however, must have a main program section that controls the general flow of the program and calls the subprograms and functions.

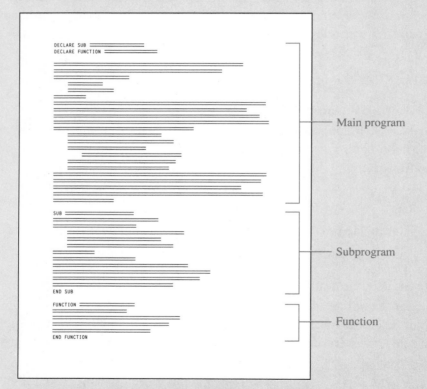

Although it might seem like a little extra work at first, learning to divide your programs into these organizational units will pay off when you start writing longer programs. Remember: No matter how many subprograms and functions a program contains, it is still a single BASIC program.

The DECLARE Statement

One of the advantages of QuickBASIC is that it helps you program properly. For example, based on the information you provide when you create a subprogram, QuickBASIC adds a DECLARE statement to the top of your main program when you save the program on disk. A DECLARE statement *declares* the existence of a subprogram to the main program. Each subprogram must have a corresponding DECLARE statement at the top of the main program.

The syntax for the DECLARE statement is as follows:

```
DECLARE SUB SubprogramName (parameters)
```

SubprogramName is the name of the subprogram, and *parameters* is a list of variables received by the subprogram.

NOTE: Although QuickBASIC generates the DECLARE statement on its own, it's up to you to maintain the parameter list. If you change the parameter list in your subprogram, you must change the parameter list in the DECLARE statement to match. See the section "Passing Arguments to a Subprogram," later in this chapter, for more information.

By convention, DECLARE statements appear after the introductory comments in a program and before constant and variable declarations. In addition, BASIC requires that the DECLARE statements precede any executable statements.

Calling a Subprogram

After you've created and declared a subprogram, you can execute (*call*) it. To call a subprogram, simply specify the subprogram name—along with any arguments the subprogram requires—in the body of the main program or another procedure.

The SONG2.BAS program (Figure 7-2) demonstrates how to declare and call the *Chorus* subprogram. SONG2.BAS is nine lines shorter and is easier to follow than SONG.BAS. Note how the subprogram *Chorus* is set off from the rest of the program starting at line 53 by SUB and END SUB statements. The main program contains five calls to the *Chorus* subprogram. Note also that the *Chorus* subprogram name begins with an uppercase letter—we'll use this convention throughout this book to distinguish procedure names from variable names and from other BASIC statements and functions.

 NOTE: Figure 7-2 contains a listing of the SONG2.BAS program as it would be printed on your printer or listed in a book—not as it appears in the QuickBASIC environment. Remember that inside the QuickBASIC Interpreter all subprograms are separated from the main program and are accessible through the SUBs command on the View menu. To type this program in from scratch, follow the instructions in the next practice session.

```
1   ' SONG2.BAS
2   ' This program displays the lyrics of the folk song "Clementine."
3
4   DECLARE SUB Chorus ()      ' declare Chorus subprogram before use
5
6   CLS
7   PRINT "------------------------ Clementine ------------------------"
8   PRINT
9
10  PRINT "In a cavern, in a canyon,"          ' first verse
11  PRINT "Excavating for a mine,"
12  PRINT "Lived a miner, forty-niner,"
13  PRINT "And his daughter, Clementine."
14
15  Chorus                                     ' call Chorus subprogram
16
17  PRINT "Light she was and like a fairy,"    ' second verse
18  PRINT "And her shoes were number nine;"
19  PRINT "Herring boxes without topses,"
20  PRINT "Sandals were for Clementine."
21
22  Chorus                                     ' call Chorus subprogram
23
```

FIGURE 7-2.   *(continued)*
SONG2.BAS: A program that prints the lyrics to the song "Clementine" using a subprogram named Chorus.

FIGURE 7-2. *continued*

```
24    INPUT "Press Enter for more...", dummy$      ' pause
25    PRINT
26
27    PRINT "Drove she ducklings to the water,"   ' third verse
28    PRINT "Ev'ry morning just at nine;"
29    PRINT "Hit her foot against a splinter,"
30    PRINT "Fell into the foaming brine."
31
32    Chorus                                      ' call Chorus subprogram
33
34    PRINT "Ruby lips above the water,"          ' fourth verse
35    PRINT "Blowing bubbles soft and fine;"
36    PRINT "But alas, he was no swimmer,"
37    PRINT "So he lost his Clementine."
38
39    Chorus                                      ' call Chorus subprogram
40
41    INPUT "Press Enter for more...", dummy$      ' pause
42    PRINT
43
44    PRINT "Then the miner, forty-niner,"        ' fifth verse
45    PRINT "Soon began to peak and pine;"
46    PRINT "Thought he oughter join his daughter,"
47    PRINT "Now he's with his Clementine."
48
49    Chorus                                      ' call Chorus subprogram
50
51    END
52
53    SUB Chorus
54
55    ' The Chorus subprogram prints the chorus of the song "Clementine."
56
57    PRINT
58    PRINT "Oh my darling, oh my darling,"        ' chorus
59    PRINT "Oh my darling, Clementine,"
60    PRINT "You are lost and gone forever,"
61    PRINT "Dreadful sorry, Clementine."
62    PRINT
63
64    END SUB
```

Figure 7-3 provides a detailed look at the *Chorus* subprogram definition and call.

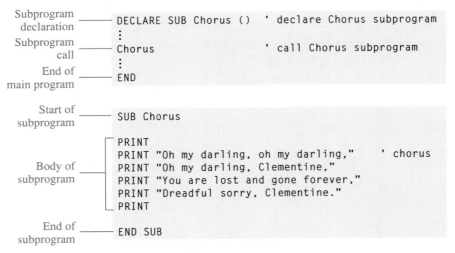

FIGURE 7-3.
The components of a typical subprogram definition and call.

Practice: Entering the SONG2.BAS program

The following exercise walks you through the steps necessary to enter the SONG2.BAS program (Figure 7-2). These steps should be adapted and followed whenever you add a new subprogram to your program.

The END Statement

Throughout this book you'll see an END statement at the end of the main program section when a program contains subprograms or functions. END is an optional instruction that tells BASIC that the last instruction in the program has been reached and that execution should stop. Although the QuickBASIC Interpreter doesn't require the END statement, END is a useful visual clue indicating exactly where the main program section ends.

1. Select New from the File menu to start a new program, and type in lines 6 through 15 of Figure 7-2.

2. Place the cursor on the call to the *Chorus* subprogram (the word "Chorus") and select New SUB from the Edit menu. The following dialog box will appear:

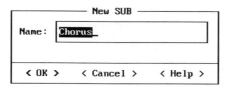

3. If some other name appeared in the New SUB dialog box, or if nothing appeared at all, you could specify a subprogram name by typing it now. The subprogram name you want (*Chorus*) is there now, so press Enter to open a new subprogram window. You'll see the following:

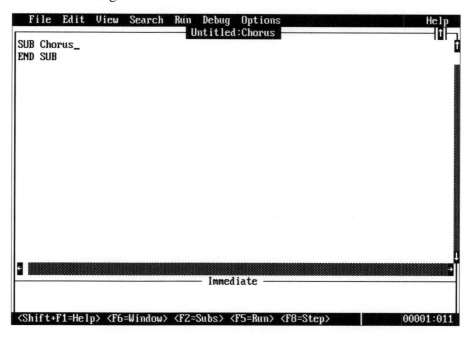

4. There are no parameters to list after the subprogram name, so press Enter to start a new line. Notice that the window title bar now displays the name of the program and the name of the procedure, separated by a colon.

5. Type in the body of the subprogram (lines 54 through 63 of Figure 7-2). Notice that QuickBASIC has added line 64 (the END SUB statement) for you. Your screen should now look like this:

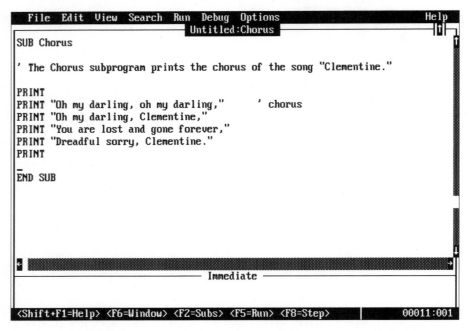

6. Select the SUBs command from the View menu to get a dialog box showing the main program, subprograms, and functions in your program.

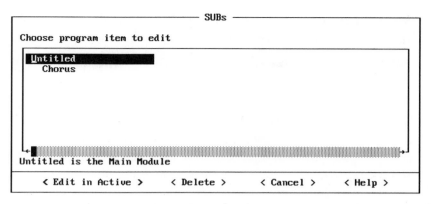

7. Use the direction keys to highlight the main program (currently *Untitled*), and press Enter. QuickBASIC displays the main program in the View window and places the cursor on the line where you left off.

8. Save your program with the name NEWSONG.BAS. (Don't save your program as SONG2.BAS or you might overwrite the copy of SONG2.BAS that is already on your disk.) Before QuickBASIC writes your program to disk, it puts a DECLARE statement at the top of your program (line 4 in Figure 7-2). Your screen should now look like this:

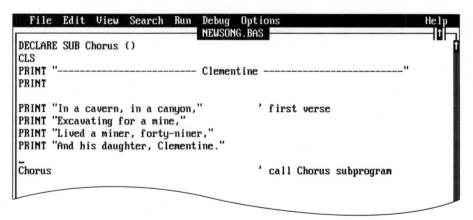

9. Move the cursor below the call to the *Chorus* subprogram and type in the rest of your program (lines 16 through 51 of Figure 7-2).

10. Add lines 1, 2, 3, and 5 to the top of your program and save it again.

After you've followed these steps, run the program by pressing Shift-F5. You should receive three screenfuls of lyrics to the song ''Clementine.'' The output should be identical to that produced by the SONG.BAS program. If your program doesn't run as expected, compare it to Figure 7-2 and fix any discrepancies. If you're still having problems, load and run the SONG2.BAS program from the CHAP07 subdirectory on disk. The SONG2.BAS program is a little longer than the ones we've seen so far in this book, so typing errors might be tougher to find.

This program illustrates a general rule: As the length of your programs increases, it takes a little more time to get them up and running. Don't be dismayed—this is to be expected. You'll learn more about debugging programs and fixing common programming mistakes in Chapter 12.

USING VARIABLES WITH PROCEDURES

The programs you've written so far have used only a handful of variables, but when you write larger programs you may need to start using lots of them. To help you keep track of large numbers of variables, QuickBASIC enforces some special rules that deal with variables in procedures. We'll discuss those rules in this section and introduce the concept of *global* and *local* variables and how variables are *passed* from one procedure to another.

Global and Local Variables

QuickBASIC classifies variables into two groups: *global variables* and *local variables*. Global variables are declared in the main program and change value as dictated by the main program and procedures. Local variables are declared in the main program or in a subprogram or function, but are valid only within the procedure in which they were declared: They are not affected by changes outside their procedure.

These classifications let you use "globally" important variables everywhere in a program at the same time you use variables of lesser importance "locally" in a procedure. And by keeping these two types of variables distinct, you can write more modular code. Because they're self-contained, programs that use local variables are more general purpose than programs that use global variables.

Declaring global variables

To declare global variables, you place a COMMON SHARED statement near the top of the main program. This declaration allows variables to be used and modified anywhere in the main program or procedures. It does not, however, assign values to the variables. Values are assigned later in the program with assignment statements. The syntax for the COMMON SHARED statement is as follows:

```
COMMON SHARED variableList
```

where *variableList* is a list of one or more variables separated by commas. You can declare any number of variables in one COMMON SHARED statement.

Practice: Using global variables

The GLOBAL.BAS program (Figure 7-4) shows how the global variable *game$* is declared in the main program and modified by the *AddGame* subprogram.

Load the GLOBAL.BAS program from disk and run it. You'll receive the following output:

```
    In the main program, game$ = Chess
In the AddGame subprogram, game$ = Chess and backgammon
 Back in the main program, game$ = Chess and backgammon
```

The program shows that any changes made to the global variable *game$* will be reflected throughout the program.

```
' GLOBAL.BAS
' This program demonstrates the use of a global variable.

DECLARE SUB AddGame ()      ' declare AddGame subprogram

COMMON SHARED game$         ' declare game$ as a global variable

game$ = "Chess"             ' initialize game$ with value of "Chess"

CLS

PRINT "     In the main program, game$ = "; game$ ' display in main prog.

AddGame                                          ' display in subprogram

PRINT " Back in the main program, game$ = "; game$ ' display in main prog.

END

SUB AddGame

game$ = game$ + " and backgammon"

PRINT "In the AddGame subprogram, game$ = "; game$

END SUB
```

FIGURE 7-4.

GLOBAL.BAS: A program demonstrating the use of a global variable in a program.

Declaring local variables

Variables are local by default, so you don't have to use any special commands to declare them. Actually you're an old hand at declaring local variables—you've been doing it all along!

Practice: Using local variables

The LOCAL.BAS program (Figure 7-5) removes the COMMON SHARED statement from the GLOBAL.BAS program to demonstrate that a local variable in the main program and a local variable in a subprogram do not interact with each other. Both variables are named *game$*, and both are string variables. Notice that although both local string variables have the same name, they are completely independent of each other.

Load the LOCAL.BAS program and run it. You'll receive the following output:

```
        In the main program, game$ = Chess
In the AddGame subprogram, game$ =  and backgammon
 Back in the main program, game$ = Chess
```

As you can see, the modification of *game$* in the *AddGame* subprogram does not affect the *game$* variable in the main program.

```
' LOCAL.BAS
' This program demonstrates the use of a local variable.

DECLARE SUB AddGame ()      ' declare AddGame subprogram

game$ = "Chess"             ' initialize game$ with value of "Chess"

CLS

PRINT "      In the main program, game$ = "; game$ ' display in main prog.

AddGame                                          ' display in subprogram

PRINT " Back in the main program, game$ = "; game$ ' display in main prog.

END

SUB AddGame

game$ = game$ + " and backgammon"

PRINT "In the AddGame subprogram, game$ = "; game$

END SUB
```

FIGURE 7-5.
LOCAL.BAS: A program demonstrating the use of a local variable in a program.

Passing Arguments to a Subprogram

You can make any number of variables accessible by declaring them globally. Although convenient, this method increases the chances that your variable will be accidentally modified somewhere in the program.

So BASIC provides a way for you to share arguments (such as variables, constants, and results of expressions and functions) with a limited number of subprograms rather than with the entire program. This method of sharing is called *passing arguments*.

Arguments passed to a subprogram are received by *parameters,* which are local variables within a subprogram. You can use these variables exactly like any other variables.

Arguments *vs* parameters

Let's formalize the difference between the terms *argument* and *parameter*:

- **An argument is a constant, a variable, or an expression that is *passed to* a subprogram.** Argument names appear after the subprogram name in a procedure call. A collection of argument names is known as an *argument list.*

- **A parameter is a variable that *receives* a value passed to a subprogram.** Parameter names appear in SUB and DECLARE statements and follow the rules that apply to standard data types. A collection of parameter names is known as a *parameter list.*

Each argument must have a corresponding parameter of the same type (but not necessarily of the same name). Figure 7-6 shows the relationship between an argument list and a parameter list.

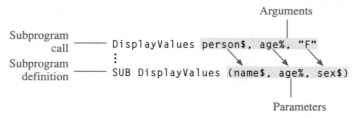

FIGURE 7-6.
The relationship between arguments and parameters.

The following list shows some valid argument-parameter pairs:

```
GetInput name$, number$, address$
  :              ↘      ↘       ↘
SUB GetInput (person$, phone$, address$)

TranslateToNorsk pig$, dog$
  :                  ↘    ↘
SUB TranslateToNorsk (gris$, hund$)

PrintHeader TIME$, DATE$, title$, pageNumber%
  :              ↘     ↘       ↘         ↘
SUB PrintHeader (currentTime$, currentDate$, title$, num%)

MixedCall testInt%, testString$, VALUE!, "Hello", 747
  :              ↘     ↙    ↙     ↙        ↙
SUB MixedCall (a%, b$, c!, d$, e%)
```

Modifying arguments

Passing arguments to a subprogram is not a one-way street. Any value that a subprogram assigns to a parameter is passed back to the matching argument when the subprogram is finished.

Let's use Figure 7-6 as an example: If *person$* contained the value *Elisabeth* at the time the program called *DisplayValues*, the parameter *name$* would receive that value.

If the subprogram then assigned the value *Vivienne* to *name$*, that value would be assigned to *person$* upon completion of the subprogram.

Keep in mind, however, that constants and expressions are inherently constant: Their values can't change. In Figure 7-6, for example, even if the *DisplayValues* subprogram modified the value of *sex$*, nothing would happen to the matching argument (*"F"*).

Practice: Passing arguments to a subprogram

The ARGUMENT.BAS program (Figure 7-7) demonstrates how two arguments are passed to the *AddInterest* subprogram. The *monthName$* parameter receives the *month$* argument, and the *amount!* parameter receives the *balance!* argument. The *AddInterest* subprogram then changes the month, multiplies the value of *amount!* by 1.05, and returns both values to the main program.

```
' ARGUMENT.BAS
' This program demonstrates passing arguments to a subprogram.

DECLARE SUB AddInterest (monthName$, amount!)

month$ = "January"                ' initialize month$ with value
                                  '    of "January"
balance! = 1500                   ' initialize balance! with value of 1500

CLS

PRINT "Before subprogram:"        ' display original values
PRINT "  month$ = "; month$
PRINT "  balance! ="; balance!
PRINT

AddInterest month$, balance!      ' call subprogram to modify values

PRINT "After subprogram:"         ' display modified values
PRINT "  month$ = "; month$
PRINT "  balance! ="; balance!

END

SUB AddInterest (monthName$, amount!)

monthName$ = "February"           ' change name of month
amount! = amount! * 1.05          ' add 5% to amount

END SUB
```

FIGURE 7-7.
ARGUMENT.BAS: A program demonstrating how to pass arguments to a subprogram.

Load the ARGUMENT.BAS program from disk and run it. You'll receive the following output:

```
Before subprogram:
  month$ = January
  balance! = 1500
```

(continued)

continued

```
After subprogram:
  month$ = February
  balance! = 1575
```

Both *month$* and *balance!* were modified without the use of global variables.

CREATING FUNCTIONS

A function is a block of code placed between FUNCTION and END FUNCTION statements. Functions follow the same general rules as subprograms, with one important exception: A function performs a task and returns a value to the main program or calling procedure. You use a function the same way you use BASIC's built-in functions—by including it in a BASIC statement. In this section you'll learn how to create your own functions—called *user-defined functions*—with QuickBASIC.

Syntax of a Function

The syntax of a function is as follows:

```
FUNCTION FunctionName (parameterList)
    local variable and constant declarations
    function statements
    FunctionName = returnValue
END FUNCTION
```

- FUNCTION is the QuickBASIC statement that marks the beginning of the function definition.

- *FunctionName* is the name of the function and must end with a type declaration character (just like a variable name). It can be up to 40 characters long and is the name used to call the function. It can't be a BASIC keyword or the same as any variable name or procedure name in your program.

- (*parameterList*) is an optional list of variables.

- *local variable and constant declarations* is an optional list of variables and constants declared and used within the function. They have no effect on variables or constants with the same name elsewhere in the program.

- *function statements* is the working part of the function. You can use almost any BASIC statements in a function.

- *FunctionName = returnValue* is an assignment statement in the body of the function (usually near the end) that sets the return value of the function. *returnValue* can be a simple variable or the result of an expression or another function. *FunctionName* and *returnValue* must be of the same type.

- END FUNCTION is the QuickBASIC statement that marks the end of the function definition.

To see how these elements work together, examine the following call, which passes three integer arguments and returns an integer value that is assigned to the *number%* variable:

```
number% = SumOfTerms%(a%, b%, c%)
```

Note that the function name *SumOfTerms%* contains an integer type-declaration character that matches the integer type-declaration character in *number%*. User-defined functions return a value in one of the five BASIC data types: string, integer, long integer, single-precision floating-point, or double-precision floating-point.

Creating a Function

Creating a user-defined function is quite similar to creating a subprogram:

1. Enter the function using the New Function command from the Edit menu, just as you used the New SUB command to enter a subprogram earlier in the chapter.

2. Examine and edit your functions by using the SUBs command from the View menu. All of your subprograms and functions will be listed together in the SUBs dialog box.

Practice: Using a user-defined function

The AVERAGE.BAS program (Figure 7-8) demonstrates several of the elements of user-defined functions in the declaration of a function named *Average!*. *Average!* is designed to return the average of three integer parameters passed to the function. After the QuickBASIC Interpreter executes the *Average!* function, the *Average!* name represents a single-precision floating-point value in the main program that can be assigned to a floating-point variable or displayed with a PRINT statement.

```
' AVERAGE.BAS
' This program prints the average of three numbers.

DECLARE FUNCTION Average! (int1%, int2%, int3%)    ' declare function

CLS

PRINT "Enter three integers to be averaged together."
PRINT
INPUT "    First integer:  ", first%
INPUT "    Second integer:  ", second%
INPUT "    Third integer:  ", third%

PRINT
PRINT "The average is"; Average!(first%, second%, third%)

END

FUNCTION Average! (int1%, int2%, int3%)

sum% = int1% + int2% + int3%     ' sum of arguments

Average! = sum% / 3                  ' return value is average of arguments

END FUNCTION
```

FIGURE 7-8.
AVERAGE.BAS: A program that prints the value returned by a function.

Load the AVERAGE.BAS program from disk and run it. You'll receive output similar to the following:

```
Enter three integers to be averaged together.

    First integer:  10
    Second integer: 20
    Third integer:  50

The average is 26.66667
```

Similarities to Subprograms

Functions have a number of characteristics in common with subprograms:

- A function call contains the same number of arguments as are present in the function parameter list.

- A function parameter list receives values passed from the main program or calling procedure and assigns them variable names so that they can be used in the body of the function.

- Functions can declare and use local variables and constants.

- Functions are declared near the top of the main program with DECLARE statements that are automatically generated by QuickBASIC.

- Functions are stored separately in the QuickBASIC environment and are accessible through the SUBs command on the View menu.

- Functions aid in modularizing your programs and avoiding repeated program code by placing often-used routines in easy-to-use modules.

WHICH SHOULD YOU USE?

By now you may be thinking that subprograms and functions are pretty much the same. After all, both subprograms and functions are flexible programming structures that can handle a variety of tasks and return one or more values to the calling module. What, then, are the real differences between subprograms and functions, and which should you use in a given programming situation?

Subprograms Are Miniprograms

Think of a subprogram as a small, self-contained program. Subprograms should complete the important tasks of a program, yet be general purpose enough to be used in other programming projects. Subprograms are often longer than functions, and are usually used when information is displayed on the screen. The following tasks are often best suited to subprograms:

- Getting input from the user
- Displaying information on the screen
- Processing several numeric values or strings
- Drawing graphic shapes and designs
- Playing musical notes or songs
- Returning multiple values to the calling module

Functions Return a Value

Functions excel in calculating and returning a single value to the main program; they are not designed to return multiple values or execute general tasks. The following tasks are often best suited for functions:

- Performing a numeric calculation
- Returning a string value
- Generating a random number
- Converting one value to another
- Evaluating logical expressions and returning a value of true or false
- Calculating one result from several arguments

The Main Program Handles Declaration and Control

What tasks are left for the main program to handle? Actually, not many if you make thorough use of subprograms and functions. The following tasks are often best suited to the main program:

- Introductory comments and explanations
- Initialization of key variables and structures

- Program code that is executed only once
- Flow-control structures that determine the path of program execution

The following declarations *must* be included in the main program if they appear in a program:

- Global variable and constant declarations
- Subprogram and function declarations

Now that you've learned about the main program, subprograms, and functions, you're ready to start writing well-organized and modular programs.

THE BOWLING.BAS PROGRAM

This section introduces a longer, more interesting program that puts together much of what we've learned in the last six chapters:

- Managing variables
- Controlling program flow
- Looping
- Working with procedures
- Working with color and sound

Although this program is quite long (almost 350 lines!), it gives you an idea of what you can really *do* with the QuickBASIC Interpreter. It also demonstrates QuickBASIC's ability to handle a number of separate procedures.

Practice: Running the BOWLING.BAS program

Load the BOWLING.BAS program from disk. When the program has been loaded, run it by pressing Shift-F5. You'll see the following on your screen.

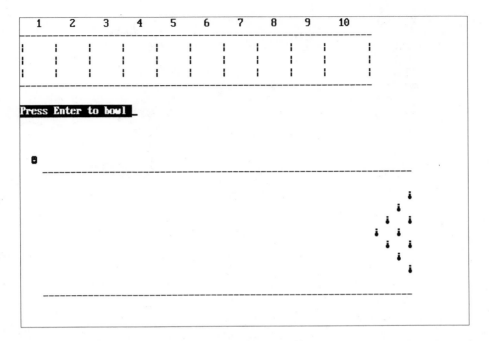

The BOWLING.BAS program is a simple 10-pin bowling game that makes use of a random-number generator, sound, and text-based graphics to simulate a 10-frame game. Play the game by pressing Enter as indicated by the prompt. Each time you bowl a new ball the program throws the ball down the lane for you, counts up the pins that fall, updates the running total on the scoreboard, and returns the ball to you. Each game is completely random, so each time you play you'll get different results. (To stop the program before the game is finished, press Ctrl-Break.) Just as in regular bowling, if you get a spare or a strike you get one or two extra balls added to your score. When you finish a game, your screen will show output similar to that on the following page.

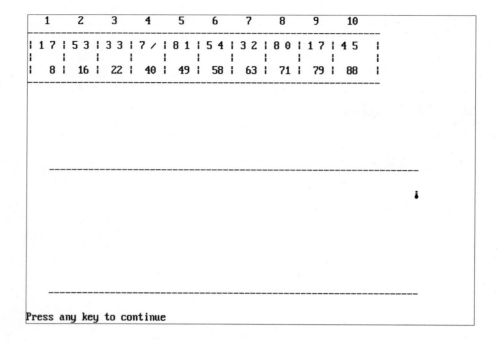

```
       1      2      3      4      5      6      7      8      9     10
     ------------------------------------------------------------------
   ¦ 1 7 ¦ 5 3 ¦ 3 3 ¦ 7 / ¦ 8 1 ¦ 5 4 ¦ 3 2 ¦ 8 0 ¦ 1 7 ¦ 4 5     ¦
   ¦     ¦     ¦     ¦     ¦     ¦     ¦     ¦     ¦     ¦           ¦
   ¦   8 ¦  16 ¦  22 ¦  40 ¦  49 ¦  58 ¦  63 ¦  71 ¦  79 ¦  88      ¦
     ------------------------------------------------------------------




             ----------------------------------------------------------

                                                                    ¡




             ----------------------------------------------------------
   Press any key to continue
```

Looking at the BOWLING.BAS Program

After you've played one or more games, take a few minutes to examine the organization of the program. (Because of its length, BOWLING.BAS does not appear in this book.) BOWLING.BAS contains seven subprograms and one function. Each subprogram is declared with a DECLARE statement near the top of the program and is accessible through the SUBs command on the View menu. The majority of the processing in BOWLING.BAS takes place in IF statements—comments are included next to each of these structures that spell out exactly what they do.

Two new statements appear in the BOWLING.BAS program: LOCATE and PRINT USING. LOCATE places the cursor at a specific row and column position on the screen in preparation for a PRINT statement. LOCATE is used often in text-based graphics programs to assist in drawing objects or character strings in different places on the screen. We'll discuss LOCATE in detail in Chapter 11.

PRINT USING is used with a string called a *template* to display a formatted pattern of characters on the screen. In the BOWLING.BAS program, the template string is named *score$* and is used with PRINT USING to print the running score in each frame of the scoreboard. We'll discuss PRINT USING in detail in Chapter 8.

Practice: Stepping through BOWLING.BAS

To give you a feeling for how QuickBASIC executes a program with many procedures, the following exercise steps through the execution of the BOWLING.BAS program using the following commands from the Debug, Run, and View menus:

Command	*Menu*	*Key*	*Purpose*
Step	Debug	F8	Execute highlighted statement
Procedure Step	Debug	F10	Execute highlighted procedure
Continue	Run	F5	Run program from highlighted statement
Output Screen	View	F4	View contents of output screen

Use these four commands whenever you want to examine the flow of a program in detail. We'll discuss them again in Chapter 12 when we learn how to track down bugs in a program. For now, appreciate how these commands give us an inside look at how procedures are called and processed in QuickBASIC.

Load the BOWLING.BAS program into the QuickBASIC Interpreter again and carry out the following steps:

1. Press the F8 key. QuickBASIC highlights the COMMON SHARED statement, the first statement in your program that will be executed. The lines above COMMON SHARED are nonexecutable comments and procedure declarations.

2. Slowly press F8 five times. QuickBASIC executes the next five executable statements in BOWLING.BAS. The fifth statement (ScoreCard) is a call to the *ScoreCard* subprogram. When QuickBASIC executes that statement it goes directly to the *ScoreCard* subprogram, where it highlights the first executable statement (COLOR 3).

Using the Split Command

The Split command on the View menu lets you view two locations in your program at once. This is particularly useful when your program has many subprograms and functions and you'd like to edit one procedure while looking at another. The following is a list of steps you should follow when you use the Split command. Because you can use the Split command in a a number of different ways, you should experiment with Split to see which you like best.

1. Select the Split command from the View menu. The View window will split horizontally into two windows. The upper window, containing the cursor, will be the active window.

2. If you need to make edits in the upper window, scroll to the correct location and make the edits. If both View windows contain the same part of the program, the edits you make in the upper View window will be reflected in the lower View window as soon as you move the cursor off the line you've edited.

3. Press F6 to make the lower View window the active window (or click on it with the mouse). If you would like to move to the upper window again, press F6 twice (or click on the window with the mouse).

4. If you want to place the contents of a procedure into one of the split windows, select the window you want to put the procedure in, press F2 to view the list of procedures, and select the procedure you want to load.

5. When you've finished using split windows, select the Split command from the View menu to switch back to one View window. The active split window will become the active single window.

3. Slowly press F8 12 times. QuickBASIC executes the statements in the *ScoreCard* subprogram one at a time until the last statement (END SUB) is highlighted.

4. Press F4. QuickBASIC displays the contents of the output screen. Because you just executed the eight PRINT statements in the *ScoreCard* subprogram, you should see a blank scorecard and the two sides of the lane. Press Enter to return to the QuickBASIC View window.

5. Press F8. QuickBASIC executes the last statement in the *ScoreCard* subprogram and returns to the main program. A call to the *DrawPins* subprogram is now highlighted.

6. Press F10. QuickBASIC executes the entire *DrawPins* subprogram and highlights the next statement in the main program. Press F4 to verify that *DrawPins* has displayed 10 pins on the screen, and press Enter to return.

7. Press F5. QuickBASIC continues execution of the program. Continue playing the game to the end or press Ctrl-Break to stop the program in midstream. If you do press Ctrl-Break, notice that the last QuickBASIC statement executed is highlighted. You can continue program execution from this point if you want to by pressing F8 (to step) or F5 (to run), or you can select the Exit command from the File menu to quit QuickBASIC.

SUMMARY

This chapter introduced subprograms and functions—two programming structures that prevent repetition and extend the BASIC language. Subprograms are defined between SUB and END SUB statements, and functions are defined between FUNCTION and END FUNCTION statements. Both kinds of procedures are entered and tracked using the QuickBASIC menu system. Both procedure types support local variables and the exchange of arguments from the calling module. Subprograms and functions, combined with the flow-control and looping structures we discussed in Chapters 5 and 6, make up a complete collection of tools that can be used to write structured, well-organized programs.

QUESTIONS AND EXERCISES

1. Which of the following are advantages to programming with procedures?

    a. Procedures can be called any number of times.

    b. Procedures let you create your own statements and functions.

    c. Procedures make program development easier.

    d. General-purpose procedures can be incorporated into other programming projects.

2. What is wrong with the following SUB statement?

    ```
    SUB EnterName$ (firstName$, lastName$)
    ```

3. What is the shortcut key for the SUBs command on the View menu?

4. What menu command can you use to execute an entire procedure in one step?

5. Write a QuickBASIC statement that declares a global variable named *total%*.

6. What is the difference between a subprogram and a function?

7. Write a subprogram named *GetCarFacts* that prompts the user for the make, model, year, and color of an automobile and returns this information to the main program in four variables. When you've finished, write a statement that calls the *GetCarFacts* subprogram.

8. Write a function named *FindLarger%* that accepts two integer arguments and returns the larger one to the calling module. When you've finished, write a statement that calls the *FindLarger%* function.

9. Write a program that uses subprograms to print a collection of characters arranged to form one of three shapes: a line, a rectangle, or a triangle. When you run the program, it should produce output similar to the following.

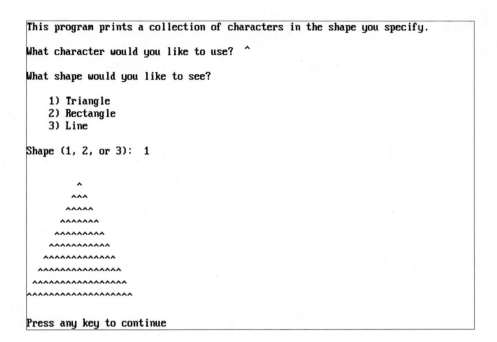

```
This program prints a collection of characters in the shape you specify.

What character would you like to use?  ^

What shape would you like to see?

    1) Triangle
    2) Rectangle
    3) Line

Shape (1, 2, or 3):  1


             ^
            ^^^
           ^^^^^
          ^^^^^^^
         ^^^^^^^^^
        ^^^^^^^^^^^
       ^^^^^^^^^^^^^
      ^^^^^^^^^^^^^^^
     ^^^^^^^^^^^^^^^^^
    ^^^^^^^^^^^^^^^^^^^


Press any key to continue
```

Working with Large Amounts of Data

Now that you've learned how to work with both simple data types and variables, it's time for you to expand your knowledge—to learn how QuickBASIC deals with larger amounts of data in a program. By using the skills you learn in this chapter, you'll be able to create data structures—collections of individual data items—that help you organize large amounts of information and speed up operations involving many variables.

STORING AND RETRIEVING INFORMATION

You've learned three ways to store values in a program:

- By assigning values to a constant:

  ```
  CONST PRICE! = 12.95
  ```

- By assigning values to a variable:

  ```
  firstName$ = "Duncan"
  ```

- By assigning values to a variable with INPUT:

  ```
  INPUT "Enter number of home runs:  ", homers%
  ```

These are all single values. But what if you have many values—values that you plan to use repeatedly, in a specific order? That's when the DATA and READ statements come in handy.

Using the DATA and READ Statements

The DATA and READ statements work together to let you store and retrieve information within a program. Values are first stored in one or more DATA statements and are then assigned to variables with one or more READ statements. Use the DATA and READ statements as follows:

```
READ variableList
DATA constantList
```

variableList is a list of one or more variables separated by commas and *constantList* is a list of one or more numeric or string values separated by commas. Each value in the DATA statement must have a corresponding variable of the proper type in the READ statement. For example, the following is a valid pair of DATA and READ statements. Note how the values appear in the same order as the variables.

```
READ name$, age%  ◄───┐
     ▲                │
DATA Beaver Cleaver, 9
```

A simple example best demonstrates how DATA and READ work together. In the following program, the READ statement assigns the first DATA value to the string variable *name$* and the second DATA value to the integer variable *age%*. The PRINT statement then makes use of the variables.

```
READ name$, age%
PRINT name$; " is"; age%; "years old."
DATA Beaver Cleaver, 9
```

When you run this program, your output screen displays the following result:

```
Beaver Cleaver is 9 years old.
```

Figure 8-1 shows how data values are assigned to variables.

```
READ name$, age%  ◄───┐
PRINT▲name$; " is"; age%; "years old."
DATA Beaver Cleaver, 9
```

FIGURE 8-1.
Values stored in a DATA statement are assigned to variables with a READ statement.

DATA and READ statements: Helpful hints

Keep the following points in mind as you begin to use the DATA and READ statements to store and retrieve information:

■ You can create multiple DATA and READ statements; just be sure that each READ variable has a matching DATA value, as follows:

```
READ month$, numberOfDays%
READ holidays%

DATA November
DATA 30, 3
```

■ If a value in the DATA statement contains a comma, a colon, or significant trailing or leading spaces, the entire value must be enclosed in quotation marks, as follows:

```
DATA "    Leading spaces", "Address, City"
```

■ DATA statements must appear within the main program. (They are commonly placed at the bottom of the main program.) READ statements must be located *above* DATA statements in the main program, but they can appear anywhere in any of the program's procedures.

What if the types don't match?

Each value in a DATA statement must be assigned to a corresponding variable of the proper type in a READ statement. If the types don't match, QuickBASIC makes the following conversions:

If DATA value is	But READ variable is	Conversion result is
string	integer/floating-point	syntax error
integer/floating-point	string	string
integer	floating-point	floating-point
floating-point	integer	round to integer

A syntax error is indicated by the following dialog box:

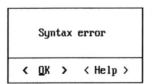

```
 ┌─────────────────────────┐
 │                         │
 │   Syntax error          │
 │                         │
 ├─────────────────────────┤
 │  < OK >    < Help >      │
 └─────────────────────────┘
```

The following program demonstrates a type mismatch between a string DATA value and an integer READ variable.

```
READ name$
PRINT "Name:   "; name$
READ address$
PRINT "Address:  "; address$
READ age%
PRINT "Age:  "; age%

DATA Beaver Cleaver, "211 Pine Street, Mayfield", nine
```

When you run the program, your output screen briefly displays the following result:

```
Name:  Beaver Cleaver
Address:  211 Pine Street, Mayfield
```

The *Syntax error* message then appears because the READ statement cannot assign a string value (*nine*) to an integer variable (*age%*). To fix the program, change *nine* to *9* to accommodate the integer variable *age%*, or change *age%* to *age$* to accommodate the string value *nine*.

Typical DATA Statement Values

DATA and READ statements are most appropriate when you know the value of the variables ahead of time and if you know that the values will always appear in the same order. The following values are tailor-made for the DATA/READ method of storage and retrieval:

- Days of the week (Sunday through Saturday)
- Months of the year (January through December)
- Names of persons, places, or organizations
- Numeric data for calculation or analysis
- Numeric values for musical notes

Practice: Storing several values

The ADDTHEM.BAS program (Figure 8-2) shows how to use a READ statement within a FOR loop to assign several DATA values to variables. Note that the integer constant *ITEMS%* controls the number of items read from the DATA statements. By changing *ITEMS%* you can change the number of items read.

1. Load the ADDTHEM.BAS program from the CHAP08 subdirectory on disk and run it.

```
' ADDTHEM.BAS
' This program reads and adds values stored in DATA statements.

CONST ITEMS% = 20                ' set the number of items to be read

CLS

FOR i% = 1 TO ITEMS%             ' for each item to be read
    READ number!                 '   assign the next DATA item to number!
    sum! = sum! + number!        '   add the item to the running total
NEXT i%

PRINT "The sum of the"; ITEMS%; "numbers is"; sum!

DATA 1, 2, 3, 4, 5, 6, 7, 8, 9, 10
DATA 88.2, 25, 3.3, 100, -74.2, 0, 20, 0.34, -89, 5.4567
```

FIGURE 8-2.
ADDTHEM.BAS: A program that uses READ to assign 20 data items to variables.

Your output screen displays the following result:

```
The sum of the 20 numbers is 134.0967
```

2. Change the value of the *ITEMS%* constant to *4* and run the program again. Your output screen displays the following result:

```
The sum of the 4 numbers is 10
```

The end-of-data marker

Unless your program can identify the last DATA value, it might keep executing READ statements—trying to assign a value to a variable. The result is the following error message, which indicates that no more data is available for assignment:

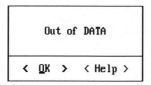

To prevent this error, use an *end-of-data marker* as the final entry in your final DATA statement. The end-of-data marker is a value that your program tests against to determine the end of the DATA values. When it reads this final value, it moves on to execute the rest of the program. This technique is useful when you have a long list of values in DATA statements that will be processed only once. The ADDTHEM.BAS program works around this potential problem by using a constant containing the exact number of values as the upper limit for the FOR loop. Many times you won't have such a luxury. In the following program ADDTHEM.BAS is revised to check for an end-of-data marker.

Tracking DATA Values: The Data Pointer

To help the READ statement assign values to variables, QuickBASIC uses a *data pointer* to point to the next DATA statement value to be assigned. When a program begins, the data pointer points to the first value in the first DATA statement. As program execution continues, and as DATA values are assigned, the data pointer points to the next unassigned DATA statement value.

Practice: Checking for an end-of-data marker

The ADDTHEM2.BAS program (Figure 8-3) uses an end-of-data marker (−9999) to represent the last DATA entry in the program. Load the ADDTHEM2.BAS program from disk and run it.

```
' ADDTHEM2.BAS
' This program reads and adds values stored in DATA statements
'   until an end-of-data marker (-9999) is detected.

CLS

DO WHILE (number! <> -9999)        ' loop until end-of-data marker read
    READ number!                   ' assign next DATA item to number!
    IF (number! <> -9999) THEN     ' if not end-of-data marker then
        sum! = sum! + number!      '   keep a running total
        items% = items% + 1        '   count the number of values read
    END IF
LOOP

PRINT "The sum of the"; items%; "numbers is"; sum!

DATA 1, 2, 3, 4, 5, 6, 7, 8, 9, 10
DATA 88.2, 25, 3.3, 100, -74.2, 0, 20, 0.34, -89, 5.4567
DATA -9999
```

FIGURE 8-3.
ADDTHEM2.BAS: A program that reads data until an end-of-data marker is reached.

Your output screen displays the following result:

```
The sum of the 20 numbers is 134.0967
```

Rereading DATA values with the RESTORE statement

At times you might want to read repeatedly through the list of DATA values in a program. (For example, you might want to perform a number of different calculations on the same set of values.) At the point where you want to return to the first DATA value, use the RESTORE statement, which resets the data pointer to the first DATA statement value in the program. You can use RESTORE as often as you like in a program.

The RESTORE statement has the following syntax:

```
RESTORE
```

 Practice: Using RESTORE to repeat a list of values
The TVHOURS.BAS program (Figure 8-4) uses RESTORE, DATA, and READ to track how many hours a person watches television during a three-week period. A pair of nested FOR loops cycles through each day of the week three times (to simulate three weeks), tracking the total number of viewing hours. The RESTORE statement at the end of each cycle returns the data pointer to Monday.

NOTE: To brighten up the output screen, the COLOR statement displays the total number of viewing hours in flashing red. You will see this only if you have a color monitor.

1. Load the TVHOURS.BAS program from disk and run it.
    You receive three sets of input prompts similar to the following:

```
How many hours of TV did you watch during the last 3 weeks?

Monday, Week 1 --> 0
Tuesday, Week 1 --> 1
Wednesday, Week 1 --> 0
Thursday, Week 1 --> 2
Friday, Week 1 --> 0
Saturday, Week 1 --> 2.5
Sunday, Week 1 --> 2
```

2. Respond to the prompts. After you enter all 21 values, the output screen displays the final result, which appears in the following form:

```
You watched 23.5 hours of television during the last three weeks!
```

Now that you've learned how to store and retrieve large numbers of values in your program, it's time to learn an efficient way to work with them. The following section introduces the *array,* a powerful structure that can help you handle large amounts of data of the same type.

```
' TVHOURS.BAS
' This program uses DATA, READ, and RESTORE statements to track
'    the number of TV hours viewed over a three-week time period.

CLS

PRINT "How many hours of TV did you watch during the last 3 weeks?"
PRINT

FOR i% = 1 TO 3        ' for each of the last 3 weeks
    FOR j% = 1 TO 7    '   and for each day in the week
        READ day$                  ' read day name from DATA list
        PRINT day$; ", Week"; i%;  ' prompt with day and week
        INPUT "--> ", hours!       ' get TV hours for that day
        totalHours! = totalHours! + hours!   ' total all the hours
    NEXT j%
    PRINT              ' print a blank line after each week
    RESTORE            ' move data pointer to Monday for next iteration
NEXT i%

PRINT "You watched";                ' display total number of hours
COLOR 20                            '    in blinking red for fun
PRINT totalHours!; "hours";
COLOR 7                             ' return foreground color to white
PRINT " of television during the last three weeks!"

DATA Monday, Tuesday, Wednesday, Thursday, Friday, Saturday, Sunday
```

FIGURE 8-4.
TVHOURS.BAS: A program demonstrating the RESTORE statement.

WORKING WITH ARRAYS

When you want to organize variables of the same type under one name, use an array. Much as an egg carton organizes a number of individual eggs, an array lets you group many values under one name.

An array can contain any one of the data types you've worked with so far in this book; that is, you can have

- String arrays
- Integer arrays

- Long integer arrays
- Single-precision floating-point arrays
- Double-precision floating-point arrays

You cannot mix types within an array; that is, a string array can contain only strings, an integer array can contain only integers, and so on.

Let's look at an example that organizes data into three types of arrays: string arrays, integer arrays, and single-precision floating-point arrays.

Tracking Information with Arrays: Erin's Bike Market

Erin's Bike Market, a large downtown bicycle shop, has a staff of seven salespersons. Erin wants to track two values every month:

- The number of bikes sold by each salesperson
- The number of dollars brought in by each salesperson

When she writes down this information, it falls naturally into three lists, as shown in Figure 8-5:

Salesperson	Bikes sold	Total sales
Megan	6	$ 1350.12
Eric	5	$ 1578.55
Ron	12	$ 2343.84
Mary Ann	7	$ 1256.36
Barbara	11	$ 2613.79
Jack	2	$ 489.00
Nancy	5	$ 1356.03

FIGURE 8-5.
A sample of salesperson data at Erin's Bike Market.

- A list of string values (salespersons' names)
- A list of integer values (bicycle sales for each salesperson)
- A list of floating-point values (total dollar sales for each salesperson)

By making these lists, Erin has already worked with arrays. In fact, she has created three of them: a string array for the salespersons' names, an integer array for the number of bicycle sales, and a single-precision floating-point array for the total dollar sales. Each list, with its distinct type of information, qualifies as an array. And each array contains seven *elements,* or individual values. Now that Erin has organized her arrays on paper, she can begin to convert them into a program with the help of the DIM statement.

The DIM Statement: Making Reservations for Your Array

When you make a reservation at a restaurant, you provide particular information in exchange for a guaranteed table. That is, by giving your name, specifying which meal you intend to eat (breakfast, lunch, or dinner), and indicating the number of people in your party, you ensure that space is available for you. Well, in the world of arrays, the DIM statement serves the same purpose as a reservation. It provides you with memory space for an array—and all it asks in return is three pieces of information:

- The name you've selected for the array
- The type of data you plan to store in the array
- The maximum number of elements the array will contain

This process of space allocation is called *dimensioning.*

The DIM statement has the following syntax:

```
DIM arrayName(subscript)
```

arrayName is the name you select for the array and *subscript* is the maximum number of elements in the array. The final character of *arrayName* must be the type-declaration character that identifies the data type of the array: *$* for strings, *%* for integers, *&* for long integers, *!* for single-precision floating-point numbers, or *#* for double-precision floating-point numbers.

For example, examine the following DIM statement, which dimensions a string array that can contain up to 50 elements numbered 0 through 49:

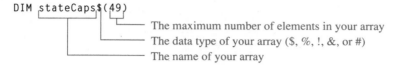

```
DIM stateCaps$(49)
```
— The maximum number of elements in your array
— The data type of your array ($, %, !, &, or #)
— The name of your array

When you execute this DIM statement, BASIC reserves memory space for a 50-element array to contain the names of the state capitals.

> *NOTE: A typical computer has room for many arrays, each containing thousands of elements. But because computer memory is not unlimited, you shouldn't set aside more array elements than you think you'll need.*

Erin, for example, would create the three arrays she needs by using these DIM statements:

■ For the names of the salespersons, a seven-element string array called *salesGroup$*:

```
DIM salesGroup$(6)
```

■ For the number of bicycles sold, a seven-element integer array called *bikesSold%*:

```
DIM bikesSold%(6)
```

■ For the total sales per salesperson, a seven-element floating-point array called *totalSales!*:

```
DIM totalSales!(6)
```

Note that in all three arrays the number 6 sets aside memory space for seven elements numbered 0 through 6.

Each element in the array is associated with a number. By default, QuickBASIC associates the first element of an array with the number 0, the second element of an array with the number 1, and so on for each element of the array, as shown in Figure 8-6.

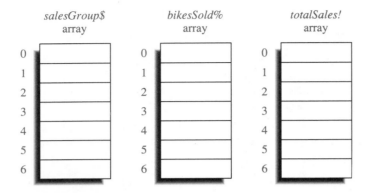

FIGURE 8-6.
Each element of a dimensioned array is associated with a number.

Working with Array Elements

Once you've dimensioned an array with the DIM statement, it's easy to refer to any of the elements within the array. To reference an element of an array, you use the array name and an array *index* surrounded by parentheses. The index must be an integer value; for example, it can be a simple number or an integer variable. The following statement assigns the string value *Tomato* to element 3 in the *shoppingList$* array:

```
shoppingList$(3) = "Tomato"
```

The OPTION BASE Statement

If you think your program would be clearer conceptually if the first element in each array were 1 instead of 0, use the OPTION BASE statement. The OPTION BASE statement associates the first element—or *base*—of all arrays in a program with the number 1. To use OPTION BASE, simply place the following statement near the top of your program, before any DIM statements:

```
OPTION BASE 1
```

The programs throughout this chapter use the OPTION BASE statement this way.

Practice: Storing values in an array

The GETNAMES.BAS program (Figure 8-7) demonstrates how information is stored in an array and printed out using two FOR loops. GETNAMES uses the constant PERSONS% to hold the number of salespersons in Erin's bicycle shop and OPTION BASE to make the first element of all arrays in the program number 1 instead of 0.

Load the GETNAMES.BAS program from disk and run it.

```
' GETNAMES.BAS
' This program reads string information into an array.

CONST PERSONS% = 7          ' number of salespersons
OPTION BASE 1               ' set base of all arrays to 1

DIM salesGroup$(PERSONS%)   ' dimension salesGroup$ string array

CLS

FOR i% = 1 TO PERSONS%      ' use i% to access array elements
    INPUT "Enter salesperson name: ", salesGroup$(i%)
NEXT i%

PRINT
PRINT "You entered the following names:"
PRINT

FOR i% = 1 TO PERSONS%      ' print entire contents of array
    PRINT salesGroup$(i%)
NEXT i%
```

FIGURE 8-7.
GETNAMES.BAS: A program demonstrating loading and printing an array.

You'll be prompted to supply names for the salespeople. You'll receive output similar to the following:

```
Enter salesperson name:  Megan
Enter salesperson name:  Eric
Enter salesperson name:  Ron
Enter salesperson name:  Mary Ann
```

(continued)

Formatting Your Output:
The PRINT USING Statement

The PRINT USING statement lets you design how you want your output to appear on the screen. PRINT USING is particularly helpful if you need to display large amounts of data in tabular form. To create the design you want, you use a *template* string. The syntax for the PRINT USING statement is as follows:

```
PRINT USING template; argumentList
```

template is a string and *argumentList* is a collection of one or more values to be displayed, separated by semicolons. *template* specifies how the values in *argumentList* should be displayed. The formatting characters in *template* must match up one for one with the characters of the values in *argumentList*. The following table describes a few of the useful formatting characters that can be included in *template*:

Character(s)	Description
#	Represents one digit of a numeric value
.	Represents the decimal point in a numeric value
$$	Cause a dollar sign to be displayed with a number
\ \	Represent one or more spaces that can be filled with string data

The following program creates a formatting template named *tmp$* and uses it in a PRINT USING statement to display a string variable and a dollars-and-cents floating-point value:

```
tmp$ = "Name: \          \ Payment: $$####.##"
name$ = "Duncan Hund"
payment! = 2496.33
PRINT USING tmp$; name$; payment!
```

When you execute the statements you receive the following output:

```
Name:  Duncan Hund      Payment:  $2496.33
```

continued

```
Enter salesperson name:  Barbara
Enter salesperson name:  Jack
Enter salesperson name:  Nancy

You entered the following names:

Megan
Eric
Ron
Mary Ann
Barbara
Jack
Nancy
```

Practice: Using multiple arrays in a program

The BIKEINFO.BAS program (Figure 8-8) demonstrates how a number of arrays can be used together in a program to track related information. BIKEINFO is a revision of the GETNAMES program, which is designed for use in Erin's Bike Market. This version tracks the salesperson names with the *salesGroup$* array, the number of bikes sold with the *bikesSold%* array, and the total value of sales with the *totalSales!* array. The three arrays are designed to be used together—each contains a piece of information about the salespersons in the bike shop, as shown in Figure 8-6. If you reference the array indexes together in a FOR loop, related items can be accessed at the same time. The PRINT USING statement and the template *tmp$* display the data in each array.

Load the BIKEINFO.BAS program from disk and run it.

```
' BIKEINFO.BAS
' This program reads information into three arrays and prints it.

CONST PERSONS% = 7        ' number of salespersons
OPTION BASE 1             ' set base of all arrays to 1
```

FIGURE 8-8. *(continued)*
BIKEINFO.BAS: A program demonstrating the use of three arrays in a FOR loop.

FIGURE 8-8. *continued*

```
DIM salesGroup$(PERSONS%)     ' dimension salesGroup$ string array
DIM bikesSold%(PERSONS%)      ' dimension bikesSold% integer array
DIM totalSales!(PERSONS%)     ' dimension totalSales! floating-point array

CLS

FOR i% = 1 TO PERSONS%         ' get salesperson name and sales data
    INPUT "Enter salesperson name: ", salesGroup$(i%)
    INPUT "   Bikes sold: ", bikesSold%(i%)
    INPUT "   Total sales:  $", totalSales!(i%)
    PRINT
NEXT i%

PRINT "You entered the following sales data:"
PRINT
PRINT "Salesperson     Bikes sold     Total sales"
PRINT "-------------------------------------------"
PRINT

' initialize tmp$, a formatting template for PRINT USING
tmp$ = "\              \ ###           $$####.##"

FOR i% = 1 TO PERSONS%          ' print contents of each array
    PRINT USING tmp$; salesGroup$(i%); bikesSold%(i%); totalSales!(i%)
NEXT i%
```

You'll receive output similar to the following:

```
Enter salesperson name:  Megan
   Bikes sold:  6
   Total sales:  $1350.12

Enter salesperson name:  Eric
   Bikes sold:  5
   Total sales:  $1578.55

Enter salesperson name:  Ron
   Bikes sold:  12
   Total sales:  $2343.84
```

(continued)

continued

```
Enter salesperson name:  Mary Ann
   Bikes sold:  7
   Total sales:  $1256.36

Enter salesperson name:  Barbara
   Bikes sold:  11
   Total sales:  $2613.79

Enter salesperson name:  Jack
   Bikes sold:  2
   Total sales:  $489

Enter salesperson name:  Nancy
   Bikes sold:  5
   Total sales:  $1356.03

You entered the following sales data:

Salesperson      Bikes sold     Total sales
------------------------------------------------


Megan               6           $1350.12
Eric                5           $1578.55
Ron                12           $2343.84
Mary Ann            7           $1256.36
Barbara            11           $2613.79
Jack                2            $489.00
Nancy               5           $1356.03
```

Filling Part of an Array

You needn't fill an array to the brim. In fact, allowing a little room for future growth is often a good idea. If you intend to do this, however, you need a way to signal QuickBASIC that the user is finished entering data. One way to do this is by using an end-of-data marker, as discussed earlier in the chapter. You can have the user add elements to the array as part of a WHILE loop that continually checks for the end-of-data marker. As soon as QuickBASIC sees the marker, it exits the loop and executes the rest of the program. The end-of-data marker should be the same data type as the array being filled, and it should be a value that the user is unlikely to type during the normal execution of the program. A typical end-of-data marker for a string array is *QUIT* or *END*. A typical end-of-data marker for a numeric array is *−9999*.

Practice: Using an end-of-data marker

The DATAEND.BAS program (Figure 8-9) demonstrates how to fill an array with different amounts of data. The program fills and prints three arrays again, but this time dimensions the arrays with 50 elements each and uses an end-of-data marker of *END* to indicate that the user is finished entering data. (Note that *END* must be entered in all capital letters.)

Load the DATAEND.BAS program from disk and run it.

```
' DATAEND.BAS
' This program reads information into three arrays and prints it.
'   The maximum number of names that can be entered is 50; fewer
'   can be entered by typing "END" for the salesperson name.

OPTION BASE 1                  ' set base of all arrays to 1

DIM salesGroup$(50)            ' dimension salesGroup$ string array
DIM bikesSold%(50)             ' dimension bikesSold% integer array
DIM totalSales!(50)            ' dimension totalSales! floating-point array

CLS

PRINT "Follow prompts to enter bike shop data.  Type END to quit."
PRINT

count% = 1                     ' initialize an array counter variable

WHILE (salesGroup$(count%) <> "END")  ' continue until name = "END"
    INPUT "Enter salesperson name:  ", salesGroup$(count%)
```

FIGURE 8-9. *(continued)*
DATAEND.BAS: A program that uses an end-of-data marker to determine when input is complete.

FIGURE 8-9. *continued*

```
    IF (salesGroup$(count%) <> "END") THEN
        INPUT "   Bikes sold: ", bikesSold%(count%)
        INPUT "   Total sales: $", totalSales!(count%)
        PRINT
        count% = count% + 1              ' increment the array counter
    END IF
WEND


PRINT
PRINT "You entered the following sales data:"
PRINT
PRINT "Salesperson    Bikes sold    Total sales"
PRINT "-----------------------------------------"
PRINT

' initialize tmp$, a formatting template for PRINT USING
tmp$ = "\                \ ###              $$####.##"

FOR i% = 1 TO count% - 1      ' print contents of each array
    PRINT USING tmp$; salesGroup$(i%); bikesSold%(i%); totalSales!(i%)
NEXT i%
```

You'll receive output similar to the following:

```
Follow prompts to enter bike shop data.  Type END to quit.

Enter salesperson name:  Nancy
   Bikes sold:  5
   Total sales:  $1356.03

Enter salesperson name:  Barbara
   Bikes sold:  11
   Total sales:  $2613.79

Enter salesperson name:  END

You entered the following sales data:

Salesperson    Bikes sold    Total sales
-----------------------------------------

Nancy              5          $1356.03
Barbara           11          $2613.79
```

217

Creating Flexible Arrays

As you've learned, when you use the DIM statement you must inform QuickBASIC of the intended number of elements in your array so that it can reserve an adequate amount of space in memory. But what if you're not sure how many elements your array will contain? For example, if your program is dependent on user input for the contents of the array, the number of elements entered might vary each time the program is run. How can you tell QuickBASIC how much memory to reserve?

The DIM statement is actually quite accommodating. In fact, it can create two kinds of arrays depending on the type of information you provide: *static arrays* and *dynamic arrays*.

Static arrays

A static array is an array of a specific size—a size that you know in advance. For example, in the BIKEINFO.BAS program, the number of salespersons is known in advance and placed into the program as a constant:

```
CONST PERSONS% = 7
```

The DIM statement then uses the constant PERSONS% as the number of elements in the array:

```
DIM salesGroup$(PERSONS%)
```

Dynamic arrays

A dynamic array is an array whose size can change. A dynamic array is dimensioned only when the user of the program defines the number of elements the array is to contain. To create a dynamic array, you would follow these steps:

1. Use the INPUT statement to prompt the user for the number of elements.

2. Assign the value entered by the user to an integer variable.

3. Use the integer variable with the DIM statement to dimension the array.

Use a static array when you know in advance how big the array should be. Use a dynamic array when the array size will be determined anew each time the program is run.

Practice: Using a variable to set array size

The DYNAMIC.BAS program (Figure 8-10) uses the *persons%* variable to dimension the three dynamic sales arrays. Note the IF statement that checks the value of *persons%*: If *persons%* is less than or equal to 0, no arrays are dimensioned.

Load the DYNAMIC.BAS program from disk and run it.

```
' DYNAMIC.BAS
' This program reads information into three dynamic arrays and prints it.

OPTION BASE 1                    ' set base of all arrays to 1

CLS

INPUT "How many salesperson names would you like to enter?  ", persons%
IF (persons% > 0) THEN           ' must be at least one salesperson

    DIM salesGroup$(persons%)  ' dimension salesGroup$ string array
    DIM bikesSold%(persons%)   ' dimension bikesSold% integer array
    DIM totalSales!(persons%)  ' dimension totalSales! floating-pt. array

    PRINT

    FOR i% = 1 TO persons%          ' get salesperson name and sales data
        INPUT "Enter salesperson name:  ", salesGroup$(i%)
        INPUT "   Bikes sold:  ", bikesSold%(i%)
        INPUT "   Total sales:  $", totalSales!(i%)
        PRINT
    NEXT i%

    PRINT "You entered the following sales data:"
    PRINT
```

FIGURE 8-10.   *(continued)*

DYNAMIC.BAS: A program demonstrating the use of three dynamic arrays.

FIGURE 8-10. *continued*

```
    PRINT "Salesperson     Bikes sold     Total sales"
    PRINT "-----------------------------------------------"
    PRINT

    ' initialize tmp$, a formatting template for PRINT USING
    tmp$ = "\                \ ###            $$####.##"

    FOR i% = 1 TO persons%      ' print contents of each array
    PRINT USING tmp$; salesGroup$(i%); bikesSold%(i%); totalSales!(i%)
    NEXT i%

END IF
```

You'll receive output similar to the following:

```
How many salesperson names would you like to enter?

Enter salesperson name:  Megan
   Bikes sold:  6
   Total sales:  $1350.12

Enter salesperson name:  Eric
   Bikes sold:  5
   Total sales:  $1578.55

You entered the following sales data:

Salesperson     Bikes sold     Total sales
---------------------------------------------

Megan              6            $1350.12
Eric               5            $1578.55
```

Searching for an Element in an Array

At times you might want to perform a search within an array. You generally do this to find a specific array element or to find an array element based on comparison. Both operations involve stepping through an array one element at a time and keeping track of matches to a search string.

- QuickBASIC compares a search string with each element of the array until a match is found or until all array elements have been examined.

- If a comparison search is in effect, you use one or more temporary variables to track the progress of the comparison. Comparisons usually take one of the following forms:

  ☐ Find the largest number in the array.

  ☐ Find the smallest number in the array.

The following exercises demonstrate typical methods for finding a specific array element and for finding the largest number in an array.

Practice: Finding an array element

The SEARCH.BAS program (Figure 8-11) demonstrates how to search an array for a specific element. The program prompts the user for salesperson data and then asks which salesperson's data the user would like to examine. A FOR loop steps through each element of the *salesGroup$* array until a match is found or all the array entries have been examined:

- If a match is found, the corresponding elements from the *bikesSold%* and *totalSales!* arrays are displayed, and then the loop is exited with an EXIT FOR statement.

The EXIT FOR Statement

The EXIT FOR statement lets you exit a FOR loop early—before the loop finishes on its own. EXIT FOR is useful when you want to loop a specific number of times *unless* a certain condition is met. The following program asks for names until the user has entered 10 names or until the user enters *QUIT*, whichever occurs first:

```
FOR i% = 1 TO 10
    INPUT "Enter a name:  ", firstName$
    IF (firstName$ = "QUIT") THEN EXIT FOR
    PRINT firstName$
NEXT i%
```

- If no match is found, the message *Name not found* is displayed.

  Load the SEARCH.BAS program from disk and run it.

```
' SEARCH.BAS
' This program reads data into three arrays and searches for a name.
'   The maximum number of names that can be entered is 50; fewer
'   can be entered by typing "END" for the salesperson name.

OPTION BASE 1                    ' set base of all arrays to 1

DIM salesGroup$(50)              ' dimension salesGroup$ string array
DIM bikesSold%(50)               ' dimension bikesSold% integer array
DIM totalSales!(50)              ' dimension totalSales! floating-point array

CLS
PRINT "Follow prompts to enter bike shop data.  Type END to quit."
PRINT


count% = 1                       ' initialize an array counter variable
WHILE (salesGroup$(count%) <> "END") ' continue until name = "END"
    INPUT "Enter salesperson name:  ", salesGroup$(count%)

    IF (salesGroup$(count%) <> "END") THEN
        INPUT "   Bikes sold:  ", bikesSold%(count%)
        INPUT "   Total sales:  $", totalSales!(count%)
        PRINT
        count% = count% + 1  ' increment the array counter
    END IF
WEND

PRINT                            ' prompt user for search string
INPUT "What name would you like to search for?  ", search$
PRINT

' initialize tmp$, a formatting template for PRINT USING
tmp$ = "\                   \  ###              $$####.##"
```

FIGURE 8-11.   *(continued)*

SEARCH.BAS: A program demonstrating how an array can be searched for a specific element.

FIGURE 8-11. *continued*

```
' compare each array element with search string until a match is
'    found, then display the record and exit the loop;  display
'    message if search string is not found

FOR i% = 1 TO count% - 1     ' count% - 1 is the last array element
    IF (salesGroup$(i%) = search$) THEN
        PRINT "Salesperson    Bikes sold    Total sales"
        PRINT "-------------------------------------------"
        PRINT
        PRINT USING tmp$; salesGroup$(i%); bikesSold%(i%); totalSales!(i%)
        EXIT FOR              ' this statement breaks out of a FOR loop
    END IF
    IF (i% = count% - 1) THEN PRINT "** Name not found **"
NEXT i%
```

You'll receive output similar to the following:

```
Follow prompts to enter bike shop data.  Type END to quit.

Enter salesperson name:  Jack
    Bikes sold:  2
    Total sales:  $489.00

Enter salesperson name:  Ron
    Bikes sold:  12
    Total sales:  $2343.84

Enter salesperson name:  Mary Ann
    Bikes sold:  7
    Total sales:  $1256.36

Enter salesperson name:  END

What name would you like to search for?  Ron

Salesperson    Bikes sold    Total sales
-------------------------------------------

Ron              12           $2343.84
```

Practice: Finding the largest number in an array

The MAXSALES.BAS program (Figure 8-12) demonstrates how the largest element in an array can be extracted with a FOR loop. The program prompts the user for salesperson data and then examines each element of the *totalSales!* array. The largest sales figure is stored in the variable *largest!* and is compared with each element of *totalSales!*. If an array element is larger than *largest!*, that array element becomes the new *largest!*. (The *lg%* variable stores the array index associated with *largest!*.) After it examines all array elements, the program displays the largest sales figure and the related elements in the *salesGroup$* and *bikesSold%* arrays.

Load the MAXSALES.BAS program from disk and run it.

```
' MAXSALES.BAS
' This program reads salesperson data into three arrays and displays
'    the salesperson with the highest total sales.  The maximum number
'    of names that can be entered is 50; fewer can be entered by
'    typing "END" for the salesperson name.

OPTION BASE 1                   ' set base of all arrays to 1

DIM salesGroup$(50)             ' dimension salesGroup$ string array
DIM bikesSold%(50)              ' dimension bikesSold% integer array
DIM totalSales!(50)             ' dimension totalSales! floating-point array

CLS

PRINT "Follow prompts to enter bike shop data.  Type END to quit."
PRINT

count% = 1                      ' initialize an array counter variable

WHILE (salesGroup$(count%) <> "END")  ' continue until name = "END"
    INPUT "Enter salesperson name:  ", salesGroup$(count%)
```

FIGURE 8-12.   *(continued)*

MAXSALES.BAS: A program demonstrating the extraction of the largest element in an array.

FIGURE 8-12. *continued*

```
        IF (salesGroup$(count%) <> "END") THEN
            INPUT "    Bikes sold:  ", bikesSold%(count%)
            INPUT "    Total sales:  $", totalSales!(count%)
            PRINT
            count% = count% + 1  ' increment the array counter
        END IF
WEND

largest! = totalSales!(1)    ' first array element is largest so far
lg% = 1                      ' save array index

' compare remaining array elements for something bigger--if one is
'   found, assign it to largest! and save the array index in lg%; if
'   there is a tie for the largest, return the first element found

FOR i% = 2 TO count% - 1
    IF (totalSales!(i%) > largest!) THEN
        largest! = totalSales!(i%)  ' save new largest value
        lg% = i%                    ' save array index
    END IF
NEXT i%

' initialize tmp$, a formatting template for PRINT USING
tmp$ = "\            \ ###           $$####.##"

PRINT
PRINT "** "; salesGroup$(lg%); " has the highest total sales **"
PRINT
PRINT "Salesperson    Bikes sold    Total sales"
PRINT "-------------------------------------------"
PRINT
PRINT USING tmp$; salesGroup$(lg%); bikesSold%(lg%); totalSales!(lg%)
```

You'll receive output similar to the following:

```
Follow prompts to enter bike shop data.  Type END to quit.

Enter salesperson name:  Megan
   Bikes sold:  6
   Total sales:  $1350.12

Enter salesperson name:  Eric
   Bikes sold:  5
   Total sales:  $1578.55

Enter salesperson name:  Nancy
   Bikes sold:  5
   Total sales:  $1356.03

Enter salesperson name:  Mary Ann
   Bikes sold:  7
   Total sales:  $1256.36

Enter salesperson name:  END

** Eric has the highest total sales **

Salesperson     Bikes sold     Total sales
----------------------------------------

Eric                5            $1578.55
```

Two-Dimensional Arrays

QuickBASIC also lets you declare arrays of two dimensions. A two-dimensional array represents a table of values with rows and columns, such as a scoreboard, an accounting ledger, or a gameboard. In this section we'll discuss how to declare and use a two-dimensional array in a QuickBASIC program.

Let's start with an example. Sam, the local soda distributor, wants to track sales for his top four brands over the last 12 months. He wants to put the information in a table that uses brand names for row titles and months for column titles, as shown in Figure 8-13.

	Jan	Feb	Mar	Apr	May	Jun	Jul	Aug	Sep	Oct	Nov	Dec
Orca Spray	64	63	58	45	36	32	41	39	50	67	69	103
Fizzy Delite	35	41	60	57	38	29	25	19	26	37	43	36
Alki Seltzer	15	9	12	21	24	32	46	42	37	22	18	13
Schpritz	30	30	30	35	42	44	49	48	38	35	31	30

FIGURE 8-13.
A table of values showing soda sales over the last 12 months.

Using Arrays with Procedures

In Chapter 7 you learned how variables can be declared locally or globally and how variable arguments are passed to subprograms and functions. A similar set of rules applies to arrays used in programs that contain procedures:

- By default, arrays are local to the main program or procedure they are declared in.

- Arrays are declared global with the COMMON SHARED statement in the main program; for example:

```
DIM stores$(20)
COMMON SHARED stores$()
```

- A single array element can be passed to a procedure; for example:

```
GetInput stores$(12)
```

- An entire array can be passed to a procedure by specifying no subscript; for example:

```
PrintAllStores stores$()
```

As the programs you write become larger, you'll want to use arrays right along with subprograms and functions to keep your code organized and efficient.

Tabular information of this nature is perfectly suited to a two-dimensional array. In this example one dimension of the array corresponds to the brand name rows and the other dimension corresponds to the month columns. Items in a two-dimensional array are identified with row *and* column subscripts. Figure 8-14 shows how row and column subscripts would be assigned to each dimension if the base of the array were set at 1. A one-dimensional array requires one subscript to identify an array element. A two-dimensional array requires two subscripts to identify an array element. In Figure 8-14, for example, the number of cases of Orca Spray sold in May would be identified by row 1, column 5.

Row subscripts

Column subscripts

	1	2	3	4	5	6	7	8	9	10	11	12
1 **Orca Spray**	64	63	58	45	36	32	41	39	50	67	69	103
2 **Fizzy Delite**	35	41	60	57	38	29	25	19	26	37	43	36
3 **Alki Seltzer**	15	9	12	21	24	32	46	42	37	22	18	13
4 **Schpritz**	30	30	30	35	42	44	49	48	38	35	31	30

FIGURE 8-14.
Assigning two-dimensional array subscripts to the soda sales table.

Declaring a two-dimensional array

To dimension a two-dimensional array, use the DIM statement as follows:

```
DIM arrayName(rows, columns)
```

arrayName is the name of the array, *rows* is the number of rows in the array (the first dimension), and *columns* is the number of columns in the array (the second dimension). *rows* and *columns* must be integers and can be expressed as numbers, constants, or variables. The final character of *arrayName* must be the type-declaration character that identifies the data type of the array: $ for strings, % for integers, & for long integers, ! for single-precision floating-point numbers, or # for double-precision floating-point numbers. As with one-dimensional arrays, every element in a two-dimensional array must be of the same data type.

NOTE: The first element in each dimension of the array is numbered 0 unless you use the OPTION BASE 1 statement before you dimension the array.

For example, the following statements dimension an array named *sodaSales%* with 4 rows and 12 columns:

```
OPTION BASE 1
DIM sodaSales%(4, 12)
```

The following statements dimension a dynamic two-dimensional array named *sodaSales%*:

```
OPTION BASE 1
INPUT "Enter number of soda brands sold:  ", brands%
INPUT "Enter number of months to track:  ", months%
DIM sodaSales%(brands%, months%)
```

Practice: Building a table of values

The SALES.BAS program (Figure 8-15) demonstrates how the two-dimensional array *sodaSales%* is filled and displayed on the screen. SALES gets the numbers of rows and columns in the soda sales table from the user, stores those numbers in the *brands%* and *months%* integer variables, and uses them to dimension the *sodaSales%* array. SALES uses two nested FOR loops to fill and display the array and uses DATA and READ statements to store and retrieve the months of the year. Use this program as a guide for filling and printing any two-dimensional dynamic array.

Load the SALES.BAS program from disk.

```
' SALES.BAS
' This program tracks the sales of soda over a given number of months.

CLS

PRINT "** Soda sales tracking program **"
PRINT
DO
    INPUT "How many brands of soda do you sell?  ", brands%
LOOP WHILE (brands% < 1)
```

FIGURE 8-15. *(continued)*
SALES.BAS: A program that uses a dynamic two-dimensional array to track soda sales.

FIGURE 8-15. *continued*

```
DO
    INPUT "How many months would you like to record (1-12)?  ", months%
LOOP WHILE (months% < 1) OR (months% > 12)
PRINT


OPTION BASE 1                       ' set first array element at 1
DIM sodaSales%(brands%, months%)  ' dimension soda sales array
DIM brandNames$(brands%)           ' dimension brand name array


' get names of soda brands sold

PRINT "Enter the"; brands%; "brands of soda you sell"
PRINT
FOR i% = 1 TO brands%
    INPUT "Brand name:  ", brandNames$(i%)
NEXT i%


' get soda sales for each month

PRINT
PRINT "Enter soda sales in cases"
PRINT

FOR i% = 1 TO brands%           ' for each brand of soda...
    PRINT "** "; brandNames$(i%); " **"
    PRINT                       '   print name of brand
    FOR j% = 1 TO months%       ' for each month...
        READ mo$                '   read month name from DATA list
        PRINT "  "; mo$;        '   print month name and prompt for input
        INPUT ": ", sodaSales%(i%, j%)  ' store input in array
    NEXT j%
    PRINT
    RESTORE                     ' rewind DATA list to first month
NEXT i%


' print out soda sales table

CLS
```

(continued)

FIGURE 8-15. *continued*

```
PRINT "Soda sales in cases for"; months%; "months"
PRINT
PRINT "-----------------------------------------------------------"
PRINT "Brand/Month   ";

FOR i% = 1 TO months%
    PRINT " ";
    READ mo$                 ' read month name from DATA list
    PRINT mo$;               ' print month names across top of table
NEXT i%

PRINT
PRINT "-----------------------------------------------------------"

' templates for PRINT USING

nameTmp$ = "\             \"   ' for brand name (up to 12 digits)
salesTmp$ = " ###"             ' for cases sold (up to 3 digits)

FOR i% = 1 TO brands%          ' fills in the table
    PRINT USING nameTmp$; brandNames$(i%);
    FOR j% = 1 TO months%
        PRINT USING salesTmp$; sodaSales%(i%, j%);
    NEXT j%
    PRINT
NEXT i%

PRINT "-----------------------------------------------------------"

' data for READ statements above

DATA Jan, Feb, Mar, Apr, May, Jun, Jul, Aug, Sep, Oct, Nov, Dec
```

When you run SALES.BAS, you are prompted for input in the following manner:

```
** Soda sales tracking program **

How many brands of soda do you sell?  4
How many months would you like to record (1-12)?  12
```

(continued)

continued

```
Enter the 4 brands of soda you sell

Brand name:  Orca Spray
Brand name:  Fizzy Delite
Brand name:  Alki Seltzer
Brand name:  Schpritz

Enter soda sales in cases

** Orca Spray **

  Jan:  64
  Feb:  63
  Mar:  58
   ⋮
```

After the data for each brand name and month has been entered, you'll receive output similar to the following:

```
Soda sales in cases for 12 months

-------------------------------------------------------------
Brand/Month    Jan Feb Mar Apr May Jun Jul Aug Sep Oct Nov Dec
-------------------------------------------------------------
Orca Spray      64  63  58  45  36  32  41  39  50  67  69 103
Fizzy Delite    35  41  60  57  38  29  25  19  26  37  43  36
Alki Seltzer    15   9  12  21  24  32  46  42  37  22  18  13
Schpritz        30  30  30  35  42  44  49  48  38  35  31  30
-------------------------------------------------------------
```

 NOTE: To print a copy of the final table on your printer, be sure that your printer is on, and then hold down the Shift key and press the PrtSc key. The Shift-PrtSc key combination sends all the text on the screen to the printer.

Array Troubleshooting

Although arrays are a great boon to your programs, they also increase the potential for error. This section examines some typical programming errors associated with arrays and with processing large amounts of data and provides ways to avoid them when possible.

Mistake 1: Not using an integer to define a subscript

The number of elements and dimensions in an array is determined by integer subscripts in the DIM statement. *Be sure the subscripts are integer values or variables.* The following array declaration, for example, is valid:

```
DIM grades%(students%, 15)
```

The subscripts *students%* and *15* are both integer values. The following declaration is not valid because *items$* and *quantity$* are string values:

```
DIM costTable!(items$, quantity$)
```

When you attempt to dimension an array with invalid subscripts, you receive the following error message:

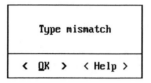

If you supply a floating-point number as a subscript, QuickBASIC rounds the value to the nearest integer value and then dimensions the array. For example, the following statement successfully dimensions an array with 6 elements (0 through 5):

```
DIM values%(4.6)
```

 NOTE: Using a floating-point value as an array subscript will be confusing to a person reading your program. Avoid dimensioning an array with such.

Mistake 2: Using a DIM statement in a loop

Be sure DIM statements are outside any loops in your program. The following program fragment demonstrates the incorrect use of a DIM statement to declare a dynamic array:

```
OPTION BASE 1
size% = 5
CLS
```

(continued)

continued

```
FOR i% = 1 to size%
    DIM names$(size%)
    INPUT "Enter a name:  ", names$(i%)
NEXT i%

PRINT
FOR i% = 1 to size%
    PRINT names$(i%)
NEXT i%
```

If you run the program, you receive the following error message when the DIM statement is executed a second time:

```
┌─────────────────────────────────┐
│                                 │
│   Duplicate definition          │
│                                 │
├─────────────────────────────────┤
│   <  OK  >    < Help >          │
└─────────────────────────────────┘
```

To avoid this error, dimension the *names$* array before the loop, as follows:

```
OPTION BASE 1
size% = 5
DIM names$(size%)
CLS

FOR i% = 1 to size%
    INPUT "Enter a name:  ", names$(i%)
NEXT i%

PRINT
FOR i% = 1 to size%
    PRINT names$(i%)
NEXT i%
```

Mistake 3: Confusing array index with array value

It's easy to confuse the value used to *index* an array element with the value *in* the array element. Remember that the array index is always in parentheses and that it follows the array name that describes the location of the array value (Figure 8-16).

```
DIM roomRate!(roomStyles%, daysRented%)
   :
roomRate!(5, 3) = 45.85
```

Array index   Array value

FIGURE 8-16.
Array index and array value.

The following statement tries to assign the string value ''Orcas Hotel''
to the fifth element in the *vacationSpots$* array but fails because the array
index and the array value are in the wrong locations:

```
vacationSpots$("Orcas Hotel") = 5
```

The correct array assignment is as follows:

```
vacationSpots$(5) = "Orcas Hotel"
```

Mistake 4: Mismatching array types

Every element in an array must be of the same data type. If you attempt to
assign a variable or value to an array that does not match the array type
specified in the DIM statement, you'll receive an error message. For example, the following assignment statement generates an error because
cost! is a single-precision array and the value *"57.36"* is a string type. (A
correct assignment would be *57.36* without the quotation marks.)

```
cost!(i%) = "57.36"
```

This type of assignment error produces the following message:

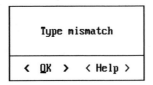

```
Type mismatch

< OK >   < Help >
```

A similar type mismatch occurs while the program is running if the user
enters a value that does not match the array element receiving input. The
following loop, for example, prompts the user to enter several integers.

```
DIM values%(5)
FOR i% = 1 to 5
    INPUT "Enter a number:  ", values%(i%)
NEXT i%
```

If the user enters a string value, the following message will appear:

```
Enter a number:  ten

Redo from start
Enter a number:
```

Redo from start is QuickBASIC's way of prompting the user for data of the correct type. Usually this message is enough to get users back on track. As we've mentioned before, however, the best way to avoid input problems is to spell out with your input prompt exactly what you want.

Mistake 5: Making out-of-range errors

Attempting to reference an element that does not exist in an array generates an *out-of-range* error when the program is run. For example, QuickBASIC generates an error when the third of the following statements is executed, because *testScores%* can contain only 25 elements and a reference is made to a 30th element.

```
OPTION BASE 1
DIM testScores%(25)
testScores%(30) = 92
```

The out-of-range error is most common in a looping structure, as shown in the following program fragment:

```
OPTION BASE 1
DIM colors$(4)
count% = 0
CLS

DO
    count% = count% + 1
    INPUT "Enter a color name:  ", colors$(count%)
LOOP UNTIL (colors$(count%) = "QUIT")
```

When you run the program fragment, you receive the following output:

```
Enter a color: yellow
Enter a color: red
Enter a color: blue
Enter a color: green
Enter a color: white
```

After the fifth color is entered (filling the last element in the array), the *count%* loop counter is incremented and the INPUT statement (now referencing an element beyond the end of the array) triggers the *Subscript out of range* error.

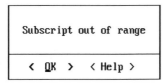

The solution for out-of-range problems is to determine the upper and lower bounds of the array and not go past them. QuickBASIC provides the UBOUND and LBOUND functions to return the bounds of any array in your program so that you can handle this potential problem.

The UBOUND and LBOUND functions

The UBOUND and LBOUND functions return integer values corresponding to the upper and lower bounds of an array. UBOUND and LBOUND should be used in the following manner:

```
UBOUND(arrayName, dimension)
```

```
LBOUND(arrayName, dimension)
```

arrayName is the name of the array you want to determine bounds for and *dimension* is the dimension you want to check (not required if you're evaluating a one-dimensional array). Both functions return integer values that can be assigned to variables or used in expressions.

The following program fragment uses the UBOUND and LBOUND functions to check a one-dimensional array named *players$*.

```
OPTION BASE 1
DIM players$(9)
PRINT "Upper bound is"; UBOUND(players$)
PRINT "Lower bound is"; LBOUND(players$)
```

When you run the program fragment, you receive the following output:

```
Upper bound is 9
Lower bound is 1
```

When the bounds of a two-dimensional array are checked, a dimension number is required: 1 for the first dimension or 2 for the second dimension. The following program fragment uses UBOUND and LBOUND to check the bounds of both dimensions in a two-dimensional array named *janSales%*:

```
OPTION BASE 1
DIM janSales%(3, 4)
PRINT "Upper bound of first dimension is"; UBOUND(janSales%, 1)
PRINT "Lower bound of first dimension is"; LBOUND(janSales%, 1)
PRINT "Upper bound of second dimension is"; UBOUND(janSales%, 2)
PRINT "Lower bound of second dimension is"; LBOUND(janSales%, 2)
```

When you run the program fragment, you receive the following output:

```
Upper bound of first dimension is 3
Lower bound of first dimension is 1
Upper bound of second dimension is 4
Lower bound of second dimension is 1
```

Practice: Avoiding the subscript-out-of-range message

The BOUNDS.BAS program (Figure 8-17) demonstrates how to use UBOUND and LBOUND to check the bounds of an array in a DO loop and thus avoid out-of-range errors. The program dimensions a one-dimensional string array named *party$*, which is designed to hold party game ideas. BOUNDS.BAS then fills the array and prints it out.

NOTE: The DO loop in the BOUNDS program makes use of the EXIT DO statement, which exits the loop if the user enters QUIT before all the elements of the array are filled. Use EXIT DO in your programs when you need to terminate a DO loop before the WHILE or UNTIL condition is met.

Load the BOUNDS.BAS program from disk and run it.

```
' BOUNDS.BAS
' This program loads data into an array until QUIT is typed or
'   the array boundaries are exceeded.

OPTION BASE 1                   ' set array base to 1
DIM party$(5)                   ' dimension array with 5 elements

count% = 1                      ' initialize loop counter to 1

CLS                             ' display intro message and QUIT note
PRINT "Enter party game ideas; type QUIT to stop"
PRINT
                                ' loop while count% is within array bounds
DO WHILE (count% >= LBOUND(party$)) AND (count% <= UBOUND(party$))
    INPUT "Party game:  ", party$(count%)     ' read input into array
    IF (party$(count%) = "QUIT") THEN EXIT DO ' if user types QUIT,
    count% = count% + 1                       '   then exit loop
LOOP

PRINT
PRINT "You entered the following games:"
PRINT

FOR i% = 1 TO count% - 1     ' print array contents
    PRINT party$(i%)         ' count% - 1 contains last value entered
NEXT i%
```

FIGURE 8-17.
BOUNDS.BAS: A program that uses LBOUND and UBOUND to avoid referencing an array element that is out of bounds.

You'll receive output similar to the following:

```
Enter party game ideas; type QUIT to stop

Party game:  Blindman's bluff
Party game:  Bingo
Party game:  Pin the tail on the donkey
Party game:  Spin the bottle
Party game:  Moonlight bowling
```

(continued)

239

continued
```
You entered the following games:

Blindman's bluff
Bingo
Pin the tail on the donkey
Spin the bottle
Moonlight bowling
```

SUMMARY

This chapter has introduced the important structures, functions, statements, and techniques provided by QuickBASIC for working with large amounts of data in a program. We covered the following topics:

- Using DATA, READ, and RESTORE to assign data stored in a program to variables

- Creating and using a one-dimensional array

- Searching for elements in an array

- Formatting tabular information with PRINT USING

- Creating and using a two-dimensional array

- Troubleshooting common array-related programming errors

In the next chapter you'll learn the many functions and techniques specially designed for working with strings.

QUESTIONS AND EXERCISES

1. Which comes first in a program, a DATA statement or a READ statement?

2. What type of information is well suited to the DATA/READ/RESTORE approach to working with data?

3. Write a program that displays each of the values in the following DATA statement with a FOR loop:

```
DATA Beaver, Wally, Lumpy, Whitey, Gus, Eddie, Larry
```

4. True or False: More than one type of data can be stored in an array.

5. Write a statement that sets aside memory for an array of 100 single-precision floating-point values.

6. What is an end-of-data marker?

7. Write a program that declares, fills, and then prints a dynamic one-dimensional array containing the major characters of your favorite television show or movie.

8. What is an out-of-range error?

9. Write a program that uses a two-dimensional array to keep score for a nine-inning baseball game. Your program should initialize the array, prompt the user for the baseball teams' names and mascots, get the runs scored for each inning, determine the final score and winner of the game, and display the results.

Working with Strings

Chapters 3 and 4 introduced the string data type and let you practice creating strings and displaying them on your screen. This chapter continues that discussion and introduces many of the functions available in QuickBASIC for working with strings. We'll describe

- Assigning user input to a string
- Combining strings
- Selecting characters from a string
- Comparing strings
- Sorting strings

When combined with the skills you've developed in preceding chapters, these functions can help you perform a wide variety of tasks.

STRINGS: AN OVERVIEW

A string is a series of consecutive characters that you use as a unit. Typically, you store information as a string when you can't easily store it as a numeric data type. For example, because of its textual nature, the title of a book—let's say *The Original Mother Goose*—would be stored as a string rather than as a numeric data type.

You might find it helpful to think of a string as occupying a series of memory locations in a computer. You can think of the memory locations as little boxes set side by side—each box holding one character of the string, as shown in Figure 9-1. The memory locations, or boxes, are fixed in place, but the characters can be moved between the boxes at will. Characters, or boxes, can also be added to or removed from the string as the need arises.

FIGURE 9-1.
A string is a series of characters.

You can use the following characters in a string:

- Uppercase letters of the alphabet (A though Z)
- Lowercase letters of the alphabet (a through z)
- Numerals (0 though 9)
- Punctuation symbols (. , ; : ' ' ? !)
- Mathematical symbols (# % ( ) − + = \ / < >)
- Miscellaneous symbols (~ @ $ ^ & * _ ¦ { } [ ])
- Characters in the IBM extended character set

TWO TYPES OF STRINGS

QuickBASIC supports two types of strings for use in your programs:

- *String constants* are declared within your program. As the name suggests, the characters in a string constant never change.
- *String variables* are also declared within your program. The characters in a string variable can change at any time.

Let's examine why and how you use these types of strings in QuickBASIC.

String Constants

String constants are strings that don't change while a program is running. QuickBASIC separates string constants into two groups: *literal string constants* and *symbolic string constants*.

Literal string constants

A literal string is a string surrounded by quotation marks. You generally assign literal strings to a variable or use them as arguments to a statement or function. For example, the following statements contain literal strings.

```
cheer$ = "Go Seahawks!"

PRINT "1313 Mockingbird Lane"

goal$ = CenterString$("Today I shall fly a kite")

birthDate$ = "11-19-63"
```

Literal strings are also known as *string values.*

Symbolic string constants

A symbolic string constant is a name assigned to a literal string:

```
CONST DI$ = "Her Royal Highness, Diana, Princess of Wales"
```
        Constant   Literal string

Once you've assigned a constant, you can use the constant anywhere you would otherwise have to use the literal string (much as you can call someone by a nickname as well as by a full name).

As you learned in Chapter 4, you assign a constant in a CONST statement, usually near the beginning of a program. In this book, constants are written in all-uppercase letters to distinguish them from variables:

```
CONST DI$ = "Her Royal Highness, Diana, Princess of Wales"

PRINT "Charles's wife is now called "; DI$
```

Once you declare a constant, you cannot change its value. For example, a program containing the following two statements would generate the error message *Duplicate definition* when you run the program because the value of a constant cannot change during the execution of a program:

```
CONST DI$ = "Her Royal Highness, Diana, Princess of Wales"
DI$ = "Lady Diana Spencer"
```

This is the difference between a constant and a variable: The value of a variable can change as a program runs; the value of a constant cannot.

Practice: Using string constants

Constants are particularly useful when you have repetitive patterns in a program. The PIG.BAS program (Figure 9-2) declares the constant *PIG$* and assigns to it the literal string *This little piggy*.

Load the PIG.BAS program from the CHAP09 subdirectory on disk and run it.

```
' PIG.BAS
' This program demonstrates the use of string constants.

CLS

CONST PIG$ = "This little piggy "

PRINT PIG$; "went to market"
PRINT PIG$; "stayed home"
PRINT PIG$; "had roast beef"
PRINT PIG$; "had none"
PRINT PIG$; "cried 'Wee wee wee' all the way home"
```

FIGURE 9-2.
PIG.BAS: A simple demonstration of symbolic and literal string constants.

You'll receive the following output:

```
This little piggy went to market
This little piggy stayed home
This little piggy had roast beef
This little piggy had none
This little piggy cried 'Wee wee wee' all the way home
```

String Variables

Unlike string constants, string variables can change at any time during the execution of a program. QuickBASIC supports two types of string variables: *variable-length strings* and *fixed-length strings*.

In this book, variable-length and fixed-length string variables begin with a lowercase letter to distinguish them from subprograms, functions, statements, and constants.

Variable-length strings

Variable-length strings let you obtain and store information from the user of a program. A variable-length string can contain from 0 through 32,767 characters (although the typical range is 0 through 80 because of the width of the screen) and can grow or shrink in length during the execution of a program. Variable-length strings can be declared in three ways:

- By placing the string type-declaration character (*$*) at the end of the variable name. For example, the following statement gets a string from the user and assigns it to the string variable *firstName$*.

```
INPUT "Enter your first name:  ", firstName$
```

  As you examine the examples in this book, you'll see many instances in which variable-length strings are used with INPUT to assign meaningful variable names to particular words and phrases. We also use these variable-length strings as arguments to statements and functions such as PRINT.

- By using the DEFSTR statement. For example, the following statement directs QuickBASIC to regard as a variable-length string any variable that begins with the letter *S* and does not have a type-declaration character (*%*, *&*, *!*, *#*, or *$*):

```
DEFSTR S
```

- By using AS STRING with the DIM statement. For example, the following statement declares the variable *fullName* to be a variable-length string:

```
DIM fullName AS STRING
```

  Note that *fullName* does not end with a *$*. Whenever you declare a string using the AS STRING keywords, you cannot use the string type-declaration character.

  As you learned in the previous chapter, you can also use the DIM statement to declare an *array* of variable-length strings. For example, the following statement declares an array of 10 variable-length strings:

```
DIM names$(10)
```

Practice: Using variable-length strings

The PHONE.BAS program (Figure 9-3) uses INPUT statements and a two-dimensional variable-length string array named *contacts$* to store a list of friends and telephone numbers. (Because telephone numbers often contain characters that are not numerals, such as dashes and letters, it's a good idea to store them in strings.)

Load the PHONE.BAS program from disk and run it.

```
' PHONE.BAS
' This program uses a variable-length string array to record names and
'    telephone numbers.

OPTION BASE 1                    ' set lower bound of array to 1

CLS

INPUT "How many names would you like to enter?  ", names%
PRINT

DIM contacts$(names%, 2)   ' declare array for names and phone numbers

FOR i% = 1 TO names%        ' read names into contacts$ array
    INPUT "Enter name:  ", contacts$(i%, 1)
    INPUT "Enter phone number:  ", contacts$(i%, 2)
    PRINT
NEXT i%

PRINT "You entered the following contact list:"
PRINT

FOR i% = 1 TO names%         ' print contents of array
    PRINT "Name:  "; contacts$(i%, 1), "Phone:  "; contacts$(i%, 2)
NEXT i%
```

FIGURE 9-3.
PHONE.BAS: A demonstration of variable-length strings.

You'll receive output similar to the following:

```
How many names would you like to enter?  3

Enter name:  Little Bo-Peep
Enter phone number:  555-LAMB

Enter name:  Little Jack Horner
Enter phone number:  555-PLUM

Enter name:  Little Boy Blue
Enter phone number:  555-HORN

You entered the following contact list:

Name:  Little Bo-Peep       Phone:  555-LAMB
Name:  Little Jack Horner   Phone:  555-PLUM
Name:  Little Boy Blue      Phone:  555-HORN
```

Note that the alignment of the phone number column is achieved by using a comma between the two columns in the PRINT statement. In this case, advancing to the next print zone was enough to align the items. If the string values differ greatly in size, however, a different solution is needed. Try entering some names of widely differing lengths to see why.

Fixed-length strings

Fixed-length strings let you declare a string variable of a certain length. Although the contents of a fixed-length string can change at any time, the length remains constant. In general, it is a good idea to use fixed-length strings whenever you are sure of the length of a string of characters or when you need to align groups of strings.

To declare a fixed-length string, you add a string variable name and a string length to the DIM statement, as follows:

```
DIM strName AS STRING * n
```

strName is the name of the fixed-length string and *n* is the string length. For example, the following statement declares a fixed-length string named *address* that is 25 characters long:

```
DIM address AS STRING * 25
```

You can also dimension an *array* of fixed-length strings by including the number of array elements and a dimension. For example, the following statement declares a one-dimensional fixed-length string array named *fullNames*:

```
DIM fullNames(25) AS STRING * 25
```

Fixed-length strings are left-justified by default and are padded with blank spaces on the right side if the length of the string value assigned to the string is less that the total length of the string (Figure 9-4). Note that you cannot use the string type-declaration character (*$*) when you declare a fixed-length string.

```
DIM address AS STRING * 25
```

Storage is allocated for the fixed-length variable *address*.

```
address = "1012 Daisy Lane"
```

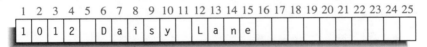

A string value is assigned to *address*.

```
address = "4250 W Lk Coppalice Parkway NE"
```

|1|2|3|4|5|6|7|8|9|10|11|12|13|14|15|16|17|18|19|20|21|22|23|24|25|
|4|2|5|0| |W| |L|k| |C|o|p|p|a|l|i|c|e| |P|a|r|k|w|

A string value that is too long is truncated.

FIGURE 9-4.
Alignment of characters in a fixed-length string.

Practice: Fixed-length strings

The PHONEFIX.BAS program (Figure 9-5) revises the PHONE.BAS program to include two one-dimensional fixed-length string arrays to track the phone list. Two separate arrays are required because the string length in each array is different. If the string length were the same, one two-dimensional fixed-length string array could be used.

Load the PHONEFIX.BAS program from disk and run it.

```
' PHONEFIX.BAS
' This program uses two fixed-length string arrays to record names and
'    telephone numbers.

OPTION BASE 1                              ' set lower bound of array to 1

CLS
                                           ' get number of names
INPUT "How many names would you like to enter? ", names%
PRINT

DIM fullNames(names%) AS STRING * 18   ' 18 characters each for names
DIM phones(names%) AS STRING * 14      ' 14 characters each for phones

FOR i% = 1 TO names%                       ' read values into both arrays
    INPUT "Enter name: ", fullNames(i%)
    INPUT "Enter phone number: ", phones(i%)
    PRINT
NEXT i%

PRINT "Name                  Phone"
PRINT "-----------------------------------"

FOR i% = 1 TO names%                       ' print contents of both arrays
    PRINT fullNames(i%); " "; phones(i%)
NEXT i%
```

FIGURE 9-5.
PHONEFIX.BAS: A demonstration of fixed-length strings.

252

You'll receive output similar to the following:

```
How many names would you like to enter?  3

Enter name:  Little Bo-Peep
Enter phone number:  555-LAMB

Enter name:  Little Jack Horner
Enter phone number:  555-PLUM

Enter name:  Little Boy Blue
Enter phone number:  555-HORN

Name                    Phone
------------------------------------
Little Bo-Peep          555-LAMB
Little Jack Horner      555-PLUM
Little Boy Blue         555-HORN
```

Note that although the alignment of the phone-number column is now predictable, if one of the names or phone numbers were longer than the allotted number of characters, it would be truncated.

Combining Strings

One of the simplest things you can do with strings is combine them to form larger strings. This process is called *concatenation*. You concatenate strings primarily to prepare text for output on the screen or printer or for storage in a data structure or file. A concatenated string generally should be 80 characters or less in length. This limitation prevents the string from wrapping (spilling over onto the next line).

Both string constants and string variables can be concatenated in any combination, and the result can be assigned to a string variable or supplied as an argument to a statement or function that expects string values (such as PRINT).

For example, the following statement combines the literal strings *Microsoft*, *QuickBASIC*, and *Interpreter* and assigns the result to the *language$* string variable:

```
language$ = "Microsoft" + "QuickBASIC" + "Interpreter"
```

The plus-sign operator (+) is the concatenation operator. It combines the three literal strings and forms one string. The assignment operator (=) then assigns the result to the string variable *language$*. Note that there are no spaces in the literal strings in this statement. (The spaces surrounding the operators don't count.) If you were to print out the value of *language$* with the PRINT statement, the following output would appear:

```
MicrosoftQuickBASICInterpreter
```

The concatenation operator combines the strings exactly as they are, without adding spaces. To include spaces, you must add spaces to the literal strings themselves; that is, a space needs to appear *within* the quotation marks. Each of the following statements would accomplish this goal:

- ```
  PRINT "Microsoft" + " QuickBASIC" + " Interpreter"
  ```
- ```
  PRINT "Microsoft " + "QuickBASIC " + "Interpreter"
  ```
- ```
  PRINT "Microsoft" + " " + "QuickBASIC" + " " + "Interpreter"
  ```

The result of a concatenation can also be supplied as an argument to some QuickBASIC statements directly—without assigning the results to an intermediate variable:

```
PRINT "Microsoft" + "QuickBASIC" + "Interpreter"
```

The result of the preceding statement is the same as the result of

```
language$ = "Microsoft" + "QuickBASIC" + "Interpreter"
PRINT language$
```

Practice: Concatenating strings

The NEWS.BAS program (Figure 9-6) demonstrates a number of the options available to you through string concatenation.

Load the NEWS.BAS program from disk and run it.
```

```
' NEWS.BAS
' This program demonstrates string concatenation.

CONST STRUCTURE$ = "Bridge"

DIM action AS STRING * 10
action = "is falling"

direction$ = "down"

CLS

INPUT "Please enter the name of a city:  ", cityName$

PRINT
PRINT "News Flash: ";
PRINT cityName$ + " " + STRUCTURE$ + " " + action + " " + direction$ + "!"
```

FIGURE 9-6.
NEWS.BAS: A program demonstrating string concatenation.

If you respond to the city prompt with *London*, you'll receive the following output:

```
Please enter the name of a city:  London
News Flash:  London Bridge is falling down!
```

PUTTING STRING FUNCTIONS TO WORK

So far we've declared string constants and variables, combined strings in a process called concatenation, and used strings as arguments in INPUT and PRINT statements. In this section you'll learn about QuickBASIC functions that are specifically designed to manipulate and return values from literal strings and string variables. You'll learn how to

■ Change the case of a string.

■ Determine the length of a string.

■ Take strings apart.

Changing the Case of a String

It's easy to change a string's letters to all uppercase or all lowercase. Simply use the UCASE$ or LCASE$ function. These functions are handy if you need to ensure that all data in your program is in the same format and you're not sure whether the user entered uppercase or lowercase text. (When you learn how strings are compared, you'll understand the importance of this information.)

Using the UCASE$ function

To change a string's letters to all uppercase, use the UCASE$ function, as follows:

```
UCASE$(stringexpression)
```

stringexpression is any variety of string. The value returned by UCASE$ can be assigned to a string variable or supplied as an argument to a statement or function that accepts string values. UCASE$ affects only the lowercase letters of *stringexpression.*

Practice: Using the UCASE$ function

The UPPER.BAS program (Figure 9-7) demonstrates how the UCASE$ function works. UPPER.BAS declares one string constant and two string variables and then uses the UCASE$ function to display them in uppercase. Note that the UCASE$ function affects only the output of the PRINT statement—it doesn't change the content of the *WRITER$* constant or the *address$* variable. (It's a good thing too, because—as you've learned—assigning a new value to a constant would be an error.) When the strings are displayed again at the end of the program, only the *borough$* variable retains uppercase letters, by virtue of its original string assignment.

Load the UPPER.BAS program from disk and run it.

```
' UPPER.BAS
' This program demonstrates the UCASE$ function.

CONST WRITER$ = "Sir Arthur Conan Doyle"
address$ = "1326 Serpentine Avenue"
borough$ = UCASE$("St. John's Wood")

CLS

PRINT UCASE$(WRITER$)
PRINT UCASE$(address$) + ", " + borough$
PRINT
PRINT WRITER$
PRINT address$ + ", " + borough$
```

FIGURE 9-7.
UPPER.BAS: A demonstration of the UCASE$ function.

You'll receive the following output:

```
SIR ARTHUR CONAN DOYLE
1326 SERPENTINE AVENUE, ST. JOHN'S WOOD

Sir Arthur Conan Doyle
1326 Serpentine Avenue, ST. JOHN'S WOOD
```

Using the LCASE$ function

To change a string's letters to all lowercase, use the LCASE$ function, as follows:

LCASE$(*stringexpression*)

stringexpression is any variety of string. The value returned by LCASE$ can be assigned to a string variable or supplied as an argument to a statement or function that accepts string values. LCASE$ affects only the uppercase letters of *stringexpression*.

Practice: Using the LCASE$ function

The LOWER.BAS program (Figure 9-8) demonstrates how the LCASE$ function works. LOWER.BAS converts the uppercase letters in a string to lowercase and assigns the resulting string to a variable and the PRINT statement.

Load the LOWER.BAS program from disk and run it.

```
' LOWER.BAS
' This program demonstrates the UCASE$ and LCASE$ functions.

CLS

character$ = "Sherlock Holmes"
PRINT character$

character$ = UCASE$(character$)
PRINT character$

character$ = LCASE$(character$)
PRINT character$
```

FIGURE 9-8.
LOWER.BAS: A program demonstrating the LCASE$ function.

You'll receive the following output:

```
Sherlock Holmes
SHERLOCK HOLMES
sherlock holmes
```

Determining the Length of a String

Often you'll want to know how many characters are in a string. This knowledge can be particularly handy with variable-length strings, especially those entered from the keyboard.

To determine how many characters (including spaces) are in a string, use the LEN function, as follows:

LEN(*stringexpression*)

stringexpression once again is any kind of string. The value returned by LEN can be assigned to an integer variable or supplied as an argument to a statement or function that accepts integer values.

The following statements show how the LEN function determines the number of characters in a string and assigns the number to an integer variable:

```
fullName$ = "Old Mother Hubbard"
nameLength% = LEN(fullName$)
PRINT fullName$; " is"; nameLength%; "characters long"
```

When you execute these statements, you receive the following output:

```
Old Mother Hubbard is 18 characters long
```

Practice: Using the LEN function

The MENU.BAS program (Figure 9-9) shows how the value returned by the LEN function can be used as an argument to a PRINT statement. MENU.BAS declares three variable-length strings that contain potential meal selections for the user. These strings are displayed with PRINT statements. An INPUT statement prompts the user for a meal selection. The user's selection is assigned to the *choice$* variable and is converted to uppercase with the UCASE$ function. The SELECT CASE statement then compares the *choice$* variable with the three meal variables. If a match occurs, the meal choice and its length (returned by the LEN function) are printed. If no match occurs, the CASE ELSE statement prints the message *I don't recognize that meal!*

Load the MENU.BAS program from disk and run it.

```
' MENU.BAS
' This program demonstrates the LEN function.

missMuffet$ = "Curds and Whey"          ' declare meal strings
simpleSimon$ = "Pie du Jour"
petersPlate$ = "Pumpkin Surprise"
```

FIGURE 9-9.
MENU.BAS: A program demonstrating the LEN function.

(continued)

LEARN BASIC NOW

FIGURE 9-9. *continued*

```
CLS

PRINT "Which meal would you enjoy?"      ' display meal prompt
PRINT

PRINT missMuffet$                        ' display meal choices
PRINT simpleSimon$
PRINT petersPlate$
PRINT

INPUT "Selection:  ", choice$            ' get meal choice from user
choice$ = UCASE$(choice$)                ' convert string to uppercase
PRINT

SELECT CASE choice$                      ' find variable that matches
    CASE IS = UCASE$(missMuffet$)        '    meal entered and print length
        PRINT missMuffet$; " is"; LEN(missMuffet$); "characters long"
    CASE IS = UCASE$(simpleSimon$)
        PRINT simpleSimon$; " is"; LEN(simpleSimon$); "characters long"
    CASE IS = UCASE$(petersPlate$)
        PRINT petersPlate$; " is"; LEN(petersPlate$); "characters long"
    CASE ELSE                            ' print message if no match found
        PRINT "I don't recognize that meal!"
END SELECT
```

You'll receive output similar to the following:

```
Which meal would you enjoy?

Curds and Whey
Pie du Jour
Pumpkin Surprise

Selection:  Curds and Whey

Curds and Whey is 14 characters long
```

Taking Strings Apart

Earlier in this chapter you learned that QuickBASIC lets you combine strings through concatenation. But sometimes you'll have the need to take strings apart, for example, to get only a person's last name from the full name. QuickBASIC provides six functions that allow you to do just that. The following sections describe how to use these functions to

- Get the right end of a string (RIGHT$).

- Get the left end of a string (LEFT$).

- Get the middle of a string (MID$).

- Trim the right end of a string (RTRIM$).

- Trim the left end of a string (LTRIM$).

- Find a string within a string (INSTR).

You'll also learn about statements that let you

- Get an entire line of input (LINE INPUT$).

- Print repeated characters (SPACE$, STRING$).

Getting the ends of a string

The RIGHT$ and LEFT$ functions let you retrieve one or more characters starting from one end of a string. This is useful when you want to display only part of a string or when you want to remove part of a string.

The syntax for the RIGHT$ function is as follows:

```
RIGHT$(stringexpression, n)
```

The syntax for the LEFT$ function is as follows:

```
LEFT$(stringexpression, n)
```

stringexpression is any variety of string, and *n* is an integer value (ranging from zero to the length of the string) indicating the number of characters to be returned by RIGHT$ or LEFT$. The value returned can be assigned to a string variable or supplied as an argument to a statement or function that accepts string values.

Practice: Using the RIGHT$ function

The GETRIGHT.BAS program (Figure 9-10) uses the RIGHT$ function to retrieve characters from a variable named *alphabet$*, which contains the 26 letters of the alphabet. GETRIGHT.BAS extracts the requested number of characters and displays them with a character count.

Load the GETRIGHT.BAS program from disk and run it.

```
' GETRIGHT.BAS
' This program demonstrates the RIGHT$ function.

CLS

alphabet$ = "ABCDEFGHIJKLMNOPQRSTUVWXYZ"    ' declare test string

PRINT "How many characters (from right to left) in the following"
PRINT "string would you like to display?"
PRINT
PRINT alphabet$                             ' display test string
PRINT

    ' get from user number of rightmost characters to be displayed
DO  ' loop until number is in proper range (1 through 26)
    INPUT "    Number (1-26):  ", rightNum%
LOOP WHILE (rightNum% < 1) OR (rightNum% > 26)

PRINT
rightChar$ = RIGHT$(alphabet$, rightNum%)  ' display characters
PRINT "You specified"; LEN(rightChar$); "characters:  "; rightChar$
```

FIGURE 9-10.
GETRIGHT.BAS: A program demonstrating the RIGHT$ function.

You'll receive output similar to the following:

```
How many characters (from right to left) in the following
string would you like to display?

ABCDEFGHIJKLMNOPQRSTUVWXYZ

    Number (1-26):  14

You specified 14 characters:  MNOPQRSTUVWXYZ
```

Practice: Using the LEFT$ function

The GETLEFT.BAS program (Figure 9-11) revises the GETRIGHT.BAS program to extract characters from the left side of a string with the LEFT$ function. Note that the variable names have changed slightly (*rightNum%* becomes *leftNum%* and *rightChar$* becomes *leftChar$*) and that the function RIGHT$ has been changed to LEFT$. Outside of these changes (and a few changes to the prompt and program comments), GETLEFT.BAS is identical to GETRIGHT.BAS. Because the operation of the RIGHT$ and LEFT$ functions is so similar, it's quite easy to change a program so that it modifies a string from the opposite end.

Load the GETLEFT.BAS program from disk and run it.

```
' GETLEFT.BAS
' This program demonstrates the LEFT$ function.

CLS

alphabet$ = "ABCDEFGHIJKLMNOPQRSTUVWXYZ"     ' declare test string

PRINT "How many characters (from left to right) in the following"
PRINT "string would you like to display?"
PRINT
PRINT alphabet$                              ' display test string
PRINT

    ' get from user number of leftmost characters to be displayed
DO  ' loop until number is in proper range (1 through 26)
    INPUT "    Number (1-26):  ", leftNum%
LOOP WHILE (leftNum% < 1) OR (leftNum% > 26)

PRINT
leftChar$ = LEFT$(alphabet$, leftNum%)       ' display characters
PRINT "You specified"; LEN(leftChar$); "characters: "; leftChar$
```

FIGURE 9-11.
GETLEFT.BAS: A program demonstrating the LEFT$ function.

You'll receive output similar to the following:

```
How many characters (from left to right) in the following
string would you like to display?

ABCDEFGHIJKLMNOPQRSTUVWXYZ

   Number (1-26):  14

You specified 14 characters:  ABCDEFGHIJKLMN
```

Getting the middle of a string

The MID$ function lets you retrieve one or more characters from anywhere within a string—from the left, from the middle, or (with some help from the LEN function) from the right. Its versatility makes the MID$ function one of the most useful string functions. And, as we'll see later, it also provides the processing power to solve many string-related problems.

The syntax for the MID$ function is as follows:

```
MID$(stringexpression, start, length)
```

stringexpression is any kind of string, *start* is an integer value between 1 and the length of the string (indicating the first character to be returned), and *length* is an integer value indicating the number of characters to be returned. The value returned by MID$ can be assigned to a string variable or supplied as an argument to a statement or function that accepts string values. Figure 9-12 examines the syntax of the MID$ function in detail.

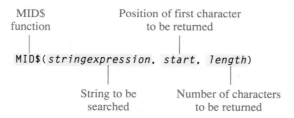

FIGURE 9-12.
The components of the MID$ function.

The following statements show some valid uses of the MID$ function. Notice the powerful possibilities that arise when you use the value returned by a function as an argument to MID$ or when you assign the value returned by MID$ to another statement or function.

```
middleName$ = MID$("Queen Victoria Belfield", 7, 8)
```
Result: *middleName$* contains Victoria

```
address$ = "1521 Plumtree Lane #25-K"
streetNameStart% = 6
length% = 13
PRINT UCASE$(MID$(address$, streetNameStart%, length%))
```
Result: PLUMTREE LANE

```
inString$ = "Making it all make sense"
rightmostWord$ = MID$(inString$, LEN(inString$) - 4, 5)
```
Result: *rightmostWord$* contains sense

```
PRINT "The current year is "; MID$(DATE$, 7, 4)
```
Result: The current year is 1990

Practice: Using the MID$ function

The GETMID.BAS program (Figure 9-13) shows how to retrieve characters from the middle of a string with the MID$ function. GETMID modifies the GETRIGHT and GETLEFT programs to include a starting point along with the number of characters in the *alphabet$* string to be displayed. GETMID uses two DO loops to get integer values in the proper range and then uses the MID$ function to assign the selected characters to the *midChar$* variable. The results of the selection are printed with the following IF statement, which appears near the end of the program:

```
IF (numToDisplay% = LEN(midChar$)) THEN
    PRINT numToDisplay%; "characters displayed:  "; midChar$
ELSE
    PRINT numToDisplay%; "characters requested,";
    PRINT LEN(midChar$); "displayed:  "; midChar$
END IF
```

265

The IF statement compares *numToDisplay%*—the variable containing the number of characters the user requested to be displayed—to the number of characters in *midChar$* (returned by the LEN function). If the two values are equal, the value of *numToDisplay%* is printed along with the contents of *midChar$*. If the two values are not equal, the LEN function is used to determine the actual number of characters, and this value is displayed along with the *midChar$* string. GETMID contains this additional message to notify the user that the display length entered exceeded the number of characters remaining in the string.

Load the GETMID.BAS program from disk and run it.

```
' GETMID.BAS
' This program demonstrates the MID$ function.

CLS

alphabet$ = "ABCDEFGHIJKLMNOPQRSTUVWXYZ"   ' declare test string

PRINT "How many characters (from left to right) in the following"
PRINT "string would you like to display?"
PRINT
PRINT alphabet$                            ' display test string
PRINT

    ' get from user number of characters to be displayed
DO  ' loop until number is in proper range (1 through 26)
    INPUT "    Number (1-26):  ", numToDisplay%
LOOP WHILE (numToDisplay% < 1) OR (numToDisplay% > 26)
PRINT                                   ' get starting number...
PRINT "What character would you like to start with?"
PRINT

DO                                      '  in proper range
    INPUT "    Starting number (1-26):  ", start%
LOOP WHILE (start% < 1) OR (start% > 26)
```

FIGURE 9-13. *(continued)*
GETMID.BAS: A program demonstrating the MID$ function.

FIGURE 9-13. *continued*

```
PRINT                                          ' get characters
midChar$ = MID$(alphabet$, start%, numToDisplay%)

    ' compare requested characters with actual characters retrieved
    '   and print an appropriate message with string
IF (numToDisplay% = LEN(midChar$)) THEN
    PRINT numToDisplay%; "characters displayed:  "; midChar$
ELSE
    PRINT numToDisplay%; "characters requested,";
    PRINT LEN(midChar$); "displayed:  "; midChar$
END IF
```

You'll receive output similar to the following:

```
How many characters (from left to right) in the following
string would you like to display?

ABCDEFGHIJKLMNOPQRSTUVWXYZ

    Number (1-26):  14

What character would you like to start with?

    Starting number (1-26):  4

 14 characters displayed:  DEFGHIJKLMNOPQ
```

If you specify a number outside the range permitted by GETMID, you receive output similar to the following:

```
How many characters (from left to right) in the following
string would you like to display?

ABCDEFGHIJKLMNOPQRSTUVWXYZ

    Number (1-26):  0
    Number (1-26):  30
    Number (1-26):  15
```

(continued)

continued

```
What character would you like to start with?

    Starting number (1-26):  W

Redo from start
    Starting number (1-26):  20

 15 characters requested, 7 displayed:  TUVWXYZ
```

If you type in a non-numeric value (such as a letter) at one of the prompts, QuickBASIC prints the message *Redo from start* and redisplays the prompt. Handling this type of response from the user is important when you are developing "break-proof" programs that other people will use.

Trimming a string

When you want to align strings or eliminate wasted space at the ends of strings, you can use the QuickBASIC trimming functions, LTRIM$ and RTRIM$.

The LTRIM$ function lets you trim the left end of a string; that is, LTRIM$ returns a string with no leading spaces or tabs. The RTRIM$ function performs a similar task on the right end of a string.

The syntax for the LTRIM$ function is as follows:

```
LTRIM$(stringexpression)
```

The syntax for the RTRIM$ function is as follows:

```
RTRIM$(stringexpression)
```

stringexpression can be any variety of string. The value returned by LTRIM$ or RTRIM$ can be assigned to a string variable or supplied as an argument to a statement or function that accepts string values.

The following statements use the LTRIM$ function to remove the three leading spaces from the string variable *englishPhrase$* before printing:

```
englishPhrase$ = "   Good evening"
englishPhrase$ = LTRIM$(englishPhrase$)

PRINT englishPhrase$; "!"
```

These statements result in the following output:

```
Good evening!
```

The following statements use the RTRIM$ function to remove the three final spaces from the string variable *germanPhrase$* before printing:

```
germanPhrase$ = "Guten Abend   "
germanPhrase$ = RTRIM$(germanPhrase$)

PRINT germanPhrase$; "!"
```

These statements result in the following output:

```
Guten Abend!
```

Practice: Using LTRIM$ and RTRIM$

The GREETING.BAS program (Figure 9-14) shows how to use the LTRIM$ and RTRIM$ functions together to trim blank spaces from both ends of a fixed-length string.

GREETING declares two fixed-length string variables named *firstName* and *lastName* and uses the INPUT statements to obtain string values for these variables. The GREETING program then displays two messages for the user of the program. The first message is not trimmed; the second is trimmed by both the LTRIM$ and RTRIM$ functions. Note that the fixed-length strings themselves are not modified—you cannot change the length of a fixed-length string.

Note how a string argument is passed from RTRIM$ to LTRIM$ to PRINT in the following statement from GREETING:

```
PRINT "I think "; LTRIM$(RTRIM$(firstName)); " ";
```

The RTRIM$ function processes the variable *firstName* and passes the resulting string value to the LTRIM$ function. LTRIM$ then processes the string and passes a string value to the PRINT statement. The PRINT statement then combines the string value with two other string values and displays them on your screen.

Load the GREETING.BAS program from disk and run it.

```
' GREETING.BAS
' This program demonstrates the LTRIM$ and RTRIM$ functions.

DIM firstName AS STRING * 12  ' declare fixed-length strings
DIM lastName AS STRING * 15

CLS
                             ' get first and last names
INPUT "Enter your first name:  ", firstName
INPUT "Enter your last name:  ", lastName

PRINT                        ' print greeting without trimming
PRINT "Nice to meet you, "; firstName; " "; lastName; "!"
                             ' print compliment with trimming
PRINT "I think "; LTRIM$(RTRIM$(firstName)); " ";
PRINT LTRIM$(RTRIM$(lastName)); " has a nice ring to it."
```

FIGURE 9-14.
GREETING.BAS: A program demonstrating the LTRIM$ and RTRIM$ functions.

You'll receive output similar to the following:

```
Enter your first name:  Jack
Enter your last name:  Sprat

Nice to meet you, Jack          Sprat           !
I think Jack Sprat has a nice ring to it.
```

Getting an entire line from the user

Throughout this chapter we've used the INPUT statement to get input from the user. The INPUT statement is quite versatile—it can assign input to one or more variables of different types and supply an optional prompt to spell out exactly what the user should enter. One thing we haven't discussed, however, is how the INPUT statement processes a comma in the input line. Consider the following statement, which prompts the user to enter a name and address:

```
INPUT "Enter name and address:  ", mailingAddress$
```

If the user responds to the prompt with a string containing commas, the error message *Redo from start* appears, as shown in the following dialog:

```
Enter name and address:  Jon Victor, 1118 Skyridge, Lacey, WA, 98503

Redo from start
Enter name and address:
```

As discussed in Chapter 4, the INPUT statement has a special use for the comma character in the input line: The comma separates the values assigned to variables. But what happens when unexpected commas appear in the input—as shown above? In this case you could solve the problem by assigning parts of the input string to different variables. For example, the following INPUT statement assigns the string value entered to five string variables:

```
INPUT "Enter name and address:  ", name$, address$, city$, state$, zip$
```

But there are times when it would be a lot simpler to have one variable name associated with a line of input. QuickBASIC provides a solution to this problem with the LINE INPUT statement. The LINE INPUT statement gets an entire line of text from the keyboard and assigns it to a string variable, even if commas are present.

The syntax for the LINE INPUT statement is as follows:

```
LINE INPUT [;] ["promptstring";] stringvariable
```

promptstring is a literal string that prompts the user for input, and *stringvariable* is any string variable.

- A semicolon immediately after LINE INPUT keeps the cursor on the same line after the user presses Enter.

- If *promptstring* is included, a semicolon is required to separate *promptstring* from *stringvariable*.

- Unlike the INPUT statement, the LINE INPUT statement prints no question mark unless it is included in *promptstring*.

The following statements demonstrate the usefulness of LINE INPUT with long lines of input containing the comma character:

```
LINE INPUT ; "Enter name and address:  "; mailingAddress$
PRINT mailingAddress$
```

When you execute the statements and enter the information shown in the sample output above, you'll receive the following output:

```
Enter name and address:  Jon Victor, 1118 Skyridge, Lacey, WA, 98503
Jon Victor, 1118 Skyridge, Lacey, WA, 98503
```

You'll see the LINE INPUT statement from time to time in the chapters to come.

Printing repeated characters

QuickBASIC provides two useful functions that generate strings of repeated characters: the SPACE$ function, which returns a string of spaces, and the STRING$ function, which returns a string of characters. Both functions provide fast ways to build strings for use in formatting and aligning your output.

The syntax of the SPACE$ function is as follows:

```
SPACE$(n)
```

n is an integer value specifying the number of spaces to be included in the string. The value returned by SPACE$ can be assigned to a string variable or supplied as an argument to a statement or function that accepts string values.

The most common use of the SPACE$ function is in formatting output, as shown in the following statements:

```
blank$ = SPACE$(15)
PRINT blank$; "Big sale on bunnies today!"
```

You can use SPACE$ whenever you consistently indent text a set number of spaces.

The syntax of the STRING$ function is as follows:

```
STRING$(m, stringexpression)
```

m is an integer value specifying the length of the string to be returned, and *stringexpression* is the character to be repeated. The value returned by STRING$ can be assigned to a string variable or supplied as an argument to a statement or function that accepts string values.

Practice: Using SPACE$ and STRING$

The most common use of the STRING$ function is for headings used in program output. The HEADER.BAS program (Figure 9-15) uses STRING$ to display a header message in the middle of the screen. Note that using a constant to specify the number of repeated characters makes it easy to modify the program later and that the variables created by STRING$ and SPACE$ make excellent candidates for concatenation.

Load the HEADER.BAS program from disk and run it.

```
' HEADER.BAS
' This program demonstrates the SPACE$ and STRING$ functions.

CONST LENGTH% = 16

fileName$ = "SWEETPEA.DOC"
blank$ = SPACE$(LENGTH%)
asterisk$ = STRING$(LENGTH%, "*")
banner$ = blank$ + asterisk$ + " " + fileName$ + " " + asterisk$

CLS

PRINT banner$
```

FIGURE 9-15.
HEADER.BAS: A program demonstrating the SPACE$ and STRING$ functions.

You'll see the filename *SWEETPEA.DOC* in the middle of the top line of the screen, surrounded by equal numbers of asterisks and blank spaces.

Finding a string within a string

We've used the LEFT$, RIGHT$, and MID$ functions in this chapter to return characters from the left, right, and middle portions of a string. These functions are quite effective at extracting characters from a set place in a string, but they are less effective at searching for and extracting a specific pattern from a string. QuickBASIC fills this gap with the INSTR function, which searches for one string within another string. The INSTR function, combined with LEFT$, RIGHT$, MID$, and the support functions we've discussed in this section (UCASE$, LCASE$, LEN$, RTRIM$, LTRIM$, SPACE$, and STRING$), provide a complete collection of tools for working with strings.

The syntax for the INSTR function is as follows:

```
INSTR([start, ]basestring, searchstring)
```

start is an optional integer value specifying the character at which the search should begin, *basestring* is the string being searched, and *searchstring* is the string being sought. The value returned by INSTR can be assigned to an integer variable or supplied as an argument to a statement or function that accepts integer values. The following table lists the values that the INSTR function can return:

Condition	*Integer value returned*
searchstring found in *basestring*	Position in *basestring* at which match is found
searchstring not found in *basestring*	0
start is greater than length of *basestring*	0
basestring contains no characters	0
searchstring contains no characters	*start* (if given); otherwise, 1

Practice: Using the INSTR function

The HUNT.BAS program (Figure 9-16) uses the INSTR function to search for the string *iddle* in the string *High, diddle, diddle, the cat and the fiddle.*

Load the HUNT.BAS program from disk and run it.

```
' HUNT.BAS
' This program demonstrates the INSTR function.

CLS

search$ = "iddle"
base$ = "High, diddle, diddle, the cat and the fiddle"
strLocation% = INSTR(1, base$, search$)

IF (strLocation% <> 0) THEN
    PRINT search$; " first appears starting at character"; strLocation%
ELSE
    PRINT search$; " not found"
END IF
```

FIGURE 9-16.
HUNT.BAS: A program demonstrating the INSTR function.

When you run the program you receive the following output:

```
iddle first appears starting at character 8
```

Although the pattern *iddle* appears three times in *base$*, the INSTR function returns the location of only the first occurrence. However, you can use INSTR within a loop to find multiple occurrences of a pattern.

It's a good idea to check the value returned by INSTR whenever you use the INSTR function. This will allow your program to take appropriate action if the search string is not found, or if either the search string or the base string is empty.

For example, in the HUNT program, if *iddle* were not found, the INSTR function would assign a value of 0 to the *strLocation%* variable, and the IF statement would display the following message to indicate that *iddle* did not exist in *base$*:

```
iddle not found
```

Practice: Finding multiple occurrences of a pattern

The REPEAT.BAS program (Figure 9-17) uses the INSTR function to find multiple occurrences of a pattern in a series of lines entered from the keyboard.

The heart of REPEAT is found in the *Repeat%* function. Each time INSTR finds the search string (*search$*) in the base string (*base$*), the location of the search string is assigned to the *currentChar%* variable. The *num%* variable is then incremented and the *currentChar%* variable is moved ahead to the position just after the string match in the base string (the new starting place for the next search). This process continues until the end of the base string is reached or the search string is not found in the remainder of the base string. The *Repeat%* function then returns the total number of matches in the line to the *lineRepeats%* variable in the main program.

Load the REPEAT.BAS program from disk and run it.

```
' REPEAT.BAS
' This program prompts the user for a set number of lines and a search
'   string and then prints the lines and the number of matches found.

' set maximum number of lines that can be entered and declare string
'   array to hold lines

CONST MAXLINES% = 10
DIM inputLines$(MAXLINES%)

' declare GetText subprogram and Repeat% function

DECLARE SUB GetText (inputLines$(), numOfLines%)
DECLARE FUNCTION Repeat% (search$, base$)

CLS

' call GetText subprogram to get input from user; at return the
'   numOfLines% variable will contain number of lines received
```

FIGURE 9-17. *(continued)*
REPEAT.BAS: A program that scans lines for a pattern and prints the number of matches.

FIGURE 9-17. *continued*

```
GetText inputLines$(), numOfLines%

' get pattern to be searched for from user

PRINT
INPUT "Enter the string to be searched for:  ", pattern$
PRINT

' call Repeat% function to determine the number of matches per line;
'    totalRepeats% variable tracks number of total matches

FOR i = 1 TO numOfLines%
    lineRepeats% = Repeat%(pattern$, inputLines$(i))
    totalRepeats% = totalRepeats% + lineRepeats%
NEXT i

' display lines entered by the user...

PRINT "You entered the following lines:"
PRINT
FOR i = 1 TO numOfLines%
    PRINT inputLines$(i)
NEXT i

' and the total number of matches

PRINT
PRINT "The pattern '"; pattern$; "' appears"; totalRepeats%; "times"

END

SUB GetText (strArray$(), count%)

' The GetText subprogram fills the strArray$() array with text
'    entered at the keyboard. The number of lines that can be
'    entered is determined by the global constant MAXLINES%.
'    Both strArray$() and count% (the number of lines actually
'    entered) are returned to the main program.
```

(continued)

FIGURE 9-17. *continued*

```
PRINT "Enter up to"; MAXLINES%; "lines of text; to end, ";
PRINT "press Enter on a new line."
PRINT
count% = 0

DO
    LINE INPUT "-> "; inLine$   ' get line from user
    IF (inLine$ <> "") THEN     ' if line is not blank, copy it
        count% = count% + 1     '    to the strArray$() array
        strArray$(count%) = inLine$
    END IF
' loop until count% = MAXLINES% or an empty line is received
LOOP WHILE (count% < MAXLINES%) AND (inLine$ <> "")

END SUB

FUNCTION Repeat% (search$, base$)

' The Repeat% function returns the number of times a search string
'   is found in a base string.

searchLength% = LEN(search$)   ' determine length of search string
baseLength% = LEN(base$)       ' determine length of base string
currentChar% = 1               ' character offset in base string
num% = 0                       ' running total of matches found in base

' loop until entire string is processed or INSTR returns a 0

WHILE (currentChar% <= baseLength%) AND (currentChar% <> 0)
    currentChar% = INSTR(currentChar%, base$, search$)
    IF (currentChar% <> 0) THEN  ' if not zero, a match was found
        num% = num% + 1          ' increment number of matches
        ' new offset equals current offset plus search-string length
        currentChar% = currentChar% + searchLength%
    END IF
WEND

Repeat% = num%                 ' return total number of matches

END FUNCTION
```

You'll receive output similar to the following:

```
Enter up to ten lines of text; to end, press Enter on a new line.

-> Ten lords a-leaping,
-> Nine ladies dancing,
-> Eight maids a-milking,
-> Seven swans a-swimming,
-> Six geese a-laying,
-> Five gold rings,
-> Four calling birds,
-> Three French hens,
-> Two turtledoves, and
-> A partridge in a pear tree.

Enter the string to be searched for:  ing

You entered the following lines:

Ten lords a-leaping,
Nine ladies dancing,
Eight maids a-milking,
Seven swans a-swimming,
Six geese a-laying,
Five gold rings,
Four calling birds,
Three French hens,
Two turtledoves, and
A partridge in a pear tree.

The pattern 'ing' appears 7 times
```

COMPARING STRINGS

In Chapter 4 you learned that you can compare one string to another and branch to another place in the program based on the result of the comparison. Consider the following IF statement, which compares the variable *reply$* to the literal string *Y* and prints a message based on the comparison:

```
reply$ = "Y"
IF (reply$ = "Y") THEN
    PRINT "The two string values are equal"
ELSE
    PRINT "The two string values are not equal"
END IF
```

If you execute the above statements as is, you receive the following output:

```
The two string values are equal
```

If you change the value of *reply$* to *y* and then execute the statement, you receive a different response:

```
The two string values are not equal
```

Why is this? After all, a Y is a y.... Or is it? What criteria is QuickBASIC using for its string comparisons?

The ASCII Character Set

Before QuickBASIC can compare one character to another, it must convert each character into a number by using a translation table called the *ASCII character set*. QuickBASIC then compares the numbers, called *ASCII codes*, and returns a logical value of true if the ASCII codes are equal or false if the codes are not equal.

ASCII Is an Acronym

Like many other computer terms, ASCII is an acronym—it stands for American Standard Code for Information Interchange. The key word here is *code*: Like the Morse code used in radio and telegraphy, ASCII is an internationally accepted code for representing characters used in computers and telecommunication. Appendix B lists the complete ASCII character set.

Each character in the ASCII character set is associated with a unique number; the set contains 128 characters (codes 0 through 127) in all:

- Control characters (codes 0 through 31), including characters that correspond to special keys on your keyboard such as Enter, Backspace, and Escape

- Punctuation symbols, numbers, and mathematical symbols (codes 32 through 64)

- Uppercase letters of the alphabet (codes 65 through 90)

- Lowercase letters of the alphabet (codes 97 through 122)

- Miscellaneous symbols (codes 91 through 96 and 123 through 127)

For example, the ASCII code for the uppercase letter *A* is 65; the ASCII code for the lowercase letter *z* is 122. Following this logic, it's easy to see why QuickBASIC considers the uppercase letter *Y* and the lowercase letter *y* to be different characters.

The IBM Extended Character Set

Appendix B also contains an additional collection of characters (codes 128 through 255) known as the *IBM extended character set.* This set of symbols was developed by IBM for the IBM family of personal computers and has subsequently been adopted by most manufacturers of PC-compatible computers. The IBM extended character set (sometimes called the upper ASCII character set) contains a collection of foreign-language characters, line-drawing and box-drawing characters, and mathematical symbols. Although you can use these symbols in your programs, you can't type them through the usual means—there are no keys to press! Instead, you hold down the Alt key and type in the three-digit IBM extended character code. (Use the keys on the numeric keypad rather than the number keys near the top of your keyboard.) For example, to display the mathematical symbol π on your screen, hold down Alt and type *227* on the numeric keypad.

The following PRINT statement demonstrates a valid use of the IBM extended character set in a QuickBASIC program. The ¿ symbol was entered by holding down Alt and typing *168*.

```
PRINT "¿Como se llama?"
```

NOTE: Some older monitors cannot display characters in the IBM extended character set, and you'll have trouble printing most of the IBM extended character set symbols unless your printer is specifically set up to handle them. Be ready for some strange (but nondamaging) results when you use the extended character set.

Converting ASCII Codes to Characters

If you know a character's ASCII code but you're not sure what character it represents, you can use the CHR$ function to return the symbol to your screen or to your program.

The syntax for the CHR$ function is as follows:

```
CHR$(code)
```

code is an integer value specifying an ASCII or IBM extended character code. The value returned by CHR$ can be assigned to a string variable or supplied as an argument to a statement or function that accepts string values.

Practice: Using the CHR$ function

The ASCII.BAS program (Figure 9-18) shows how to use the CHR$ function to display the characters in the ASCII and IBM extended character sets. Note that the program skips the first 32 control

```
' ASCII.BAS
' This program displays the ASCII and IBM extended character sets.

CLS

FOR i% = 33 TO 255
    PRINT "Code"; i%; "= "; CHR$(i%)
    IF (i% MOD 23 = 0) THEN INPUT "Press Enter for more...", dummy$
NEXT i%
```

FIGURE 9-18.
ASCII.BAS: A program that uses the CHR$ function to display the ASCII and IBM extended character sets.

characters in the ASCII character set and pauses after each multiple of 23 lines (except the first and last sets) so that you can view the results at your own pace.

Load the ASCII.BAS program from disk and run it. (Because of its length, we won't show the output here.)

Converting Characters to ASCII Codes

As a complement to the CHR$ function, QuickBASIC provides the ASC function to take a character and convert it to a code in the ASCII character set or the IBM extended character set.

The syntax of the ASC function is as follows:

```
ASC(stringexpression)
```

stringexpression is a one-character string. The value returned by ASC can be assigned to an integer variable or supplied as an argument to a statement or function that accepts integer values.

Practice: Using the ASC function

The COMPARE.BAS program (Figure 9-19) uses the ASC function to show how QuickBASIC compares different characters. COMPARE asks the user for two characters and then uses a SELECT CASE statement to display one of three messages based on the values returned by ASC.

Load the COMPARE.BAS program from disk and run it.

```
' COMPARE.BAS
' This program compares any two characters.

CLS

INPUT "Enter any character:  ", firstChar$
INPUT "Enter another character:  ", secondChar$
PRINT
```

Figure 9-19. *(continued)*
COMPARE.BAS: A program that uses the ASC function to compare two characters.

FIGURE 9-19. *continued*

```
SELECT CASE ASC(firstChar$) - ASC(secondChar$)
    CASE IS < 0
        PRINT "'"; firstChar$; "' comes before '"; secondChar$; "'"
        PRINT "because"; ASC(firstChar$); "is less than"; ASC(secondChar$)
    CASE IS > 0
        PRINT "'"; firstChar$; "' comes after '"; secondChar$; "'"
        PRINT "because"; ASC(firstChar$); "is more than"; ASC(secondChar$)
    CASE ELSE
        PRINT "'"; firstChar$; "' is the same as '"; secondChar$; "'"
        PRINT "because"; ASC(firstChar$); "is equal to"; ASC(secondChar$)
END SELECT
```

You'll receive output similar to the following:

```
Enter any character:  d
Enter another character:  J

'd' comes after 'J'
because 100 is more than 74
```

Using Relational Operators with Strings

In addition to testing for equivalence in characters, QuickBASIC supports string comparisons with the following relational operators:

Operator	Meaning	Operator	Meaning
<>	Not equal	>	Greater than
=	Equal	<=	Less than or equal to
<	Less than	>=	Greater than or equal to

A single character is greater than another character if its ASCII code is greater. For example, the ASCII value of the letter *B* is greater than the ASCII value of the letter *A*, so the expression

```
"A" < "B"
```

is true, and the expression

```
"A" > "B"
```

is false.

When comparing two strings containing more than one character, QuickBASIC begins by comparing the first character in each string and then proceeds through the strings character by character until a difference is found. For example, the strings *Mike* and *Michael* are the same up to the third characters (*k* and *c*). Because the ASCII value of *k* is greater than that of *c*, the expression

```
"Mike" > "Michael"
```

evaluates to true.

If no differences are found, then (as we have seen) the strings are equal. If two strings are equal to a point, but one of the strings continues and the other one stops, the longer string is greater than the shorter string. For example, the expression

```
"AAAAA" > "AAA"
```

evaluates to true.

Sorting Strings: The STRSORT.BAS Program

The STRSORT.BAS program (Figure 9-20) uses the <= relational operator to compare array elements and uses the SWAP statement to switch any elements that are out of order.

STRSORT declares an array of strings named *inputLines$* and calls the *GetText* subprogram. The *GetText* subprogram is identical to the *GetText* subprogram in the REPEAT.BAS program (Figure 9-17): It reads lines of text into an array and then returns the array (*inputLines$*) and the number of elements in the array (*numOfElements%*) to the main program.

The program next calls the *ShellSort* subprogram. Note the following statements in the heart of *ShellSort* that compare array elements and then swap the elements if they are out of order:

```
IF strArray$(j%) <= strArray$(j% + span%) THEN EXIT FOR
' swap array elements that are out of order
SWAP strArray$(j%), strArray$(j% + span%)
```

The <= relational operator is used to compare the two array elements.

- If the value of the string expression *strArray$(j%)* is less than or equal to the value of the string expression *strArray$(j% + span%)*, the elements are already in order and the EXIT FOR statement terminates the FOR loop.

- If the value of the second string expression is greater than the value of the first, the elements are exchanged with the SWAP statement. SWAP, introduced here for the first time, exchanges the values of any two variables of the same type. In this case, two string variables are exchanged. When the array is completely sorted, it is passed back to the main program and printed in its entirety by a FOR loop.

Load the STRSORT.BAS program from disk and run it.

The Shell Sort

The logic in the *ShellSort* subprogram is based on the popular Shell Sort algorithm for sorting an array of numbers published in 1959 by Donald Shell. The Shell Sort sorts a list of elements by continually dividing the main list into smaller sublists that are smaller by half and comparing the elements at the tops and bottoms of the sublists. If the elements are out of order, they are exchanged. The end result is an array of items in descending order.

To see other sorting routines in action, load and run the SORTDEMO.BAS program from the \QBI directory of your hard disk or from the root directory of Disk 1. SORTDEMO describes the operation of six sorts, including the Shell Sort.

```
' STRSORT.BAS
' This program prompts the user for a list of names and then sorts them
'    alphabetically.

' set maximum number of lines that can be entered and declare string
'    array to hold lines

CONST MAXLINES% = 15
DIM inputLines$(MAXLINES%)

' declare GetText and ShellSort subprograms

DECLARE SUB GetText (strArray$(), numOfElements%)
DECLARE SUB ShellSort (strArray$(), numOfElements%)

CLS

' call GetText subprogram to get input from user; at return the
'    numOfElements% variable will contain number of lines received

GetText inputLines$(), numOfElements%

' call ShellSort subprogram to put inputLines$() array in
'    alphabetical order

ShellSort inputLines$(), numOfElements%

PRINT
PRINT "Sorting results:"
PRINT

FOR i% = 1 TO numOfElements%       ' print contents of sorted array
    PRINT inputLines$(i%)
NEXT i%

END
```

FIGURE 9-20.   *(continued)*

STRSORT.BAS: A program that sorts a list of strings entered by the user.

FIGURE 9-20. *continued*

```
SUB GetText (strArray$(), count%)

' The GetText subprogram fills the strArray$() array with text
'    entered at the keyboard. The number of lines that can be
'    entered is determined by the global constant MAXLINES%.
'    Both strArray$() and count% (the number of lines actually
'    entered) are returned to the main program.

PRINT "Enter up to"; MAXLINES%; "lines of text; to end, ";
PRINT "press Enter on a new line."
PRINT
count% = 0

DO
    LINE INPUT "-> "; inLine$   ' get line from user
    IF (inLine$ <> "") THEN     ' if line is not blank, copy it
        count% = count% + 1     '     to the strArray$() array
        strArray$(count%) = inLine$
    END IF
' loop until count% = MAXLINES% or an empty line is received
LOOP WHILE (count% < MAXLINES%) AND (inLine$ <> "")

END SUB

SUB ShellSort (strArray$(), numOfElements%)

' The ShellSort subprogram sorts the elements of strArray$() and
'    returns strArray$() to the main program.  The numOfElements%
'    argument contains the number of elements in strArray$().
'    ShellSort sorts elements in descending order.

span% = numOfElements% \ 2
```

(continued)

FIGURE 9-20. *continued*

```
DO WHILE span% > 0
    FOR i% = span% TO numOfElements% - 1
        j% = i% - span% + 1
        FOR j% = (i% - span% + 1) TO 1 STEP -span%
            IF strArray$(j%) <= strArray$(j% + span%) THEN EXIT FOR
            ' swap array elements that are out of order
            SWAP strArray$(j%), strArray$(j% + span%)
        NEXT j%
    NEXT i%

    span% = span% \ 2
LOOP

END SUB
```

You'll receive output similar to the following:

```
Enter up to 15 lines of text; to end, press Enter on a new line.

-> Halvorson, Mike
-> Ullom, Kim
-> Halvorson, Ken
-> Zell, Linda
-> Halvorson, Victor
-> Zell, Ben
-> Berquist, Evelyn
-> Gullikson, Emma
->

Sorting results:

Berquist, Evelyn
Gullikson, Emma
Halvorson, Ken
Halvorson, Mike
Halvorson, Victor
Ullom, Kim
Zell, Ben
Zell, Linda
```

SUMMARY

You covered a lot of ground in this chapter and added many new functions and statements to your collection of programming tools. In all, 15 new statements and functions were introduced:

- UCASE$, LCASE$
- LEN
- RIGHT$, LEFT$, MID$
- RTRIM$, LTRIM$
- LINE INPUT
- SPACE$, STRING$
- INSTR
- CHR$, ASC
- SWAP

You also learned how to declare, combine, take apart, compare, and sort strings. QuickBASIC provides such a variety of tools for working with strings because so much of what's done with personal computers revolves around working with large amounts of string data. The next chapter discusses efficient ways to manage all that data.

QUESTIONS AND EXERCISES

1. True or False: String constants are written in all-uppercase letters by convention.

2. True or False: The following declaration of a fixed-length string is a valid QuickBASIC statement:

```
DIM lastName$ AS STRING * 20
```

3. What output does the following QuickBASIC statement produce?

```
PRINT "ONE" + "TWO" + "THREE"
```

4. Which of the following values can be supplied as an argument to the LEN function?

   a. A literal string

   b. A string constant

   c. A string variable

   d. The result of a string function

5. What has happened if a call to the INSTR function returns a value of 0?

6. What does the following QuickBASIC statement display?

   ```
   PRINT CHR$(ASC("h") - 32)
   ```

7. What is the ASCII code for the letter M?

8. Write a program that prompts the user for a first name and a last name, converts the names to uppercase, and then prints them in the format *Lastname, Firstname*.

9. Write a program that gets a variable-length string from the user, reverses the order of the characters in it, and displays the new string.

10. Write a program that gets a full name from the user with one variable-length string and copies each name in the string to a separate string variable. Your program should be able to process names of any length, provided that each of the three subnames is separated by a space. Output from the program should resemble the following:

    ```
    Enter a string:  Queen Victoria Belfield

    First name:  Queen
    Middle name:  Victoria
    Last name:  Belfield
    ```

Working with Files

In Chapters 8 and 9 you learned how to manage large amounts of data in a program. In this chapter you'll learn how to save such information on disk and access it whenever you like.

CREATING AND USING SEQUENTIAL FILES

A *file* is simply a collection of data saved on disk. One type of file you can create from within a BASIC program is a *sequential file*. The contents of a sequential file must be used in order, from start to finish. (The other type of file you can create, the *random-access file*, has contents that can be accessed in any order. We won't discuss random-access files in this book.) You use the following statements and functions in your BASIC programs in order to create and work with sequential files:

Statement/Function	*Description*
OPEN	Opens a file
CLOSE	Closes a file
PRINT#	Prints unformatted data in a file
PRINT# USING	Prints formatted data in a file
WRITE#	Prints data organized into fields in a file
INPUT#	Gets data from a file
EOF	Checks for the end of a file
LINE INPUT#	Gets an entire line of data from a file

This chapter describes these statements and functions in detail and teaches you how to use sequential files to track different types of information—from a simple diary to the contents of an entire database.

 NOTE: To simplify the learning process, the files in this chapter are created on the current drive and in the current directory—no drive letters or directory paths are used. If you know enough about drives and directories to work with files outside of the current directory, feel free to do so. QuickBASIC can take full advantage of the DOS file system.

Creating and Opening a File

The OPEN statement performs double duty: You use OPEN both to create new files and to open existing files. The syntax for the OPEN statement is as follows:

```
OPEN filename FOR mode AS #filenumber
```

filename is a valid DOS filename, *mode* is a word that indicates how the file is to be used, and *filenumber* is an integer between 1 and 255 to be associated with the file that is opened.

 NOTE: By numbering your file, you can refer to it within your program simply by calling it by number. You should start numbering files within your programs with 1. The number you assign to a file is valid until you close the file.

Specifying a mode

You use the *mode* argument to specify how you intend to use the sequential file. Use one of the following words as *mode*. (You can open a file in only one mode at a time.)

Mode	*Description*
OUTPUT	Creates and opens a file that will receive output from the program. If the file already exists, its old contents are erased.
APPEND	Opens an existing file to which output from the program is appended; that is, output from the program is placed at the *end* of the file. The original contents of the file are preserved.
INPUT	Opens a file that the program can only read. The program cannot change the file, but it can use the contents as input.

Here are some sample OPEN statements:

The following statement opens the NAMES.TXT sequential file, which will store output from the program. If NAMES.TXT does not exist, it is created. If it does exist, the existing contents are erased. NAMES.TXT is associated with the number 1.

```
OPEN "NAMES.TXT" FOR OUTPUT AS #1
```

The following statement opens an existing file named NAMES.TXT and associates it with the number 1. The program stores its output at the end of the existing contents of NAMES.TXT.

```
OPEN "NAMES.TXT" FOR APPEND AS #1
```

The following statement opens an existing file named NAMES.TXT and associates it with the number 1. The contents of NAMES.TXT can be used by the program.

```
OPEN "NAMES.TXT" FOR INPUT AS #1
```

Using a string variable with OPEN

When using the OPEN statement you can even use a string variable in place of *filename*. For example, you can prompt your user to supply a file-name, and then you can assign the specified name to a variable and use the variable within the OPEN statement, as shown in the following example:

```
INPUT "What file would you like to open?  ", filename$
OPEN filename$ FOR OUTPUT AS #1
```

You'll likely want to use some of the string-evaluation skills you learned in Chapter 9 to have the program verify that the user's response (*file-name$*) is a valid DOS filename before it tries to open the file.

Closing a File

When you've finished working with a file, be sure to close it with the CLOSE statement. This ensures that all information you have written to the file is actually written to the disk. After a file is closed, the number associated with it is released and can be assigned to another file.

The syntax of the CLOSE statement is as follows:

```
CLOSE [#filenumber]
```

filenumber is the number associated with the file you want to close. If you omit the *#filenumber* argument, *all* open files are closed. Once you close a file, you must reopen it before you can use it again.

Let's look at some CLOSE examples. The following CLOSE statement closes file 1:

```
CLOSE #1
```

The following CLOSE statement closes all open files:

```
CLOSE
```

 NOTE: Although BASIC automatically closes all open files when a program terminates, you should develop the habit of closing all files as soon as you are through with them. Otherwise, an unforeseen event such as a power outage can cause your program to lose data.

Storing Data in a File

After a file is opened in OUTPUT or APPEND mode, it can receive data from your program. BASIC provides three statements that send data to an open sequential file:

- The PRINT# statement sends unformatted data to a file.

- The PRINT# USING statement sends formatted data to a file.

- The WRITE# statement sends data organized into fields to a file.

The following sections describe each of these file-storage statements in detail.

The PRINT# statement

The PRINT# statement is functionally similar to the PRINT statement, but it sends data to a file rather than to the screen. The syntax for the PRINT# statement is as follows:

```
PRINT #filenumber,[ expressionlist][,¦;]
```

filenumber is the number of the open file and *expressionlist* is the data to be sent to the file. If you omit *expressionlist*, a blank line is sent to the file.

If you put more than one item in *expressionlist*, separate the items with semicolons or commas. Semicolons and commas in the PRINT# statement work exactly as they do in the regular PRINT statement. If a semicolon is the last character in the PRINT# statement, the next item sent to the file appears at the end of the line just sent.

Practice: Storing unformatted data in a file

The CARDATA.BAS program (Figure 10-1) demonstrates how to use the PRINT# statement to send three lines of unformatted data to a file named CARDATA.TXT. Values sent to a file can be literal values, simple variables, or the results of functions or expressions.

Load the CARDATA.BAS program from the CHAP10 subdirectory on disk and run it.

```
' CARDATA.BAS
' This program uses the PRINT# statement to send three lines of
'   car information to a sequential file.

OPEN "CARDATA.TXT" FOR OUTPUT AS #1   ' open file in current drive/dir

CLS

' get some car information from the user and write it to the open file

INPUT "Enter the make of a car in your collection:   ", makeName$
INPUT "What is the model name?  ", modelName$
INPUT "What year was the car made?  ", year%

PRINT #1, makeName$, modelName$, year%

' add some literal values to the file

PRINT #1, "Mercedes-Benz", "190 SL", 1959

' add a new car to the file (RIGHT$ function returns current year
'   from DATE$ function)

PRINT #1, "Audi", "80 Quattro", " "; RIGHT$(DATE$, 4)

CLOSE #1                             ' close the file

PRINT
PRINT "Information has been successfully written to CARDATA.TXT"
```

FIGURE 10-1.
CARDATA.BAS: A program demonstrating the PRINT# statement.

You'll receive output similar to the following:

```
Enter the make of a car in your collection:  Ford
What is the model name?  Thunderbird
What year was the car made?  1956

Information has been successfully written to CARDATA.TXT
```

A file named CARDATA.TXT is also created in the current directory on the disk in the current drive. To view the file, exit the QuickBASIC Interpreter and type the following DOS command at the system prompt:

```
type cardata.txt
```

You'll receive output similar to the following:

```
Ford           Thunderbird   1956
Mercedes-Benz 190 SL         1959
Audi           80 Quattro    1990
```

The PRINT# USING statement

The PRINT# USING statement follows the same rules and uses the same special formatting characters as the PRINT USING statement, but it sends formatted data to a file rather than to the screen. PRINT# USING is helpful when you need to send large amounts of tabular data to a file. The syntax of the PRINT# USING statement is as follows:

```
PRINT #filenumber, USING template; [expressionlist][,¦;]
```

filenumber is the number of the open file, *template* is a string used to format the values in *expressionlist*, and *expressionlist* is the data to be formatted and sent to the file. (You can use comma or semicolon separators to separate the values.) The formatting characters in *template* must match up one-for-one with the characters of the values in *expressionlist*.

Practice: Storing formatted data in a file

The FRUITS.BAS program (Figure 10-2) demonstrates how to use the PRINT# USING statement to send three lines of formatted data to the FRUITS.TXT file. The formatting template in this program is the string variable *tmp$*, which uses several special formatting characters to align the data vertically before it is sent to the file.

Load the FRUITS.BAS program from disk and run it.

```
' FRUITS.BAS
' This program uses the PRINT# USING statement to send three lines
'    of formatted fruit information to a sequential file.

OPEN "FRUITS.TXT" FOR OUTPUT AS #1  ' open file in current drive/dir

CLS

' create a formatting template for the PRINT# USING statement

tmp$ = "Fruit:  \                \ Cases: ###    Price/pound:$$##.##"

' get some fruit information from the user and write it to the open file

INPUT "Enter your favorite summer fruit:  ", fruit$
INPUT "How many cases would you like to purchase?  ", cases%
INPUT "How much does it cost per pound?  $", cost!

PRINT #1, USING tmp$; fruit$; cases%; cost!

' add some literal values to the file

PRINT #1, USING tmp$; "Strawberry"; 2; 1.29

PRINT #1, USING tmp$; "Cantaloupe"; 14; .69

CLOSE #1                            ' close the file

PRINT
PRINT "Information has been successfully written to FRUITS.TXT"
```

FIGURE 10-2.
FRUITS.BAS: A program demonstrating the PRINT# USING statement.

You'll receive output similar to the following:

```
Enter your favorite summer fruit:  Pear
How many cases would you like to purchase?  10
How much does it cost per pound?  $0.89

Information has been successfully written to FRUITS.TXT
```

A file named FRUITS.TXT is also created in the current directory on the disk in the current drive. To view the file, exit the QuickBASIC Interpreter and enter the following DOS command at the system prompt:

```
type fruits.txt
```

You'll receive output similar to the following:

```
Fruit:  Pear          Cases:  10    Price/pound:  $0.89
Fruit:  Strawberry    Cases:   2    Price/pound:  $1.29
Fruit:  Cantaloupe    Cases:  14    Price/pound:  $0.69
```

The WRITE# statement

The information that the WRITE# statement sends to a sequential file is separated by commas and organized into groups called *fields*. The WRITE# statement does not format its output as the PRINT# and PRINT# USING statements do—WRITE# creates files that will be read by other programs. (We'll use this statement later in the chapter when we create and track a database file.)

The syntax for the WRITE# statement is as follows:

```
WRITE #filenumber[, expressionlist]
```

filenumber is the number of the open file and *expressionlist* is the data to be sent to the file. Elements in the list are separated by commas. If you omit *expressionlist*, a blank line is written to the file.

Figure 10-3 shows a sample WRITE# statement that sends five types of values to a file. Note how the commas between values separate the output into fields. Also note the string value that is surrounded by quotation marks: If the string contained spaces or commas, a non-BASIC program would recognize the spaces and commas as part of the string. If the file created with the WRITE# statement contains multiple lines, each line is called a *record*.

Sample program statements:

```
OPEN "TEST.TXT" FOR OUTPUT AS #1 ——— OPEN statement

a$ = "Kimberly"
b% = 25
c& = 100000                          ——— Sample variables
d! = 115.5
e# = .0123456789#

WRITE #1, a$, b%, c&, d!, e# ——— WRITE# statement
CLOSE #1 ——————————————————————————— CLOSE statement
```

Output sent to file:

```
"Kimberly", 25, 100000, 115.5, .0123456789
```

Field 1 Field 2 Field 3 Field 4 Field 5

FIGURE 10-3.
The WRITE# statement stores data in a file in fields and records.

Practice: Storing data in a file with fields

The COINS.BAS program (Figure 10-4) demonstrates how to use the WRITE# statement to store coin-collection information in a file named COINS.TXT. COINS.BAS is designed to let the user enter information about as many coins as desired. To stop entering collection information, the user simply types *END* when prompted for a country.

Load the COINS.BAS program from disk and run it.

```
' COINS.BAS
' This program uses the WRITE# statement to send coin-collection
'    information to a sequential file in fields.

OPEN "COINS.TXT" FOR OUTPUT AS #1   ' open file in current drive/dir

CLS

PRINT "This program stores coin-collection information on disk in a"
PRINT "file named COINS.TXT.  Enter coin data and type END to quit."
PRINT
```

FIGURE 10-4. *(continued)*
COINS.BAS: A program demonstrating the WRITE# statement.

FIGURE 10-4. *continued*

```
DO WHILE (country$ <> "END")          ' until the user types END...

' get coin-collection info from user and write it to the open file

    INPUT "What country is the coin from?  ", country$
    IF (country$ <> "END") THEN      ' if country$ is END don't write
        INPUT "What is the value of the coin?  ", value$
        INPUT "What is the name of the coin?   ", coinName$
        INPUT "What year was the coin minted?  ", year%

        WRITE #1, country$, value$, coinName$, year%  ' send fields
    END IF
    PRINT                              ' print blank lines between coins

LOOP

CLOSE #1                               ' close the file

PRINT "Information has been successfully written to COINS.TXT"
```

You'll receive output similar to the following:

```
This program stores coin-collection information on disk in a
file named COINS.TXT.  Enter coin data and type END to quit.

What country is the coin from?  United States
What is the value of the coin?  10 cents
What is the name of the coin?   Dime
What year was the coin minted?  1980

What country is the coin from?  Canada
What is the value of the coin?  25 cents
What is the name of the coin?   Quarter
What year was the coin minted?  1960
```

(continued)

continued

```
What country is the coin from?  Hungary
What is the value of the coin?  2 forints
What is the name of the coin?
What year was the coin minted?  1985

What country is the coin from?  Great Britain
What is the value of the coin?  1 pound
What is the name of the coin?   Pound
What year was the coin minted?  1981

What country is the coin from?  END

Information has been successfully written to COINS.TXT
```

A file named COINS.TXT is also created in the current directory on the disk in the current drive. To view the file, exit the QuickBASIC Interpreter and type the following DOS command at the system prompt:

```
type coins.txt
```

You'll receive output similar to the following:

```
"United States","10 cents","Dime",1980
"Canada","25 cents","Quarter",1960
"Hungary","2 forints","",1985
"Great Britain","1 pound","Pound",1981
```

The COINS.TXT file contains four records of four fields each, as shown in Figure 10-5:

```
Record 1 ———— "United States","10 cents","Dime",1980
Record 2 ———— "Canada","25 cents","Quarter",1960
Record 3 ———— "Hungary","2 forints","",1985
Record 4 ———— "Great Britain","1 pound","Pound",1981
```

FIGURE 10-5.
Each line in the COINS.TXT file is a record containing four fields.

Getting Data from a File

In the last section you created three files and used the DOS command TYPE to examine them. In this section you'll learn how to examine and use data files from within a BASIC program. You'll examine two statements and one function that help you work with files that have been opened for input:

- The INPUT# statement gets one or more fields of data from a file.

- The EOF function determines whether the end of the file has been reached.

- The LINE INPUT# statement gets an entire line of data from a file.

The INPUT# statement

The INPUT# statement is the primary tool you use to get data from a BASIC sequential file. The INPUT# statement gets input from a sequential file in much the same way the INPUT statement gets input from the keyboard: Both statements assign one or more data items to variables of matching types. The syntax of the INPUT# statement is as follows:

`INPUT #filenumber, variablelist`

filenumber is the number of the open file and *variablelist* is one or more variables to be assigned data from the file. Items in *variablelist* must be of the same type as items in the sequential file. Items in the sequential file can be fields of data created with the WRITE# statement or output from the PRINT# statement, from the PRINT# USING statement, or from any program that can create data files.

Practice: Getting data items from a sequential file

The FRIENDS.BAS program (Figure 10-6) demonstrates how to use the INPUT# statement in your BASIC program to get data from a sequential file. The program first opens a sequential file in the current directory for output and sends four strings to it with the WRITE# statement. The program then closes the file, opens it again for input, and reads the four strings back into the program.

Load the FRIENDS.BAS program from disk and run it.

```
' FRIENDS.BAS
' This program demonstrates the INPUT# statement.

CLS

OPEN "FRIENDS.TXT" FOR OUTPUT AS #1   ' open file for output

PRINT "Enter the names of four of your friends"
PRINT

FOR i% = 1 TO 4                       ' loop 4 times
    INPUT "Friendly name:  ", pal$    ' each time get name from user
    WRITE #1, pal$                    '    and write it to disk
NEXT i%

CLOSE #1                              ' close the file

OPEN "FRIENDS.TXT" FOR INPUT AS #1    ' reopen the file for input

PRINT
PRINT "You entered the following names:"
PRINT

FOR i% = 1 TO 4                       ' loop 4 times
    INPUT #1, pal$                    ' each time get name from file
    PRINT pal$                        '    and display it on screen
NEXT i%

CLOSE #1                              ' close the file
```

FIGURE 10-6.
FRIENDS.BAS: A program demonstrating the INPUT# statement.

You'll receive output similar to the following:

```
Enter the names of four of your friends

Friendly name:  Larry
Friendly name:  Whitey
Friendly name:  Gus
Friendly name:  Gilbert
```

(continued)

continued

```
You entered the following names:

Larry
Whitey
Gus
Gilbert
```

The file FRIENDS.TXT is also created on disk and contains the following data records:

```
"Larry"
"Whitey"
"Gus"
"Gilbert"
```

The EOF function

If your BASIC program can't tell where your sequential file ends, you might receive an end-of-file error. This error occurs when BASIC tries to read beyond the end of the file.

```
┌─────────────────────────────────┐
│                                 │
│   Input past end of file        │
│                                 │
├─────────────────────────────────┤
│   ‹ OK ›    ‹ Help ›            │
└─────────────────────────────────┘
```

To prevent this error, you must explicitly tell BASIC to quit reading values after it encounters the end of the file. To do this, use the EOF function. EOF has the following syntax:

`EOF(filenumber)`

filenumber is the number of the open file you want to check.

EOF returns a logical value of *true* if the next character to be read is past the end of the file, and *false* otherwise.

You can use the EOF function anywhere in your program to check the status of an open file, but it is most effective in a DO loop, as shown in the following practice session.

Practice: Detecting the end of a file

The COINS2.BAS program (Figure 10-7) is an enhancement of the COINS.BAS program presented earlier in the chapter: It uses the INPUT# statement to display file data and the EOF function to check for the end of the file. This new version opens the coin-collection file in APPEND mode so that coin-collection information gathered in previous runs of the program won't be overwritten by the new information; instead, all new information is placed at the end of the file.

Load the COINS2.BAS program from disk and run it.

```
' COINS2.BAS
' This program uses the WRITE# statement to send coin-collection
'    information to a sequential file and INPUT# to display it.

' open file in APPEND mode so that previous contents won't be overwritten

OPEN "COINS.TXT" FOR APPEND AS #1  ' open file in current drive/dir

CLS

PRINT "This program stores coin-collection information on disk in a"
PRINT "file named COINS.TXT.  Enter coin data and type END to quit."
PRINT

DO WHILE (country$ <> "END")         ' until the user types END...

' get coin-collection info from user and write it to the open file

    INPUT "What country is the coin from?  ", country$
    IF (country$ <> "END") THEN     ' if country$ is END don't write
        INPUT "What is the value of the coin?  ", value$
        INPUT "What is the name of the coin?   ", coinName$
        INPUT "What year was the coin minted?  ", year%

        WRITE #1, country$, value$, coinName$, year%  ' send fields
    END IF
```

FIGURE 10-7.   *(continued)*
COINS2.BAS: A program demonstrating the EOF function and the INPUT# statement.

FIGURE 10-7. *continued*

```
    PRINT                           ' print blank lines between coins

LOOP

CLOSE #1                           ' close the file

' wait for the user to press Enter to continue

INPUT "Press Enter to see the contents of your coin collection", dummy$
CLS                                ' start with a fresh screen

' open file in INPUT mode so that contents can be read by program

OPEN "COINS.TXT" FOR INPUT AS #1    ' file is in current drive/dir

' display header for tabular collection information

PRINT "Coin origin     Coin value    Coin name     Year minted"
PRINT "------------------------------------------------------------"
PRINT

' initialize formatting template for use with PRINT USING

tmp$ = "\            \ \          \ \             \ ####"

' while the end of the file has not been reached, assign file
'   items to variables and print them out

DO WHILE (NOT EOF(1))
    INPUT #1, country$, value$, coinName$, year%
    PRINT USING tmp$; country$; value$; coinName$; year%
LOOP

CLOSE #1                           ' close the file
```

You'll be prompted for input in the following manner:

```
This program stores coin-collection information on disk in a
file named COINS.TXT.  Enter coin data and type END to quit.

What country is the coin from?  Netherlands
What is the value of the coin?  2.5 guilders
What is the name of the coin?  Rijksdaalder
What year was the coin minted?  1982

What country is the coin from?  END
```

After you've entered the new information it is displayed along with the information already in the file:

```
Coin origin     Coin value    Coin name     Year minted
-----------------------------------------------------------

United States   10 cents      Dime          1980
Canada          25 cents      Quarter       1960
Hungary         2 forints                   1985
Great Britain   1 pound       Pound         1981
Netherlands     2.5 guilders  Rijksdaalder  1982
```

The LINE INPUT# statement

The INPUT# statement is an effective way to obtain individual items from files, but what do you do if you need to obtain long strings of textual information? BASIC provides the LINE INPUT# statement for this purpose. LINE INPUT# is similar to LINE INPUT; it simply obtains input from a file instead of from a keyboard. LINE INPUT# has the following syntax:

```
LINE INPUT #filenumber, variablename$
```

filenumber is the number of the open file to be read from and *variablename$* is the string variable to receive the line of input.

The LPRINT Statement

When you want to send information to the printer attached to your computer, use the LPRINT statement. LPRINT has a syntax similar to that of the PRINT statement:

```
LPRINT [expressionlist][,¦;]
```

expressionlist is a list of numeric or string expressions separated by commas or semicolons. For example, to send the string *Think Snow!* to the printer, use the following LPRINT statement:

```
LPRINT "Think Snow!"
```

To send a formfeed (page eject) command to your printer when you've finished printing, use the following statement:

```
LPRINT CHR$(12)
```

This sends ASCII character 12 to the printer to advance the paper.

Practice: Reading a diary with LINE INPUT#

The DIARY.BAS program (Figure 10-8) demonstrates how to use the LINE INPUT and LINE INPUT# statements together to track lines of textual material in a sequential file. DIARY.BAS is first opened in APPEND mode and is then marked with the current time and date from the system clock. The user can then add one or more lines to the diary, which is stored in the DIARY.TXT file in the current directory. Because the diary file is opened in APPEND mode, each entry is added to the end of the file, preserving the earlier entries. If the user requests a printout, all entries (including their time and date stamps) are sent to the printer using LPRINT statements.

```
' DIARY.BAS
' This program maintains a computer diary in a sequential file
'   named DIARY.TXT.

CLS

OPEN "DIARY.TXT" FOR APPEND AS #1    ' open file in append mode

PRINT "Enter your secret thoughts for today; type END to quit."
PRINT

PRINT #1, TIME$; " "; DATE$          ' write time and date to file
PRINT #1,                            ' write blank line to file

DO WHILE (UCASE$(line$) <> "END")    ' until user types "END",
    LINE INPUT line$                 '   get lines of text
    IF (line$ <> "END") THEN PRINT #1, line$
LOOP                                 '   and write them to the file

PRINT #1,                            ' write blank line to file
CLOSE #1                             ' close file

PRINT                                ' find out if user wants a printout
INPUT "Would you like to print out your entire diary (Y,N)? ", reply$

IF (UCASE$(reply$) = "Y") THEN       ' if yes,
    OPEN "DIARY.TXT" FOR INPUT AS #1 '   open file for input

    LPRINT STRING$(33, "-");         ' print a header at top of page
    LPRINT " My Diary ";
    LPRINT STRING$(33, "-")
    LPRINT                           '   and a blank line

    DO WHILE (NOT EOF(1))            ' until end of file is reached,
        LINE INPUT #1, line$         '   read lines from file
        LPRINT line$                 '   and send them to printer
    LOOP
```

FIGURE 10-8.   *(continued)*

DIARY.BAS: A simple diary program that demonstrates the LINE INPUT# statement.

FIGURE 10-8. *continued*

```
      CLOSE #1                        ' close file

      LPRINT CHR$(12)                 ' send formfeed character

      PRINT                           ' display message indicating diary
      PRINT "Diary sent to printer"   '   contents have been sent to
   END IF                             '   printer
```

When you run the program you are prompted for a diary entry in the following manner:

```
Enter your secret thoughts for today; type END to quit.
```

After you type in your entry and the word *END*, you'll receive the following prompt:

```
Would you like to print out your entire diary (Y,N)?
```

If you enter *Y*, the program sends a copy of the diary to the printer. Figure 10-9 shows the contents of a sample printout.

The VIEW PRINT statement

The last statement we'll discuss in this section is VIEW PRINT. VIEW PRINT isn't used directly with files but is sometimes used in combination with the INPUT#, LOCATE, and PRINT statements to display the contents of a file in different places on the screen. So far we've used the entire screen for the output of statements such as PRINT. When the 25 lines of the screen have filled up, additional PRINT statements cause the screen to scroll. With the VIEW PRINT statement, however, you can restrict printed output to only part of the screen—called a *text viewport*—while the rest remains intact. The syntax for the VIEW PRINT statement is as follows:

```
VIEW PRINT [topline TO bottomline]
```

topline is the top line of the text viewport and *bottomline* is the bottom line of the text viewport. If *topline* and *bottomline* are not included, the entire display becomes the text viewport (the default).

```
-------------------------------- My Diary ---------------------------------

11:43:12  06-07-1989

Today I met a tall, dark stranger in the jungle next to a big papaya tree.
Turned out to be a gorilla in a man suit--just my luck!

09:13:01  06-08-1989

The gorilla and I have turned out to be real chums.  He doesn't do
much--just sits around all day eating plants.  I think I'll make
him a coconut cream pie this afternoon.

15:25:10  06-09-1989

Pooluseebagumba!--I've been discovered by unfriendly natives from the
other side of the island!  This is my last entry.  I surely won't be able
to lug this computer around with me as I make my escape to the secret cave.

Signed,

ON THE RUN
```

FIGURE 10-9.
A printout produced by the DIARY.BAS program.

Once a viewport has been established, scrolling takes place only between the top and bottom lines of the viewport. This is very convenient when you want to display a list of instructions or table headings and you don't want them to scroll off the screen. Note that when a viewport is in effect you can use the statement

```
CLS 2
```

to clear only the viewport portion of the screen and leave the rest intact.

Practice: Creating a text viewport

The VIEW.BAS program (Figure 10-10) demonstrates the operation of the VIEW PRINT, LOCATE, PRINT, and CLS statements. We'll see more of these statements in the database program near the end of the chapter.

314

```
' VIEW.BAS
' This program demonstrates the VIEW PRINT statement.

CLS

PRINT "Welcome to the VIEW program!!"  ' print intro message
PRINT
PRINT "Let's watch some things scroll by..."
PRINT STRING$(80, "-");              ' print top line

LOCATE 24, 1: PRINT STRING$(80, "-");  ' print bottom line
LOCATE 25, 1: INPUT ; "Press Enter to start the program... ", dummy$

VIEW PRINT 5 TO 23                   ' enable viewport (lines 5-23)

COLOR 2                              ' set color to green
FOR i% = 1 TO 200
    PRINT "This is line"; i%          ' print message 200 times
NEXT i%
COLOR 7                              ' set color to default white

VIEW PRINT                           ' disable viewport
LOCATE 25, 1: INPUT ; "Press Enter to clear the viewport... ", dummy$
VIEW PRINT 5 TO 23                   ' enable viewport
CLS 2                                ' clear viewport only
```

FIGURE 10-10.
VIEW.BAS: A program demonstrating the VIEW PRINT statement.

Load the VIEW.BAS program from disk and run it. You'll see a screen with a divided viewport, as shown at the top of the next page.

BASIC Equivalents of DOS Commands

Many BASIC statements have counterparts in the DOS world. If you're familiar with file-related DOS commands, you might find Table 10-1 useful. It lists BASIC statements along with their DOS-command counterparts and descriptions of their purposes.

```
Welcome to the VIEW program!!

Let's watch some things scroll by...
--------------------------------------------------------------------------------
This is line 183
This is line 184
This is line 185
This is line 186
This is line 187
This is line 188
This is line 189
This is line 190
This is line 191
This is line 192
This is line 193
This is line 194
This is line 195
This is line 196
This is line 197
This is line 198
This is line 199
This is line 200


--------------------------------------------------------------------------------
Press Enter to clear the viewport... _
```

BASIC statement	*DOS equivalent*	*Description*
FILES	DIR/W	Displays a directory listing
SHELL	COMMAND	Runs a DOS command
NAME	RENAME	Changes the name of a file
KILL	DEL *or* ERASE	Deletes a file
MKDIR	MKDIR	Creates a directory
CHDIR	CHDIR	Changes the current directory
RMDIR	RMDIR	Removes an empty directory

TABLE 10-1.
BASIC equivalents of DOS commands.

The FILES statement

If you want your program to display a list of files from which a user can choose, use the FILES statement. FILES has the following syntax:

```
FILES [filename]
```

filename is the optional filename of the file you want to see a directory listing for. If you omit *filename*, BASIC displays a listing of all files in the current directory. You can use the * and *?* wildcard characters as part of *filename* in order to display a wide range of files. To display a listing for a directory or drive other than the current directory, include a drive letter or a pathname or both as part of *filename*.

Practice: Viewing the current directory

The SHOW.BAS program (Figure 10-11) demonstrates how to use the FILES command to display all files in the current directory whose names end with *.TXT*. After a directory listing is displayed, SHOW.BAS prompts the user for a filename and prints out the specified text file.

Load the SHOW.BAS program from disk and run it.

```
' SHOW.BAS
' This program lets you view a data file in the current directory.

CLS

PRINT "The current directory contains the following files with ";
PRINT "a .TXT extension:"
PRINT

FILES "*.TXT"

PRINT
INPUT "Which file would you like to display?  ", filename$

OPEN filename$ FOR INPUT AS #1

PRINT
PRINT "---------- "; UCASE$(filename$); " ----------"
PRINT
```

FIGURE 10-11.   *(continued)*
SHOW.BAS: A program demonstrating the FILES statement.

317

FIGURE 10-11. *continued*

```
DO WHILE (NOT EOF(1))
    LINE INPUT #1, line$
    PRINT line$
LOOP
```

When you run the program you get output similar to the following:

```
The current directory contains the following files with a .TXT extension:

C:\QBI
CARDATA .TXT      FRUITS .TXT      COINS  .TXT      FRIENDS .TXT
DIARY.TXT
 2080768 Bytes free

Which file would you like to display?  fruits.txt

---------- FRUITS.TXT ----------

Fruit:  Pear          Cases:  10    Price/pound:  $0.89
Fruit:  Strawberry    Cases:  2     Price/pound:  $1.29
Fruit:  Cantaloupe    Cases:  14    Price/pound:  $0.69
```

The SHELL statement

The SHELL statement lets you exit QuickBASIC temporarily and run DOS commands. The SHELL command is useful when you want to execute a command not available in QuickBASIC or when you want to give users access to DOS while a program is running. (This feature is provided by many application programs on the market today. In Microsoft Word, for example, you can exit to DOS temporarily by selecting the Library Run command.)

The syntax for the SHELL statement is as follows:

```
SHELL [commandString]
```

where *commandString* is an optional string value or string variable containing a valid DOS command line. If you include *commandString*, DOS executes the command line and returns to the BASIC program. If you omit *commandString*, DOS runs a new temporary version of itself. In nearly all respects this temporary version of DOS looks and operates just like the real version of DOS—you can enter any number of DOS commands. This version of DOS is only temporary, however: When you type *exit* and press Enter, the BASIC program continues executing.

Practice: Running a DOS command

The RUNDOS.BAS program (Figure 10-12) demonstrates how to use the SHELL command to run DOS commands from within a BASIC program. To help you track what's displayed by the program and what's displayed by DOS, the program begins by setting the foreground color to cyan. This ensures that the results of BASIC statements will appear in cyan and that the results of DOS commands will appear in white, the system default.

1. Load the RUNDOS.BAS program from disk and run it.

```
' RUNDOS.BAS
' This program executes a DOS command.

CLS

COLOR 3                 ' set color to cyan
                        ' get DOS command line from user
INPUT "Enter a DOS command line [press Enter to run DOS]:  ", dosCom$
PRINT

SHELL dosCom$           ' exit to DOS and execute the command

PRINT
PRINT "DOS command complete"

COLOR 7                 ' set color to default white
```

FIGURE 10-12.
RUNDOS.BAS: A program demonstrating the SHELL statement.

BASIC displays the following prompt:

```
Enter a DOS command line [press Enter to run DOS]:
```

319

2. To test how the SHELL statement processes one DOS command line, type *chkdsk* and press Enter. After a few moments DOS displays information similar to the following:

```
Volume MIKE          created 02-19-1990 4:36p
Volume Serial Number is 1810-1496

 21690368 bytes total disk space
    77824 bytes in 6 hidden files
   120832 bytes in 54 directories
 19410944 bytes in 1003 user files
  2080768 bytes available on disk

     2048 bytes in each allocation unit
    10591 total allocation units on disk
     1016 available allocation units on disk

   655360 total bytes memory
   361888 bytes free
```

```
DOS command complete
```

The SHELL statement processed the DOS CHKDSK command and then returned to the program.

3. Now run the RUNDOS program again, but this time simply press Enter to run a temporary version of DOS. You'll receive output of the following form. Note the way we used our time in DOS to copy a file.

```
Enter a DOS command line [press Enter to run DOS]:


Microsoft(R) MS-DOS(R) Version 4.00
          (C)Copyright Microsoft Corp 1981-1988


C:\QBI>dir *.txt

  Volume in drive C is MIKE
  Volume Serial Number is 1810-1496
  Directory of  C:\QBI
```

(continued)

continued

```
CARDATA  TXT        107 06-06-90  12:40p
FRUITS   TXT        177 06-06-90   3:56p
COINS    TXT        197 06-06-90   5:34p
FRIENDS  TXT         37 06-07-90  10:19a
DIARY    TXT        713 06-07-90   3:12p
         5 File(s)     2080768 bytes free


C:\QBI>copy diary.txt a:
         1 File(s) copied


C:\QBI>exit

DOS command complete
```

The NAME statement

The NAME statement is useful when you want rename a file or move a file from one directory to another. The syntax of the NAME statement is as follows:

```
NAME oldFileName AS newFileName
```

oldFileName is the current filename and *newFileName* is the new name you'd like the file to have. You can use directory pathnames in both *oldFileName* and *newFileName*. If the two pathnames are different, BASIC moves the file to the directory specified by *newFileName*. (You can't move files between different drives, however.) If the NAME statement cannot rename the files, the program generates an error.

Practice: Renaming a file

The NEWNAME.BAS program (Figure 10-13) demonstrates how to use the NAME statement to change the name of a file on the current drive. Note the use of the FILES statement, which displays the files in the current directory.

Load the NEWNAME.BAS program from disk and run it.

```
' NEWNAME.BAS
' This program lets you rename a data file in the current directory.

CLS

PRINT "The current directory contains the following files:"
PRINT

FILES "*.*"                    ' display files in current directory

PRINT                          ' get old and new filenames
INPUT "Which file would you like to rename?  ", oldName$
INPUT "What would you like the new name to be?  ", newName$

NAME oldName$ AS newName$  ' try to rename file

' if oldName$ does not exist or newName$ is an invalid name, the
'   NAME statement will generate a run-time error; otherwise, the
'   following lines will be executed:

PRINT                          ' print success message
PRINT UCASE$(oldName$); " renamed successfully"
```

FIGURE 10-13.
NEWNAME.BAS: A program demonstrating the NAME statement.

When you run the program you receive output similar to the following:

```
The current directory contains the following files:

C:\QBI
        .  <DIR>          ..  <DIR> FRUITS  .BAS     CARDATA .BAS
CARDATA .TXT     FRUITS  .TXT     COINS   .BAS     COINS   .TXT
COINS2  .BAS     FRIENDS .BAS     FRIENDS .TXT     DIARY   .BAS
SHOW    .BAS     NEWNAME .BAS     DIARY   .TXT     RUNDOS  .BAS

 2080013 Bytes free

Which file would you like to rename? diary.txt
What would you like the new name to be? olddiary.txt

DIARY.TXT renamed successfully
```

The KILL statement

The KILL statement is both straightforward and permanent: It deletes a file from disk. Once a file is deleted with the KILL statement it cannot be recovered. Programmers commonly use KILL to delete temporary files created during program execution, but you can also use KILL to perform general disk cleanup. The syntax of the KILL statement is as follows:

```
KILL filename
```

filename is the name of the file to be deleted. You can also use drive letters, pathnames, and the * and ? wildcard characters within a KILL statement.

NOTE: Use extreme caution with the KILL statement—especially when using wildcard characters. You might accidentally delete more files than you intended. The following practice session shows some of the safety features you should build into a program that uses the KILL statement.

Practice: Deleting a file

The KILL.BAS program (Figure 10-14) demonstrates how to use the KILL statement to delete an unwanted file. If the user includes wildcard characters in the filename entered for deletion, the program detects them with INSTR functions and displays a warning message in red, asking the user to verify the multiple deletion. If the file specified for deletion does not exist, the KILL statement generates a run-time error.

Load the KILL.BAS program from disk and run it.

```
' KILL.BAS
' This program lets you delete a file in the current directory.

CLS

PRINT "The current directory contains the following files:"
PRINT

FILES "*.*"                    ' display files in current directory
```

FIGURE 10-14.   *(continued)*
KILL.BAS: A program demonstrating the KILL statement.

FIGURE 10-14. *continued*

```
PRINT                          ' get file to delete
INPUT "Which file(s) would you like to delete?  ", filename$

' check for wildcard characters (? and *) in filename$
'    if they exist, print a warning before deleting multiple files
'    if they do not exist, proceed with deletion
'    if the file does not exist, KILL will display a run-time error

IF (INSTR(filename$, "?")) OR (INSTR(filename$, "*")) THEN
    PRINT
    COLOR 4                ' set color to red for effect
    PRINT "Danger:  Wildcards detected that can delete multiple files!"
    COLOR 7                ' set color to default white
    PRINT                  ' prompt for deletion confirmation
    INPUT "Do you want to proceed (Y,N)?  ", reply$
                           ' if reply$ is yes, then delete file
    IF (UCASE$(reply$) = "Y") THEN
        KILL filename$
        PRINT
        PRINT UCASE$(filename$); " deleted from system"
    END IF                 ' ...if not, then exit program
ELSE
    KILL filename$         ' if no wildcards exist, simply delete file
    PRINT
    PRINT UCASE$(filename$); " deleted from system"
END IF
```

You'll receive output similar to the following:

```
The current directory contains the following files:

C:\QBI

        .  <DIR>          .. <DIR> FRUITS  .BAS     CARDATA .BAS
CARDATA .TXT     FRUITS  .TXT     COINS   .BAS     COINS   .TXT
COINS2  .BAS     FRIENDS .BAS     FRIENDS .TXT     DIARY   .BAS
SHOW    .BAS     NEWNAME .BAS     OLDDIARY.TXT     KILL    .BAS
RUNDOS  .BAS
 2078419 Bytes free

Which file(s) would you like to delete?  olddiary.txt

OLDDIARY.TXT deleted from system
```

TRACKING A DATABASE
WITH SEQUENTIAL FILES

We'll conclude this chapter with a look at a simple database program, MUSICDB.BAS, which uses many of the statements and functions we've discussed to work with data stored in a sequential file. MUSICDB.BAS is designed to track the following information for each item of music in your collection:

- Title
- Recording artist
- Year released
- Style of music (rock, blues, jazz, classical, etc.)
- Medium (record, compact disc, cassette, etc.)

MUSICDB.BAS also provides a number of "database style" features to help you monitor your collection. MUSICDB.BAS lets you

- Store music-collection information permanently within a sequential file.
- Examine the music-collection records one at a time on screen.
- Print the entire music collection.
- Search for records by title or recording artist.
- Load and examine other music-collection databases.
- Exit temporarily to DOS to run DOS commands.

A sizable amount of MUSICDB.BAS is devoted to the menu-driven user interface of the program, giving you a feel for how screens typical of general-purpose application programs are created. Care has also been taken to make MUSICDB.BAS general enough so that it can easily be modified to track other types of database information. We'll discuss how this can be done after we examine how MUSICDB.BAS operates.

Tracking Information with a Database

A *database* is a collection of individual records that have a similar format. A phone book, for example, is a database: It contains an alphabetic listing of name records, each of which contains address and telephone-number elements. A database always has a fixed structure; that is, each record contains the same *type* of information, though not necessarily the same *content*.

Databases are pretty common these days—turning up in both home and professional life. Here are a few everyday examples:

- A list of employee records
- A list of student records
- A list of available products
- A music collection
- A coin collection
- A film and video collection
- A parts catalog
- A library card catalog
- A list of important dates
- Inventory information
- Team statistics
- Financial transactions

Running MUSICDB.BAS

Load the MUSICDB.BAS program from disk and run it. After a moment you'll see the first screen.

Current filename   Current mode   Current time

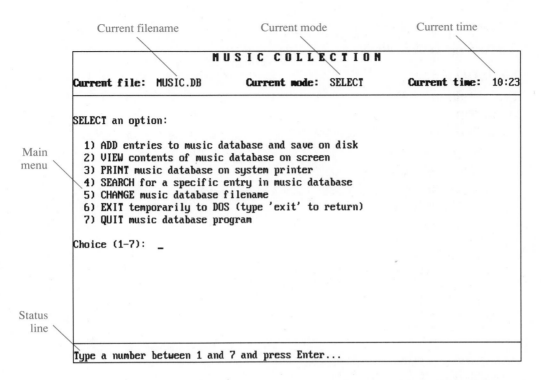

Main menu

Status line

```
            M U S I C   C O L L E C T I O N
Current file:  MUSIC.DB        Current mode:  SELECT        Current time:  10:23


SELECT an option:

    1) ADD entries to music database and save on disk
    2) VIEW contents of music database on screen
    3) PRINT music database on system printer
    4) SEARCH for a specific entry in music database
    5) CHANGE music database filename
    6) EXIT temporarily to DOS (type 'exit' to return)
    7) QUIT music database program

Choice (1-7):  _




Type a number between 1 and 7 and press Enter...
```

The following list describes the elements on the music collection screen and their significance:

■ *Current filename* describes the music database file that is currently open (MUSIC.DB is the default).

■ *Current mode* is the menu task that is currently active; this status indicator changes as different tasks are executed.

■ *Current time* is the current time as read from the system clock (updated each time the main menu is displayed).

■ *Main menu* contains the seven different tasks the program can accomplish; this is the base menu of the program and will reappear after each task has been carried out.

■ *Status line* contains instructions or information about the menu selection that is currently active.

Let's examine each of the main menu options and see what the music collection program can do.

The ADD option

Type *1* and press Enter to select the ADD menu option. When you do, MUSICDB changes the current mode to *ADD* and prompts you to enter items from your music collection. Type in the following test entries (or some of your own):

```
Item title:  The Nutcracker
   Recording artist:  Vienna Philharmonic Orchestra
   Year released:  1982
   Style of music:  Classical
   Item medium type:  Record

Item title:  Roll Out the Lefse
   Recording artist:  Norwegian Polka Boys
   Year released:  1953
   Style of music:  Polka
   Item medium type:  Record

Item title:  (T)Hanks for the Memories
   Recording artist:  The Hanks
   Year released:  1989
   Style of music:  Rock
   Item medium type:  Compact disc

Item title:  Hurried Honeymoon
   Recording artist:  The Magees
   Year released:  1988
   Style of music:  Country
   Item medium type:  Record

Item title:  Der Ring des Nibelungen (Great Scenes)
   Recording artist:  Vienna Philharmonic Orchestra
   Year released:  1985
   Style of music:  Classical
   Item medium type:  Cassette

Item title:  END
```

Notice that the middle window scrolls, leaving the top and bottom portions of the screen unchanged—this is the VIEW PRINT statement at work. When you type *END*, the program writes the information you've entered to a sequential file on disk and returns you to the main menu.

The VIEW option

Now let's have a look at the file with the VIEW option. Type *2* and press Enter to open the VIEW window and see the first record in the database. The VIEW option displays one record at a time when you press Enter, preventing information from scrolling by too quickly. Press Enter until you see the *End of file reached* message, which indicates that all records have been displayed. Notice that each record appears on the screen exactly as you entered it. Press Enter again to return to the main menu.

The PRINT option

Type *3* and press Enter to select the PRINT option from the main menu. If you have a printer attached to your system, verify that your printer is on line and ready to go, and then enter *P* to send the contents of the current file to the printer. If you don't have a printer attached to your system, don't enter *P*, or your program will begin a futile search for a printer that's not there. Instead, enter *R* to return to the main menu.

The SEARCH option

Type *4* and press Enter to select the SEARCH option from the main menu. The SEARCH option lets you search for a specific title or artist in the database. Type *2* and press Enter to indicate you want to search for an artist and then type *Vienna Philharmonic* and press Enter. If you typed in the sample entries above, your screen will look like the screen at the top of the following page.

Two albums are displayed, with the item you were searching for—in this case, the artist's name—highlighted in green. After the search is complete, press Enter to return to the main menu.

```
            M U S I C   C O L L E C T I O N
Current file:  MUSIC.DB        Current mode:  SEARCH        Current time:  10:32

   1) Search for title
   2) Search for artist

Category (1-2):  2

Enter string to be searched for:  Vienna Philharmonic

Search results:

Title:    The Nutcracker
Artist:   Vienna Philharmonic Orchestra
Year:     1982        Style:  Classical   Medium:  Record

Title:    Der Ring des Nibelungen (Great Scenes)
Artist:   Vienna Philharmonic Orchestra
Year:     1985        Style:  Classical   Medium:  Cassette


Press Enter to return to main menu..._
```

The CHANGE option

Type *5* and press Enter to select the CHANGE option from the main menu. The CHANGE option lets you change the filename you are working with so that another music database (in the same format) can be examined or created. To refresh your memory about the files you already have, CHANGE displays the contents of the current directory before it prompts you for a new filename. You can include a drive and pathname in your new file, but if you specify an invalid filename your program will terminate. If you press Enter without specifying a new filename, the default music database file MUSIC.DB will be selected.

 NOTE: Specify only music database files (new or existing) with this option. Do not specify document or program files from other applications (like those with .BAS, .BAT, or .DOC extensions) or you may damage them.

The EXIT option

Type *6* and press Enter to select the EXIT option from the main menu. The EXIT option exits to DOS temporarily so that you can carry out DOS commands or run small programs. (You won't be able to run large programs because the QuickBASIC Interpreter and the MUSICDB program are still in memory.) After you've typed a few DOS commands, type *exit* and press Enter to return to the main menu of MUSICDB.

The QUIT option

Type *7* and press Enter to select the QUIT option from the main menu. The QUIT option quits the MUSICDB program and returns you to the QuickBASIC Interpreter.

The MUSICDB.BAS Program Listing

Now that you've run the program, take a look at the program listing to see how it uses what you learned in this chapter and in previous chapters. The MUSICDB.BAS program (Figure 10-15) consists of one main program and seven subprograms. Although each subprogram handles a specific task, each is designed to be general-purpose so that it can later be adapted to a database project that's of special interest to you.

Figure 10-15 contains the complete program listing, with highlighted items indicating where you need to modify the program if you eventually decide to adapt the database to track a different type of information. Take some time to examine the listing and read the explanatory comments. As you do, notice the parts of each subprogram that are independent of the type of data being worked with: choosing a selection from the main menu; processing the selection; opening and closing files; and reading, printing, and searching for items. Changing the program to fit another type of database—a coin collection, employee records, or inventory data—simply entails removing the music-specific fields and input prompts and adding the appropriate fields of information to the new database. In other words, although the window dressing changes, the internal structure remains the same. Exercise 9 at the end of this chapter has you modify the database fields to create a home video collection program. Give Exercise 9 a try—the solution appears in Appendix D.

NOTE: Figure 10-15 shows how MUSICDB.BAS looks when it is printed out—not how it looks inside the QuickBASIC Interpreter. If you type in this program yourself, you need to use the New SUB command on the Edit menu to enter each sub-program in a separate window. For more information about this process, see Chapter 7.

```
' MUSICDB.BAS
' This is a simple database program that tracks a home music collection
'   with a sequential file and a number of general-purpose subprograms.

DECLARE SUB DisplayHeader ()              ' declare subprograms
DECLARE SUB GetMenuSelection (choice%)
DECLARE SUB AddRecords ()
DECLARE SUB ViewRecords ()
DECLARE SUB PrintRecords ()
DECLARE SUB Search ()
DECLARE SUB ChangeFilename ()

COMMON SHARED filename$, tmp$             ' declare global variables
filename$ = "MUSIC.DB"                    ' default database filename
OPEN filename$ FOR APPEND AS #1: CLOSE #1 ' ensure that file exists
tmp$ = "Year:    ####        Style: \         \ Medium: \            \"

DisplayHeader                            ' call sub to set up screen

DO
    GetMenuSelection choice%             ' call sub to get menu choice

    SELECT CASE choice%                  ' process menu choice
        CASE 1                           ' "1" means add to database
            LOCATE 3, 47: PRINT "ADD   " '   change mode to ADD
            AddRecords                   '   call sub to add items
        CASE 2                           ' "2" means view database
            LOCATE 3, 47: PRINT "VIEW  " '   change mode to VIEW
            ViewRecords                  '   call sub to view items
```

FIGURE 10-15. *(continued)*
MUSICDB.BAS: A general-purpose database program that uses a sequential file to track a home music collection. Modify the highlighted items when you adapt this program to your own needs.

332

FIGURE 10-15. *continued*

```
        CASE 3                              ' "3" means print database
            LOCATE 3, 47: PRINT "PRINT "    '   change mode to PRINT
            PrintRecords                    '   call sub to print
        CASE 4                              ' "4" means search database
            LOCATE 3, 47: PRINT "SEARCH"    '   change mode to SEARCH
            Search                          '   call sub to search
        CASE 5                              ' "5" means change filename
            LOCATE 3, 47: PRINT "CHANGE"    '   change mode to CHANGE
            ChangeFilename                  '   call sub to change it
        CASE 6                              ' "6" means exit to DOS
            CLS                             '   clear screen
            SHELL                           '   exit to DOS shell
            DisplayHeader                   '   set up screen on return
        CASE 7                              ' "7" means quit program
            LOCATE 3, 47: PRINT "QUIT  "    '   change mode to QUIT
    END SELECT

LOOP UNTIL (choice% = 7)                    ' repeat loop until QUIT chosen

END

SUB AddRecords

' The AddRecords subprogram adds new music items to the database.

LOCATE 25, 1                         ' print message on status line
PRINT "Enter music data.  Type END for title to quit...";
VIEW PRINT 5 TO 23                   ' enable viewport (lines 5-23)
PRINT                                ' prompt for data
PRINT "Enter new music item information (without commas)"
PRINT

OPEN filename$ FOR APPEND AS #1      ' open database in append mode

' get records for file until user enters END for title

WHILE (UCASE$(title$) <> "END")
    INPUT "Item title: ", title$    ' get item title
```

(continued)

FIGURE 10-15. *continued*

```basic
    IF (UCASE$(title$) <> "END") THEN
        INPUT "    Recording artist:  ", artist$    ' ...and other info
        INPUT "    Year released:  ", year%
        INPUT "    Style of music: ", style$
        INPUT "    Item medium type: ", medium$
        PRINT
                                        ' write record to database file
        WRITE #1, title$, artist$, year%, style$, medium$
    END IF
WEND

CLOSE #1                             ' close file when finished

END SUB

SUB ChangeFilename

' The ChangeFilename subprogram changes the name of the current
'   database file. If the new file does not exist, it is created.
'   If no filename is specified, the default value of MUSIC.DB is
'   assumed.  Note:  This subprogram does only minimal checking
'   for a valid DOS filename--if an invalid name is entered the
'   program will terminate.

LOCATE 25, 1: PRINT "Specify new music database filename...";
VIEW PRINT 5 TO 23              ' print message on status line

PRINT                                   ' prompt for a new filename
PRINT "Use this option to create a new music database file or open";
PRINT " an existing one."
PRINT
PRINT "The current directory contains the following files:"
PRINT
FILES "*.*"                             ' display all files in the current
PRINT                                   '    directory to help user
PRINT "What music collection data file would you like to work with?"
PRINT "(Press Enter for default database file MUSIC.DB)"
```

(continued)

FIGURE 10-15. *continued*

```
PRINT
INPUT "Filename:  ", filename$      ' assign input to global variable

IF (filename$ = "") THEN            ' if no filename entered then
    filename$ = "MUSIC.DB"          '   set filename to MUSIC.DB
ELSE                                ' otherwise trim blank spaces off
    filename$ = LTRIM$(RTRIM$(UCASE$(filename$)))
END IF                              '   both ends of file and change to
                                    '   uppercase
OPEN filename$ FOR APPEND AS #1     ' open and close file to ensure it
CLOSE #1                            '   exists on disk (this avoids file
                                    '   error when opening in INPUT mode)

END SUB


SUB DisplayHeader

' The DisplayHeader subprogram displays the status information on the
'   first three lines of the screen and the two dividing lines that set
'   off program information window.

CLS                                         ' clear screen

COLOR 9                                     ' set color to light blue

PRINT "                    M U S I C   C O L L E C T I O N"
PRINT
PRINT "Current file:              "; ' display status fields
PRINT "Current mode:         ";
PRINT "Current time:"

PRINT STRING$(80, "-")              ' print dividing lines
LOCATE 24, 1: PRINT STRING$(80, "-");    '   on lines 4 and 24

COLOR 7                             ' set color to default white

END SUB
```

(continued)

FIGURE 10-15. *continued*

```
SUB GetMenuSelection (choice%)

' The GetMenuSelection subprogram gets a menu choice from the user
'    and returns it to the main program in the choice% variable.
'    The VIEW PRINT statement is used to enable and disable the
'    viewport area (lines 5-23). The information displayed here does
'    not disturb the data in lines 1 through 4 and 24 through 25.

choice% = 0                    ' initialize choice% to zero

VIEW PRINT                     ' disable viewport to update lines 3 and 25
LOCATE 3, 16: PRINT "          ": LOCATE 3, 16: PRINT filename$
LOCATE 3, 47: PRINT "SELECT"        ' set current mode to select
LOCATE 3, 76: PRINT LEFT$(TIME$, 5)   ' update current time
LOCATE 25, 1: PRINT "Type a number between 1 and 7 and press Enter...";
VIEW PRINT 5 TO 23             ' enable viewport (lines 5-23)
CLS 2                          ' clear viewport for choice prompts

PRINT                          ' prompt user for choice
PRINT "SELECT an option:"
PRINT
PRINT "  1) ADD entries to music database and save on disk"
PRINT "  2) VIEW contents of music database on screen"
PRINT "  3) PRINT music database on system printer"
PRINT "  4) SEARCH for a specific entry in music database"
PRINT "  5) CHANGE music database filename"
PRINT "  6) EXIT temporarily to DOS (type 'exit' to return)"
PRINT "  7) QUIT music database program"
PRINT
                              ' choice must be integer between 1 and 7
DO WHILE (choice% < 1) OR (choice% > 7)
    INPUT "Choice (1-7):  ", choice%
LOOP

CLS 2                          ' clear viewport for upcoming choice
VIEW PRINT                     ' disable viewport to clear status line
LOCATE 25, 1: PRINT STRING$(80, " ");  ' print a blank line

END SUB
```

(continued)

FIGURE 10-15. *continued*

```
SUB PrintRecords

' The PrintRecords subprogram sends the entire contents of the current
'   database file to the printer.

VIEW PRINT 5 TO 23                      ' enable viewport (lines 5-23)
PRINT                                   ' display introductory message
PRINT "This option sends the contents of "; filename$;
PRINT " to your printer."

VIEW PRINT                              ' disable viewport so status
LOCATE 25, 1                            '   line can be updated
INPUT ; "Enter P to print or R to return to main menu: ", reply$
VIEW PRINT 5 TO 23                      ' enable viewport (lines 5-23)
                                        ' if user wants to print (P or p)
IF (reply$ = "P") OR (reply$ = "p") THEN
    OPEN filename$ FOR INPUT AS #1      ' open the music database file
                                        ' send header to printer
    LPRINT "------------------ Music Collection -------------------"
    LPRINT
    LPRINT "Date printed:  "; DATE$  ' print current date
    LPRINT "Filename:      "; filename$ ' print current filename
    LPRINT
    LPRINT "Collection contents:"
    LPRINT
                                        ' until file contents exhausted
    DO WHILE (NOT EOF(1))               '   read a record from file
        INPUT #1, title$, artist$, year%, style$, medium$

        LPRINT "Title:   "; title$    '  print each field of the record
        LPRINT "Artist:  "; artist$
        LPRINT "Year:    "; year%
        LPRINT "Style:   "; style$
        LPRINT "Medium:  "; medium$
        LPRINT
    LOOP
```

(continued)

FIGURE 10-15. *continued*

```
    LPRINT CHR$(12)                ' send formfeed character to printer
    CLOSE #1                       ' close file
END IF

END SUB

SUB Search

' The Search subprogram searches the entire database file for records
'    matching a search string entered by the user.  Search currently
'    supports searches for title and artist fields--additional topics
'    can be included by adding extra CASE statements.

num% = 0                            ' initialize category variable
found% = 0                          ' initialize "record found" flag

LOCATE 25, 1                        ' update status line
PRINT "Enter search category and content...";
VIEW PRINT 5 TO 23                  ' enable viewport (lines 5-23)

PRINT
PRINT "Select a search category:"   ' prompt for search topic
PRINT
PRINT "  1) Search for title"
PRINT "  2) Search for artist"
' add prompts for additional search categories here...
PRINT

DO WHILE (num% < 1) OR (num% > 2)   ' get number associated with
    INPUT "Category (1-2): ", num%  '    search topic
LOOP

PRINT                               ' get search string
INPUT "Enter string to be searched for:  ", searchStr$
PRINT
PRINT "Search results:"            ' display search results
PRINT
```

(continued)

FIGURE 10-15. *continued*

```
OPEN filename$ FOR INPUT AS #1          ' open database file

DO WHILE (NOT EOF(1))                   ' read records from file
    INPUT #1, title$, artist$, year%, style$, medium$

    SELECT CASE num% ' use num% to compare correct record field...
    CASE 1    ' if num% = 1, determine if search string in title field
        IF INSTR(UCASE$(title$), UCASE$(searchStr$)) THEN
            found% = -1                 ' if so, set found flag to true
            COLOR 2: PRINT "Title:   "; title$: COLOR 7
            PRINT "Artist: "; artist$
            PRINT USING tmp$; year%; style$; medium$
            PRINT       ' display record fields with title field in green
        END IF
    CASE 2    ' if num% = 2, determine if search string in artist field
        IF INSTR(UCASE$(artist$), UCASE$(searchStr$)) THEN
            found% = -1                 ' if so, set found flag to true
            PRINT "Title:   "; title$
            COLOR 2: PRINT "Artist:  "; artist$: COLOR 7
            PRINT USING tmp$; year%; style$; medium$
            PRINT       ' display record fields with artist field in green
        END IF
    ' add CASE statements for additional categories here...
    END SELECT
LOOP

CLOSE #1                                ' close file
IF (NOT found%) THEN                    ' if file not found display
    COLOR 2: PRINT searchStr$;          '   "not found" message
    COLOR 7: PRINT " not found in "; filename$; " database"
END IF

VIEW PRINT              ' disable viewport and update status line
LOCATE 25, 1: INPUT ; "Press Enter to return to main menu...", dummy$

END SUB
```

(continued)

FIGURE 10-15. *continued*

```
SUB ViewRecords

' The ViewRecords subprogram displays each record in the database on
'   the screen one at a time.

LOCATE 25, 1                       ' update status line
PRINT "Press Enter to continue...";

VIEW PRINT 5 TO 23                 ' enable viewport (lines 5-23)
PRINT                              ' display opening message
PRINT "This option lets you view your music collection ";
PRINT "one record at a time."
PRINT

OPEN filename$ FOR INPUT AS #1     ' open database file

DO WHILE (NOT EOF(1))              ' get record from file
    INPUT #1, title$, artist$, year%, style$, medium$

    PRINT "Title:   "; title$      ' display each field on screen
    PRINT "Artist:  "; artist$
    PRINT USING tmp$; year%; style$; medium$

    INPUT "", dummy$               ' pause after each record
LOOP

CLOSE #1                           ' close file
PRINT "** End of file reached **"  ' display EOF message
INPUT "", dummy$                   ' pause before returning
                                   '   to main program

END SUB
```

SUMMARY

In this chapter you really started putting your skills together in a useful way. You continued working with large amounts of data by learning how to read and write sequential files. You also learned the parts that DOS and DOS commands play in BASIC programming, and you practiced using a number of them in useful ways. In addition, you worked with a music-collection database program that combined the string-manipulation and user-interface techniques you developed in earlier chapters with the sequential-file skills you've learned in this chapter. The result: A general-purpose database program that can be used to track information *you* are interested in.

QUESTIONS AND EXERCISES

1. What is the difference between opening a file for OUTPUT and opening a file for APPEND?

2. Which of the following statements encloses data items in quotation marks when it sends them to a sequential file?

   a. INPUT#

   b. PRINT# USING

   c. PRINT#

   d. WRITE#

3. True or False: The filename specified in an OPEN statement must be in uppercase letters.

4. When is the LINE INPUT# statement considered more useful than the INPUT# statement?

5. What is wrong with the following QuickBASIC statement?

   ```
   SHELL COPY TEST.TXT TEST2.TXT
   ```

6. What do the following program lines display?

   ```
   searchStr$ = "Bea"
   artist$ = "The Beatles"
   IF INSTR(UCASE$(artist$), UCASE$(searchStr$)) THEN
       PRINT "Search string found!"
   ELSE
       PRINT "Search string not found"
   END IF
   ```

7. Write a program that prompts the user for a list of cities and stores the information in a sequential file. Design the program so that the user can view the contents of the file after it has been created.

8. Write a program that prompts the user for a list of names and addresses, stores them in a sequential file, and then sorts the records in a file alphabetically by name. Hint: The easiest way to solve this problem is to use an array to store the records and sort them. You might want to use the Shell Sort, which you learned in Chapter 9.

9. Use the DOS COPY command to copy the MUSICDB.BAS program to a file named VIDEO.BAS. Then modify it to track a home video collection database. The database should contain the following fields of information:

☐ Name of video

☐ Significant actors/contributors

☐ Year video was released

☐ Type of video (comedy, drama, horror, TV show)

☐ Medium (VHS, Beta, Laserdisc)

Working with Graphics and Sound

Now that you've learned the basics of BASIC, you can enhance your programs by adding graphics and sound to them. In this chapter you'll learn what kind of graphics your computer can create, and you'll learn how to use sound to jazz up your programs.

INTRODUCTION TO GRAPHICS PROGRAMMING

Your hardware dictates what type of graphics you can create. Because of this fact, it's important to know what kind of video equipment is installed in your computer.

What Is the Video Equipment?

On an IBM PC or compatible, the video equipment consists of two pieces:

- The *video adapter,* which is an electronic card installed inside your machine. (Note: On an IBM PS/2 computer or compatible, this equipment is already built into the computer—it does not come on a separate card.)

- The *monitor* (sometimes called the *video display*), which is the TV-like box that usually sits on top of your computer.

Some video equipment displays both graphics and color; some can display only graphics; some can't display graphics or color at all. And of the video equipment that displays both graphics and color, you have a wide variety of choices. Generally, the less expensive your equipment, the fewer colors and the "grainier" images you'll have. More-expensive video equipment usually displays images with many colors and a smooth, professional-looking appearance.

Video adapters

Table 11-1 lists the video adapters available for the IBM PC, IBM PC/XT, IBM PC/AT, and compatible computers: The IBM PS/2 Model 25 and Model 30 have a built-in MCGA graphics adapter; all other PS/2 models have a built-in VGA adapter.

Adapter	Multicolor display	Graphics
MDA (monochrome display adapter)	No	No
HGC (Hercules graphics card)*	No	Yes
CGA (color/graphics adapter)	Yes	Yes
EGA (enhanced graphics adapter)	Yes	Yes
MCGA (multicolor gate array)	Yes	Yes
VGA (video graphics array)	Yes	Yes

* The Hercules graphics card is not manufactured by IBM. This type of card is often referred to as a *monographics adapter* or a *monochrome graphics adapter*.

TABLE 11-1.
Video adapters for the IBM PC family of computers and compatibles.

 NOTE: You can install several types of video adapters, but most are compatible with the video adapters manufactured and sold by IBM. Therefore, this book concentrates on the equipment listed in Table 11-1.

If your computer has an MDA adapter, you won't be able to do some of the graphics exercises in this chapter. If you aren't sure what kind of adapter you have, read on. In a while, you'll load and run a program that will tell you whether you can do the exercises.

Monitors

Like video adapters, monitors come in a wide variety of types (with, of course, a wide variety of prices). Although a certain amount of mixing and matching is allowed—in other words, certain video adapters work with several different types of monitors—most computer dealers generally match the video adapter you choose to the appropriate monitor.

Text Mode *vs* Graphics Mode

All video adapters (except those that can't display graphics) can be set into two modes—*text mode* or *graphics mode*.

- In text mode, your video adapter can display alphanumeric characters—letters, numbers, and punctuation marks—but cannot display shapes (such as lines, circles, and so on).

- In graphics mode, your video adapter can still display alphanumeric characters, but it can also display non-alphanumeric items such as lines and circles.

The following sections describe these two modes in detail.

TEXT MODE

When you first start the Microsoft QuickBASIC Interpreter, your video adapter displays both the View window and the output screen in *text mode*: 25 rows of text with 80 characters per row.

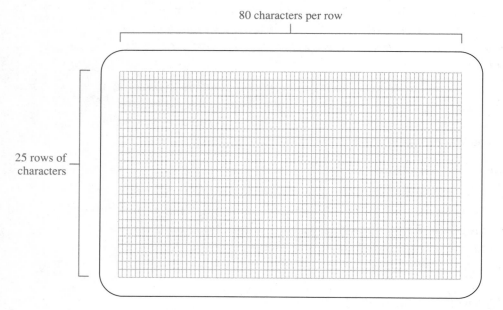

Each row and column in the output screen is numbered, giving each "box" a unique row and column coordinate, called a *screen coordinate*. Each box can hold only one alphanumeric character.

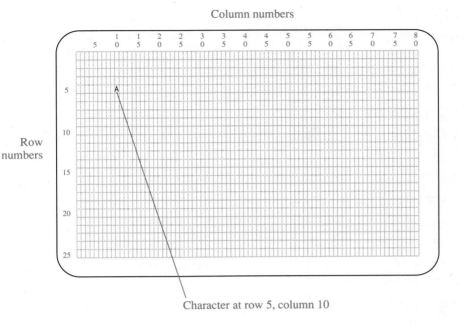

Character at row 5, column 10

The Text Cursor

You'll remember that when you write a program in the View window the blinking cursor indicates where the next character you type will appear. Well, the QuickBASIC Interpreter uses its own cursor, called the *text cursor,* to determine where characters will appear on the output screen. Unlike the blinking cursor in the View window, the text cursor is usually invisible.

Remember how the CLS statement clears the output screen? It also serves another purpose: It sets the text cursor to row 1, column 1. If the QuickBASIC Interpreter then executes a PRINT statement, the PRINT statement prints its message starting at row 1, column 1. The QuickBASIC Interpreter then moves the text cursor down to the first column of the next row (row 2, column 1).

The LOCATE Statement

But you can override the QuickBASIC Interpreter's placement of the text cursor by using the LOCATE statement. LOCATE lets you dictate within a program where the text cursor should appear.

Here's the syntax of a LOCATE statement:

```
LOCATE [row][, column]
```

row is an integer from 1 through 25 and *column* is an integer from 1 through 80.

- If you omit *row*, the text cursor remains in the current row.

- If you omit *column*, the text cursor remains in the current column.

- If you omit both *row* and *column*, QuickBASIC leaves the text cursor in its current position.

- If you specify a value outside the range of your screen size, you'll receive an error message.

NOTE: As you'll learn shortly, you can instruct your video adapter to display only 40 columns of text across the screen. In this case, column *must be no greater than 40.*

In the following example, the LOCATE statement tells the QuickBASIC Interpreter to put the cursor at row 10, column 46. When the QuickBASIC Interpreter executes the subsequent PRINT statement, it prints the message *Welcome!* beginning at row 10, column 46. After printing that message, the QuickBASIC Interpreter places the text cursor at row 11, column 1, and will print the message of the next PRINT statement beginning at that point unless your program includes another LOCATE statement that changes the position of the text cursor.

Position the text cursor at row 10, column 46.

```
LOCATE 10,46
PRINT "Welcome!"
```

Print the message starting at row 10, column 46.

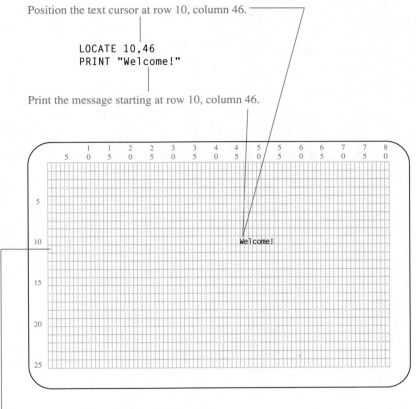

The QuickBASIC Interpreter moves the text cursor to row 11, column 1, after the message is printed.

Practice: Working with the LOCATE statement

1.   Load the LOCATE-1.BAS program (Figure 11-1) from the CHAP11 subdirectory on disk.

```
' LOCATE-1.BAS
' This program demonstrates the LOCATE statement.

CLS

INPUT "Please enter the row coordinate (1-24):  ", rowNum%
PRINT
INPUT "Please enter the column coordinate (1-80):  ", colNum%
PRINT
INPUT "Please enter a message to display:  ", message$

CLS

FOR i% = 0 TO 70 STEP 10        ' print column coordinates across
    PRINT "1234567890";         '   the top of the screen
NEXT i%

FOR i% = 2 TO 23                ' print the row numbers along the
    LOCATE i%, 1                '   left-hand side of the screen
    PRINT LTRIM$(STR$(i%))      ' don't print the blank space
NEXT i%                         '   before each number

LOCATE rowNum%, colNum%         ' print the message at the user-
PRINT message$                  '   supplied coordinates
```

FIGURE 11-1.

LOCATE-1.BAS: A program demonstrating the LOCATE statement.

2. Run the program and enter row and column values that are greater than 2 (you'll see why in a moment). After you run the program, your output screen will look something like the screen at the top of the next page.

Notice that the program prints numbers across row 1 and down columns 1 and 2. The program does this to indicate where your message begins to print so that you can verify the values you typed in for the LOCATE statement.

This example uses a row value of *5*, a column value of *20*, and the message *Hello!* Run the program a few times so that you can fully understand how the LOCATE statement works.

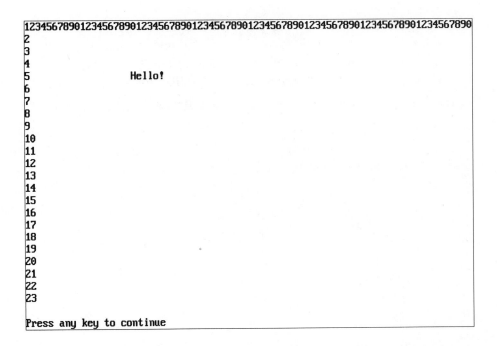

The STR$ Function

The STR$ function converts a numeric value to a string of numerals. The syntax of the STR$ function is as follows:

```
STR$(value)
```

value is any numeric expression.

You can use STR$ together with the LTRIM$ function to get rid of the space that appears to the left of non-negative numbers. This comes in handy when you position a number using the LOCATE statement. For example, the following statements display the number *12.34* with no leading space:

```
number! = 12.34
PRINT LTRIM$(STR$(number!))
```

3. Next, try running the program with a relatively large column value and a fairly long message. For example, try using a row value of *5*, a column value of *70*, and the message *Where will this be displayed?* Your output screen should look like this:

```
1234567890123456789012345678901234567890123456789012345678901234567890123456789012345678901234567890
2
3
4
5
Where will this be displayed?
7
8
9
10
11
12
13
14
15
16
17
18
19
20
21
22
23

Press any key to continue
```

Notice that the QuickBASIC Interpreter displayed the message starting at row 6, column 1, even though you had asked QuickBASIC to display it on row 5. Because the message exceeded the 80-character boundary, QuickBASIC knew it couldn't fit the entire message on row 5, so it started at the beginning of the next row. Keep this in mind as you use the LOCATE statement, and plan accordingly.

You may be curious about one thing. The program asks you for a row value from 1 through 23 and numbers the rows on the screen only up through row 23. However, earlier we explained that the row value can be 1 through 25. Why did we limit the program to 23 rows?

4. Run the program again and use a row value of *24*. Your output screen will look something like this:

```
2
3
4
5
6
7
8
9
10
11
12
13
14
15
16
17
18
19
20
21
22
23
          What will happen?

Press any key to continue
```

After printing the message, the QuickBASIC Interpreter moved the cursor down to the first column of the next row. When it moved the cursor down, QuickBASIC had to shift the contents of the screen up one row so that the next row would be displayed. Doing this, as you can see, caused the topmost row to be pushed up off the screen.

You can solve this problem by adding a semicolon to the end of the PRINT statement to keep the cursor on the same line. The following statements, for example, display the message *This is line 24* on row 24 without shifting the contents of the screen:

```
LOCATE 24, 1
PRINT "This is line 24";
```

You can use this same technique to place text on line 25. (You might remember this from the MUSICDB.BAS program in the previous chapter.) Remember, however, that the QuickBASIC Interpreter uses line 25 to display its *Press any key to continue* message, so any characters displayed on that line will be overwritten when your program ends.

Using LOCATE to Create Animation

When you started reading this book, the first program you loaded from the disk and ran was called WELCOME.BAS. This program caused the words *Welcome to Learn BASIC Now!* to "fall" from the top of the screen. All of this animation was created with the LOCATE statement.

On a computer screen, you create animation by presenting the user with the *illusion* of movement. One way to do this is by printing a character repeatedly in the direction you want the character to move, and at the same time replacing the previous occurrence of the character with a space, as shown in Figure 11-2. Although the characters don't actually move, the result has the illusion of movement.

1. Print a character.

2. Print the same character in an adjacent location.

3. Print a space where the first character was.

FIGURE 11-2.
Animating a character on the screen.

Practice: Working with text-based animation

Say you want to write a program that causes the letter X to "move" across the screen. The following steps show how you would accomplish this.

1. Load the LOCATE-2.BAS program (Figure 11-3) from disk.

```
' LOCATE-2.BAS
' This program demonstrates the first step in creating animation.

CLS

FOR i% = 1 to 80
    LOCATE 10, i%
    PRINT "X"
NEXT i%
```

FIGURE 11-3.
LOCATE-2.BAS: The first step in animating a character.

2. Run the program. When you do, the program prints a solid row of Xs across row 10 of your screen. This doesn't give the illusion of movement, but you have accomplished the first step—you've caused the letter X to "move" across the screen. Because the QuickBASIC Interpreter executes the program quickly, it prints the row of Xs almost instantaneously. Use the techniques you learned in Chapter 6 to put a delay loop in the program to slow the rate at which the QuickBASIC Interpreter prints the Xs. (The next program includes a delay loop, but try to create one yourself before moving on.)

Next you need to create the illusion of making a *single* letter X move across the screen, even though the program will actually be printing 80 separate Xs. To do this you print an X, print a second X immediately to the right of the first, and then erase the first X by overwriting it with a space.

3. Load the LOCATE-3.BAS program (Figure 11-4) from disk.

```
' LOCATE-3.BAS
' This program demonstrates simple animation.

CLS

LOCATE 10, 1              ' position the first X
PRINT "X"
FOR i% = 2 to 80         ' loop through the rest
    LOCATE 10, i%
    PRINT "X"            ' print an X next to the previous X
    LOCATE 10, i% - 1
    PRINT " "           ' "erase" the previous X

    FOR j = 1 TO 300    ' delay loop
    NEXT j

NEXT i%
```

FIGURE 11-4.
LOCATE-3.BAS: A program that animates a character.

Notice that the first X is printed before the loop begins. The reason for this lies in how the Xs are erased. The LOCATE values given to print a space are *10, i% − 1*. If the loop started with a value of 1, the first time the program tried to print a space it would try to print it at row 10, column 0. Since 0 is not a valid value, the QuickBASIC Interpreter would stop and display an error message.

4. Run the program. When you do, you should see the letter X "move" right across the screen! If you'd like, stop for awhile and experiment with the program. Including such animation in your own programs can *really* get the user's attention! (Remember the bowling ball from Chapter 7?)

The WELCOME.BAS program

Now that you've learned the basics of text-based animation, let's re-examine the WELCOME.BAS program.

Practice: Working with WELCOME.BAS
Load the WELCOME.BAS program (Figure 11-5) from disk.

```
' WELCOME.BAS
'
'             Welcome to the QuickBASIC Interpreter!
'
' To run this program, drop down the Run menu and choose Start
' or hold down either Shift key and press the F5 function key.

CLS

FOR i% = 1 TO 5

    READ column%, word$

    FOR row% = 2 TO 18
        LOCATE row%, column%
        PRINT word$
        LOCATE row% - 1, column%
        PRINT SPACE$(LEN(word$))
        SOUND (2400 / row%), 1
    NEXT row%

NEXT i%

LOCATE 1, 1

DATA 25, "Welcome", 33, "to", 36, "Learn", 42, "BASIC", 48, "Now!"
```

FIGURE 11-5.
WELCOME.BAS: The introductory program from Chapter 2.

Instead of printing only a single letter, as in the previous example, this program uses entire words. Also, to "erase" the previous word, this program uses a string of spaces to cover the entire word at once.

In addition, this program uses sound to reinforce the "falling" illusion of each word. Notice how the SOUND statement uses the current value of *row%* as a divisor of the value *2400*. As the value of *row%* increases, the result of the division operation decreases and the resulting pitch of the tone becomes lower. (You'll learn more about the SOUND statement later in this chapter.)

GRAPHICS MODE

As you've seen, text mode can be an interesting and relatively straightforward medium for presenting information on the screen. You can add both text-based "graphics" and simple animation to your programs without too much programming effort.

The downside of text-based programming is its limitations. Even the smallest character on the screen, such as a period, takes up an entire character's "box," meaning that smooth, well-defined graphics are difficult if not impossible to create. Also, text-based animation often seems jumpy because the item you animate has to jump the width of a character "box" each time your program "moves" it.

Output such as smoothly drawn shapes and flowing animation is better accomplished if your video adapter is in graphics mode and if you take advantage of the graphics tools that BASIC has to offer.

What Is Graphics Mode?

If you look closely at one of the characters on your screen, you'll see that it's actually made up of tiny dots that collectively form the letter. In fact, each of these "boxes" that we've been talking about is actually a matrix (a grid) of 8 dots by 8 dots, as shown on the next page.

In the sample matrix, the letter A is filled in to show how a matrix of dots displays a character. Although not all the dots are used, *all* the dots in the matrix—filled in or not—appear on the screen when your video adapter is in text mode. This is why an entire "box" is needed for each character.

In graphics mode the rules change. In graphics mode you can access each individual dot.

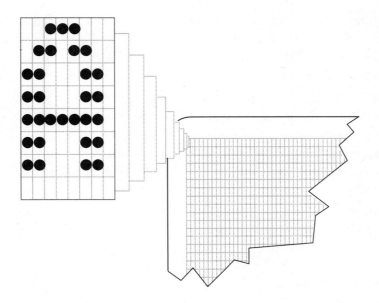

 NOTE: Some video adapters can display matrices of different sizes. For example, some can display matrices 8 dots wide and 9 dots high; others can display matrices 9 dots wide and 14 dots high, and so forth. We'll use an 8-by-8 matrix for this discussion.

Graphics resolution

In computer graphics terminology, the word *resolution* is defined as the fineness of detail in an image. Generally speaking, a low-resolution image has a grainy appearance, and a high-resolution image has a smooth, almost photographlike appearance. The higher the resolution, the better the image quality. If you look closely at a newspaper photograph, you'll see that the picture is actually made up of thousands of tiny dots. Hold the picture far away, and collectively these seemingly random dots form a recognizable image.

A computer screen (or a regular television set, for that matter) also forms pictures by displaying tiny dots that collectively form an image. The smaller the dots—that is, the greater the resolution—the better the picture quality.

On a computer screen, each of these dots is called a *pixel,* which is short for *picture element.* Unlike the dots in a newspaper photograph (which uses different-sized dots for lighter and darker areas), all of the pixels on a computer screen are the same size.

 NOTE: Remember that the video adapter, not the monitor, determines the display resolution. The video adapter is also responsible for displaying the actual characters and pictures on the screen. Therefore, when we talk about the graphics hardware and capabilities of your computer, we're really focusing on the video adapter.

Before you can start taking advantage of graphics mode, you must first switch your video adapter into graphics mode. In BASIC, you do this by using the SCREEN statement.

The SCREEN Statement

The SCREEN statement causes the QuickBASIC Interpreter to place your video adapter in graphics mode when it displays the output screen. The simplest format of the SCREEN statement is as follows:

```
SCREEN mode
```

mode is a number from 0 through 13 (except 5 and 6) that tells QuickBASIC what graphics mode you want it to switch your video adapter to. Although 12 graphics modes are available, your video adapter can use only some of them. In addition, your video adapter can display only one mode at a time.

Each mode is unique in terms of its resolution and the number of colors it supports: Some modes display 25 rows and 80 columns of text; others display 25 rows and 40 columns. And some modes display more than the usual 25 rows of text.

Table 11-2 summarizes the 14 screen modes. The resolutions shown represent the maximum possible resolutions for particular modes. The values are given as *horizontal × vertical,* so a value of 320 × 200 means the display is 320 pixels wide and 200 pixels high.

The number of colors shown for each mode represents the maximum number of colors available in that mode. Note that some adapters may be unable to display the maximum number of colors for a particular mode, even if the adapter is capable of displaying that mode.

Screen mode	Resolution	Number of colors	Text resolution
0	(Text only)	16	80 × 25
1	320 × 200	4	40 × 25
2	640 × 200	2	80 × 25
3*	720 × 348	1	80 × 25
4†	640 × 400	1	80 × 25
5	Not supported		
6	Not supported		
7	320 × 200	16	40 × 25
8	640 × 200	16	80 × 25
9	640 × 350	16	80 × 25
10	640 × 350	4‡	80 × 25
11	640 × 480	2	80 × 30
12	640 × 480	16	80 × 30
13	320 × 200	256	40 × 25

* Hercules graphics cards and compatibles only.

† Olivetti personal computers and AT&T 6300 personal computers only.

‡ Mode 10 shows different *attributes* instead of different colors. In other words, images are shown in a regular, bright, or blinking form instead of in different colors.

TABLE 11-2.
The available screen modes and their characteristics.

The text resolution shown for each mode indicates the text size that will be displayed if you use PRINT statements in your program. Note that most modes use 25 rows; more important at this point is the number of columns of text a particular mode will display.

Practice: Identifying the adapter in your computer

Load the TEST-VID.BAS program from disk and run it. This program provides you with a list of the mode settings you can use with the SCREEN statement. You might want to make a mark in Table 11-2 beside each mode supported by your particular video adapter.

NOTE: We don't list the TEST-VID.BAS program in this book because it requires the use of certain BASIC statements that, because of space limitations, we don't cover. Once you've completed the book, however, don't be afraid to load the program again and examine it. Use on-line help to find out more about keywords you don't recognize.

Understanding Graphics-Mode Coordinates

With the LOCATE statement you learned that by specifying row and column coordinates you could dictate where text would appear on the output screen. In graphics mode, the output screen actually has two types of coordinates, depending on the type of information you want to display:

- Text coordinates, which work the same in graphics mode as they do in text mode

- Graphics coordinates, which you use to place nontext information (such as lines and circles) on the screen

Let's examine the coordinate system for screen mode 1. As you saw in Table 11-2, screen mode 1 has a graphics resolution of 320×200 and a text resolution of 40×25, as shown on the screen at the top of the next page.

First, notice one very important difference between the graphics coordinate system and the text coordinate system. The upper-left pixel on the graphics screen is at coordinate (0, 0), and the upper-left character on the text screen is at coordinate (1, 1).

Another important difference is in how you specify the coordinates: In text mode, you give the coordinates as *row, column*; in graphics mode, you specify the coordinates as *column, row*.

Notice also that in graphics mode, just as in text mode, each screen location has a unique coordinate.

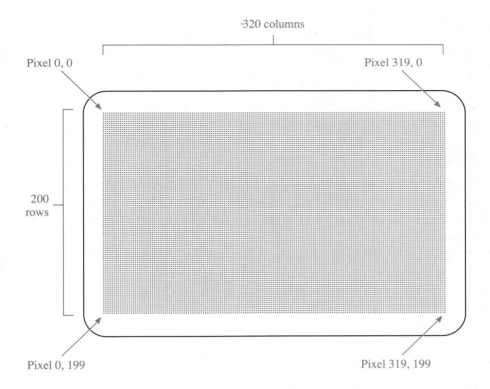

Working with Individual Pixels

After you've used the SCREEN statement to put your video adapter into graphics mode, you can use two BASIC statements to place individual pixels on the screen at specific locations: PSET and PRESET.

The PSET statement

In its simplest form, the syntax of a PSET statement is as follows:

```
PSET (xcoordinate, ycoordinate)[, color]
```

xcoordinate is the number of the column you want the pixel to appear in. The range of values you can use depends on the graphics screen mode you've set with the SCREEN statement. For example, if you chose screen mode 1, the *xcoordinate* value would be from 0 through 319 because the maximum number of columns in screen mode 1 is 320.

ycoordinate is the number of the row you want the pixel to appear in. Again, the range of values you can use depends on the graphics screen mode you've set using the SCREEN statement. For example, if you set screen mode to 1, the *ycoordinate* value would be from 0 through 199 because the maximum number of rows in screen mode 1 is 200.

NOTE: The parentheses around the xcoordinate *and* ycoordinate *values are not optional. They must appear whenever you use the PSET statement.*

color is a value representing the color of the pixel. Again, the range of color values you can choose from depends on the graphics screen mode you've set with the SCREEN statement. If you omit *color*, the current foreground color is used.

A PSET statement sets only one pixel at a time, but you can put a PSET statement inside a loop to draw several pixels in a row.

To erase a pixel drawn with the PSET command, use another PSET command with the coordinates of the pixel you want to erase, specifying the background color for the *color* value.

Practice: Using the PSET statement

1. Load the PSET.BAS program (Figure 11-6) from disk.

```
' PSET.BAS
' This program demonstrates the PSET statement.

CLS

INPUT "Please enter the screen mode (0-13):  ", modeNum%
SCREEN modeNum%

LOCATE 22, 23
PRINT "Col: Row:"
```

FIGURE 11-6.   *(continued)*
PSET.BAS: A demonstration of the PSET statement.

FIGURE 11-6. *continued*

```
FOR i% = 0 TO 200 STEP 20        ' values for xcoordinate
    FOR j% = 0 TO 135 STEP 15    ' values for ycoordinate
        PSET (i%, j%)            ' use default foreground color
        LOCATE 23, 1            ' position text cursor
        PRINT "Current coordinates: ("; i%; ","; j%; ")"

        FOR k% = 1 TO 2000       ' delay loop
        NEXT k%

        PSET (i%, j%), 0         ' use background color to erase
        LOCATE 23, 22
        PRINT SPACE$(13)         ' erase printed coordinates
    NEXT j%
NEXT i%
```

2. Run the program and enter a screen value from the list of values you can use with your particular video adapter (the list you obtained in the last practice). The program will then begin "moving" a pixel in regular jumps across the screen. After the program places each pixel on the screen, the program updates the message at the bottom of the screen to show you the pixel's coordinates.

If you can use more than one screen mode with your adapter, run the program again and enter a different mode number. Notice the difference in resolution—the program will almost cover a low-resolution screen (such as 320 × 200) with pixels but will cover only the upper-left corner of a high-resolution screen (such as 640 × 480).

Illegal Function Calls

Inevitably, you'll try to run a program that includes graphics or sound statements only to have the QuickBASIC Interpreter return you to the View window and display the following dialog box:

```
┌──────────────────────────────┐
│                              │
│  Illegal function call       │
│                              │
├──────────────────────────────┤
│  <  OK  >   < Help >         │
└──────────────────────────────┘
```

In addition, the QuickBASIC Interpreter will highlight the statement it had trouble executing. For example, if you had tried to run the preceding program with a screen mode of 0, the QuickBASIC Interpreter would have stopped the program, returned you to the View window, displayed the dialog box, and then highlighted the first PSET statement. Why?

If you look at Table 11-2, you'll notice that screen mode 0 is text-only, meaning you can't use graphics statements (such as PSET) with your video adapter in that mode.

Other conditions can cause a similar error:

■ Trying to use a COLOR statement value that is not supported by the screen mode

■ Trying to use a LOCATE statement value of 0 or a value greater than the available number of rows or columns

■ Trying to use a SCREEN statement value that your video adapter does not support

If you see this dialog box, review Table 11-2, examine the list of valid video modes that you obtained from the TEST-VID.BAS program, and then correct your program.

Changing the foreground and background colors

Chapter 6 provided a brief introduction to the COLOR statement. A quick review is in order at this point.

The COLOR statement has the following syntax:

```
COLOR [foreground][, background]
```

foreground and *background* are values for the foreground and background colors, respectively. The range of values you can use depends entirely on the graphics mode your video adapter is in. (See Table 11-2.) If you omit either value, the current value is used. If you omit *foreground*, you must precede *background* with a comma.

The foreground value determines the color of the text and graphics shapes. You can change the foreground color at any point in the program without affecting text or shapes already displayed on the screen.

The background value specifies the background color. (You can change the background color in modes 0, 7, 8, 9, and 10 only.) Note that changing the background color will not have an immediate effect. To change the color of the entire background to the new color, you must include an instruction in your program that updates the background color. The CLS statement is an excellent candidate, although you should do this early in your program because a CLS statement will erase any text or graphics already displayed on the screen.

The PRESET statement

The PRESET statement works like the PSET statement, with one important difference: If you omit the *color* argument, the current background color is used. This lets you erase pixels simply by omitting *color*. The PRESET statement has the following syntax:

```
PRESET (xcoordinate, ycoordinate)[, color]
```

Note that the PRESET statement erases whatever happens to be located at (*xcoordinate, ycoordinate*). For example, if you use a PRINT statement to print a message and then use a PRESET statement whose coordinates are in the same area, the PRESET statement might "take a bite" out of a letter in the message.

Practice: Working with the PRESET statement

1. Load the PRESET.BAS program (Figure 11-7) from disk.

```
' PRESET.BAS
' This program demonstrates the PRESET statement.

CLS

INPUT "Please enter a screen mode (0-13):  ", modeNum%
INPUT "Press Enter to begin the hailstorm...", dummy$

SCREEN modeNum%
PRINT "Press any key to stop"

DO
    RANDOMIZE TIMER
    randCol% = INT(RND(1) * 320)  ' random column number for "hailstones";
                                  '   assumes horizontal resolution of 320;
                                  '   change for higher-resolution modes

    FOR i% = 1 TO 199             ' assumes vertical resolution of 200;
                                  '   change for higher-resolution modes

        PSET (randCol%, i%)
        PRESET (randCol%, i% - 1)

        FOR j% = 1 TO 35          ' delay loop
        NEXT j%

    NEXT i%
LOOP UNTIL INKEY$ <> ""
```

FIGURE 11-7.
PRESET.BAS: A demonstration of the PRESET statement.

2. Run the program. If your video adapter allows it, enter a value of *1*, *7*, or *13* for maximum effect. The comments in the program show you what to change if you want the program to take advantage of higher-resolution screen modes.

As the program runs you can observe one of the interesting side effects of PRESET. Just before the "hailstones" appear, the program prints the message *Press any key to stop*. As the program continues to run, you'll see the PRESET statements demolish this message as the "hailstones" pass over it.

Note the use of the INKEY$ function, introduced here for the first time. INKEY$ checks the keyboard to see if a key has been pressed. If so, INKEY$ returns the ASCII code associated with the key; if not, it returns an empty string. Unlike the INPUT and LINE INPUT statements, INKEY$ doesn't wait for the user to press Enter before continuing.

Positioning Pixels with Coordinates

You can use two coordinate systems to position pixels on the screen: *absolute coordinates* and *relative coordinates*.

Absolute coordinates

The coordinate system you've used so far is the absolute coordinate system. In this system, all coordinate values are based on the upper-left-corner coordinate of (0, 0). To position a pixel on the screen, you count (or, more likely, guess) the number of columns over and the number of rows down in order to come up with the coordinate values.

As you've seen, this coordinate system works fine, but if you want to use individual pixels to create a particular shape, you're in for a lot of guesswork and counting. There is, however, another coordinate system that makes the job of determining coordinate values much easier.

Relative coordinates

With relative coordinates, the coordinates you specify for a specific pixel are *relative* to the last pixel you placed on the screen.

The screen at the top of the next page demonstrates this. To place the first pixel on the screen you must use the absolute coordinate system because no relative pixel location exists. For the second and subsequent pixels, however, you can use the relative coordinate system.

To use the relative coordinate system, you use the STEP keyword within a PSET or PRESET statement.

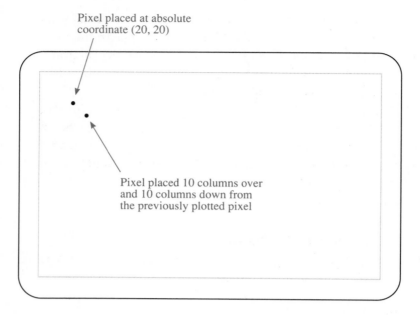

Pixel placed at absolute
coordinate (20, 20)

Pixel placed 10 columns over
and 10 columns down from
the previously plotted pixel

The STEP keyword

The syntax of a PSET statement with the STEP keyword is as follows:

```
PSET STEP(xcoordinate, ycoordinate)[, color]
```

(The syntax is identical for PRESET; simply substitute the PRESET keyword for the PSET keyword.)

The *xcoordinate* and *ycoordinate* values are positive or negative numbers that tell the QuickBASIC Interpreter where to position the pixel in relation to the last pixel it positioned with a PSET or PRESET statement. If no previous pixel exists, the QuickBASIC Interpreter uses the coordinates (0, 0).

The screen at the top of the next page demonstrates this. Notice the "daisy-chain" effect: Each pixel's location is dependent on the previous pixel's location. Always keep in mind that the STEP keyword causes the QuickBASIC Interpreter to position a pixel relative to the *last* pixel it positioned.

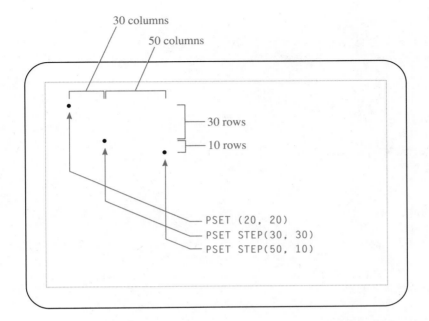

Practice: Working with the STEP keyword

1. Load the STEP-1.BAS program (Figure 11-8) from disk.

2. Run the program and enter a screen value. The program assumes a resolution of 320 × 200, so use a value of *1*, *7*, or *13* if possible. (Check what's supported by your video adapter.) Press any key to stop the program.

This program gives the illusion of traveling through space by simulating "stars" zooming by. Inside the DO loop, the program sets an "invisible" pixel at the center of the screen. This is the reference point that later PSET statements base their coordinates on.

Next, the random number *quad%* determines which quadrant the star will zoom through. Note the two IF statements—one for quadrants 0 and 1 and another for quadrants 0 and 3. (Quadrant 2 uses positive values, so no modification is necessary.) The values modified in the IF statements affect the PSET coordinates inside the FOR loop—some use positive coordinates, some use negative coordinates, and some use both.

371

```
' STEP-1.BAS
' This program uses the illusion of zooming through space
'   to demonstrate the STEP keyword.

CLS

CONST DELAY% = 200                      ' controls how fast stars "shoot"

INPUT "Please enter a screen mode (0-13):  ", modeNum%
SCREEN modeNum%

DO
    PSET (160, 100), 0                  ' set center (assumes 320 by 200
                                        '   resolution)
    quad% = INT(RND(1) * 4)             ' random number for quadrant from
                                        '   which the "star" will shoot
    randX% = INT(RND(1) * 10)           ' random number for column movement
    randY% = INT(RND(1) * 10)           ' random number for row movement

    IF quad% = 0 OR quad% = 1 THEN      ' normal movement is down;
        randY% = -randY%                '   reverse y value to move up
    END IF
    IF quad% = 0 OR quad% = 3 THEN      ' normal movement is to right;
        randX% = -randX%                '   reverse x value to move to left
    END IF

    FOR i% = 1 TO 20
        PSET STEP(-randX% * i%, randY% * i%)  ' draw "star"

        FOR j% = 1 TO DELAY%            ' delay loop
        NEXT j%

        PRESET STEP(0, 0)              ' erase "star"
    NEXT i%

LOOP UNTIL INKEY$ <> ""
```

FIGURE 11-8.
STEP-1.BAS: Zooming through space using the STEP keyword.

In the PSET statement, a random number is multiplied by the current value of the loop variable *i%*. With each loop the resulting value increases in size, causing the "star" to move farther from the center of the screen. The "star" starts off slowly in the center and accelerates as it gets closer to the edge of the screen.

Finally, note how the PRESET statement is used. The STEP keyword causes the PRESET statement to use relative coordinates—coordinates determined by the PSET statement. Because the coordinates provided are (0, 0), the PRESET statement causes the QuickBASIC Interpreter to place the PRESET pixel at the same location as the preceding PSET pixel— effectively erasing it.

Just for fun, think about how you might write this program with absolute coordinates. You can do it (you might even enjoy the challenge), but as you'll soon discover, this particular program is better suited to the use of relative coordinates.

CREATING COMPLEX SHAPES

Plotting individual pixels gives you precise control when creating graphics on the output screen. However, for complex shapes such as lines, boxes, circles, or polygons, you would have a lot of coordinate calculating to do. For lines, you could use a loop to quickly plot a series of individual points, but you'd still be faced with a lot of calculation. Fortunately, BASIC provides a set of tools that make the job of creating complex shapes a snap.

The LINE Statement

The LINE statement offers a single-statement solution for creating lines. With the LINE statement, the QuickBASIC Interpreter performs most of the work for you.

Drawing a simple line

In its simplest form, the LINE statement uses the following syntax:

```
LINE (x1, y1)-(x2, y2)[, color]
```

Note that unlike the PSET and PRESET statements, which use only a single coordinate set, a LINE statement uses *two* sets of coordinates:

■ *x1* and *y1* are the column and row coordinates of the starting point of the line.

■ *x2* and *y2* are the column and row coordinates of the ending point of the line.

Here's an example of how the LINE statement works:

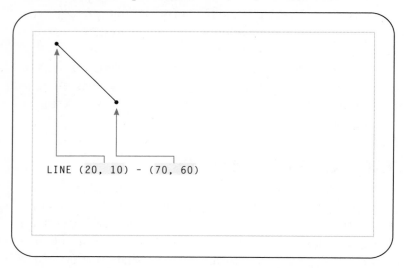

The starting point needn't be to the left of the ending point. In fact, you can start the line in the lower-right corner of the screen and work upward and to the left if you want. Simply specify the coordinates, and the Quick-BASIC Interpreter "connects the dots."

As with any other graphics command, the range of valid values for *x1*, *y1*, *x2*, and *y2* is based on the mode of your video adapter. You must enclose the coordinates in parentheses and separate the sets with a hyphen.

Practice: Working with the LINE statement

    1. Load the LINE-1.BAS program (Figure 11-9) from disk.

```
' LINE-1.BAS
' This program demonstrates the LINE statement.

CLS

INPUT "Please enter a screen mode (0-13):  ", modeNum%
INPUT "How many colors?  ", numColors%
SCREEN modeNum%

CONST DELAY% = 100                          ' controls delay between
                                            '   each line drawn
DO
    shade% = INT(RND(1) * numColors%) + 1   ' line color
    x1pos% = INT(RND(1) * 320)              ' start coordinates
    y1pos% = INT(RND(1) * 200)
    x2pos% = INT(RND(1) * 320)              ' end coordinates
    y2pos% = INT(RND(1) * 200)
    LINE (x1pos%, y1pos%)-(x2pos%, y2pos%), shade%

    FOR i% = 1 TO DELAY%                     ' delay loop
    NEXT i%

LOOP WHILE INKEY$ = ""
```

FIGURE 11-9.
LINE-1.BAS: Drawing random lines with the LINE statement.

2. Run the program. The program asks you for a screen mode and a maximum number of colors and then prints random lines on the screen in various colors. Press any key to stop the program.

Drawing a box

Drawing a box, hollow or filled, is as easy as drawing a single line. You could use four LINE statements to accomplish the job, but the inventors of BASIC figured that boxes were common enough to warrant their own feature in the BASIC language—saving you considerable time and calculation.

Interestingly enough, you use a LINE statement to create a box:

```
LINE (x1, y1)-(x2, y2)[, [color][, [B[F]]]]
```

This is the same LINE statement you just learned about, with one important difference. If you add the B option at the end of the statement, the QuickBASIC Interpreter draws a box using the start and end positions as opposite corners of the box. Here's how this works:

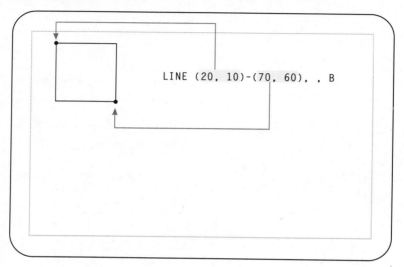

```
LINE (20, 10)-(70, 60), , B
```

Notice that the QuickBASIC Interpreter does *not* draw a line directly between the start and end points as it would for a normal LINE statement.

If you choose to include the F option immediately after the B option, QuickBASIC fills the box with the current foreground color. You can use the F option only if you use the B option.

 Practice: Working with hollow and filled boxes

1. Load the LINE-2.BAS program (Figure 11-10) from disk.

2. Run the program. Based on your responses, the program creates either a random pattern of hollow boxes or a random pattern of filled boxes. This program shows that the boxes can be any size or shape and that you can put them anywhere on the screen.

```
' LINE-2.BAS
' This program demonstrates the box-drawing capabilities
'   of the LINE statement.

CLS

INPUT "Please enter a screen mode (0-13):  ", modeNum%
INPUT "How many colors?  ", numColors%
INPUT "Hollow or solid boxes (H or F)?  ", box$
SCREEN modeNum%

CONST DELAY% = 800

DO
    shade% = INT(RND(1) * numColors%) + 1      ' line color
    x1pos% = INT(RND(1) * 320)                 ' start coordinates
    y1pos% = INT(RND(1) * 200)
    x2pos% = INT(RND(1) * 320)                 ' end coordinates
    y2pos% = INT(RND(1) * 200)

    IF UCASE$(box$) = "H" THEN
        LINE (x1pos%, y1pos%)-(x2pos%, y2pos%), shade%, B
    ELSEIF UCASE$(box$) = "F" THEN
        LINE (x1pos%, y1pos%)-(x2pos%, y2pos%), shade%, BF
    END IF

    FOR i% = 1 TO DELAY%                        ' delay loop
    NEXT i%

LOOP UNTIL INKEY$ <> ""
```

FIGURE 11-10.
LINE-2.BAS: Drawing random boxes with the LINE statement.

Drawing complex shapes

The lines, hollow boxes, and filled boxes you just worked with all used absolute coordinates. As with PSET and PRESET, you can use the STEP keyword to specify relative coordinates for a line or a box. Or you can omit the starting point of the line—forcing the QuickBASIC Interpreter to use the ending point of the last-drawn object (pixel or line) as the starting point for the new line.

Here is the syntax of a LINE statement that uses relative coordinates:

```
LINE [[STEP](x1, y1)]-[STEP](x2, y2)[, [color][, [B[F]]]]
```

Using relative coordinates allows you to create complex line drawings that might take awhile to calculate using absolute coordinates. Figure 11-11 shows some sample LINE statements that use relative coordinates and explains the result of each. In each case, assume that the last point was set at (20, 20).

LINE statement	*Result*
`LINE -(30, 50)`	Draws from (20, 20) to (30, 50)
`LINE -STEP(30, 50)`	Draws from (20, 20) to (50, 70)
`LINE (40, 40)-STEP(60, 60)`	Draws from (40, 40) to (100, 100)
`LINE STEP(30, 50)-(70, 70)`	Draws from (50, 70) to (70, 70)
`LINE STEP(30, 50)-STEP(70, 70)`	Draws from (50, 70) to (120, 140)

FIGURE 11-11.
The results of LINE statements when used with relative coordinates.

Here is a summary of relative coordinates and the LINE statement:

■ If you omit the starting coordinate set, the QuickBASIC Interpreter uses the last plotted point as the starting point.

■ If you omit the starting coordinate set and include the STEP keyword with the ending coordinate set, the QuickBASIC Interpreter positions the ending point *relative* to the last plotted point.

■ If you include the starting coordinate set and include the STEP keyword with the ending coordinate set, the QuickBASIC Interpreter positions the ending point *relative* to the specified starting coordinate set.

■ If you include the STEP keyword with the starting coordinate set and do not include the STEP keyword with the ending coordinate set, the QuickBASIC Interpreter positions the starting coordinate point *relative* to the last plotted point and positions the ending point at the specified location.

■ If you include the STEP keyword with both the starting and ending coordinate sets, the QuickBASIC Interpreter positions the starting location *relative* to the last plotted point and positions the ending coordinate point *relative* to the starting point it just calculated.

Using the relative coordinates allows you to "daisy chain" lines and boxes together, simplifying the job of drawing complex shapes.

 Practice: Working with LINE and relative coordinates

1. Load the STEP-2.BAS program (Figure 11-12) from disk:

```
' STEP-2.BAS
' This program demonstrates the use of the STEP keyword in
'   the LINE statement.

CLS

INPUT "Please enter a screen mode (0-13):  ", modeNum%
SCREEN modeNum%

blank$ = SPACE$(39)

PRINT "Enter 0 and 0 to quit"
PSET (150, 50)                    ' establish a starting point

DO
    LOCATE 22, 1
    INPUT "Horizontal movement (+ or -): ", horiz%
    INPUT "  Vertical movement (+ or -): ", vert%
    LINE -STEP(horiz%, vert%)
    LOCATE 22, 1
    PRINT blank$
    PRINT blank$
LOOP UNTIL horiz% = 0 AND vert% = 0
```

FIGURE 11-12.
STEP-2.BAS: A simple line-drawing program.

2. Run the program. This program is actually a simple drawing pro-
    gram. The program begins by plotting a pixel at (150, 50), the
    starting point for your drawing. The bulk of the work is done in
    the DO loop. The program asks you to enter horizontal and verti-
    cal values, which can be positive or negative. Once you've entered
    these values, the program uses the LINE statement along with the
    STEP keyword to draw the line.

The CIRCLE Statement

The QuickBASIC Interpreter also lets you create circles. By using the
CIRCLE statement, you can create a wide variety of circles that, in con-
junction with the other graphics tools at your disposal, allow you to create
interesting and useful graphics with your program.

In its simplest form, the syntax of a CIRCLE statement is as follows:

```
CIRCLE (xcoordinate, ycoordinate), radius[, color]
```

xcoordinate and *ycoordinate* are the same horizontal and vertical screen
coordinates you've been working with. These values tell QuickBASIC
where to position the center of the circle. *radius* is a value that specifies, in
pixels, the radius of the circle. (The radius of a circle is one-half its diame-
ter.) *color* is an integer that tells QuickBASIC what color to make the
circle. If you omit *color*, QuickBASIC uses the current foreground color.

As with any other graphics statement, the coordinates you use depend
entirely on the graphics mode you set using the SCREEN statement.

Practice: Working with the CIRCLE statement

1. Load the CIRCLE-1.BAS (Figure 11-13) program
    from disk.

2. Run the program and enter an appropriate screen mode. The pro-
    gram then asks you to enter a column value, a row value, and a
    radius value. The CIRCLE statement in the middle of the program
    draws a circle based on the numbers you entered. Then, when you
    press Enter to continue, the CLS statement "wipes the slate
    clean," and the process repeats until you enter *q* or *Q* to quit.

```
' CIRCLE-1.BAS
' This program demonstrates the CIRCLE statement.

CLS

INPUT "Please enter a screen mode (0-13):  ", modeNum%
SCREEN modeNum%

DO
    LOCATE 21, 1
    INPUT "Please enter the column number:  ", colNum%
    INPUT "   Please enter the row number:  ", rowNum%
    INPUT "        Please enter the radius:  ", radius%
    CIRCLE (colNum%, rowNum%), radius%
    INPUT "Press Enter to continue or Q to quit: ", dummy$
    CLS
LOOP UNTIL UCASE$(dummy$) = "Q"
```

FIGURE 11-13.
CIRCLE-1.BAS: A simple circle-drawing program.

Try entering values greater than the maximum screen coordinates, or enter a relatively large radius value. This technique is to create a particular effect, such as an arc near one edge of the screen.

Drawing arcs

The CIRCLE statement also lets you draw arcs, which are segments of a circle. Use a CIRCLE statement of the following form to draw an arc:

CIRCLE (*xcoordinate*, *ycoordinate*), *radius*[, [*color*][, [*start*][, *end*]]]

This is the same syntax as the simple CIRCLE statement except for the addition of the *start* and *end* values. The *start* and *end* values are the measurements, in radians, of the starting point and the ending point of the arc.

Radians: Measuring Arcs

Although you might be more accustomed to measuring arcs in terms of *degrees,* the CIRCLE statement requires that starting and ending measurements be given in *radians.* Figure 11-14 illustrates the radian measurement system. When drawing an arc of your own, simply refer to Figure 11-14 and determine the start and end points of your own arc. We've included conversion information that you'll find helpful if you know the measurements in degrees.

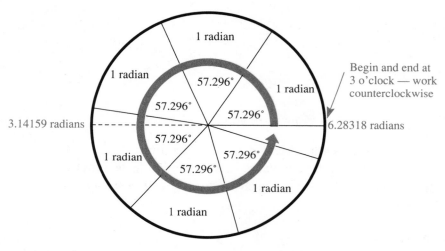

Radians = (3.14159 × (angle of degree)) ÷ 180
1 degree = 0.0174532 radian

FIGURE 11-14.
Measuring an arc in radians.

■ Measurements start at 0 (3 o'clock) and progress counterclockwise to a maximum of 6.28. The starting point of 0 and the ending point of 6.28 are the same location.

■ The values you provide for *start* and *end* are numbers from 0 through 6.28. (Note: The value 6.28 is technically $2 \times \pi$; we're using rounded numbers for simplicity.)

- If you put a minus sign in front of a value, the QuickBASIC Interpreter draws a line from that point to the center of the ''circle.''

Here is a sample arc:

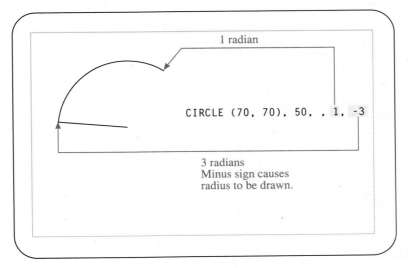

Practice: Working with arcs

1. Load the CIRCLE-2.BAS program (Figure 11-15) from disk.

```
' CIRCLE-2.BAS
' This program demonstrates how to create arcs with the CIRCLE statement.

CLS

INPUT "Please enter a screen mode (0-13):  ", modeNum%
SCREEN modeNum%
```

FIGURE 11-15.   *(continued)*
CIRCLE-2.BAS: A program that creates arcs and pie wedges.

FIGURE 11-15. *continued*

```
DO
    CLS
    PSET (150, 30): PSET (150, 125)    ' draw top and bottom points
    PSET (95, 78): PSET (205, 78)      ' draw left and right points
    LOCATE 2, 18: PRINT "1.57"         ' label for top point
    LOCATE 10, 7: PRINT "3.14"         ' label for left point
    LOCATE 18, 18: PRINT "4.71"        ' label for bottom point
    LOCATE 10, 28: PRINT "0 or 6.28"   ' label for right point

    LOCATE 20, 1
    PRINT "Enter values between 0 and 6.28"
    PRINT "(A negative value draws a radius.)"
    INPUT "Please enter starting point: ", starting!
    INPUT "Please enter ending point: ", ending!
    CIRCLE (150, 78), 50, , starting!, ending!    ' no color value
    INPUT "Press Enter to continue or Q to quit: ", dummy$

LOOP UNTIL UCASE$(dummy$) = "Q"
```

2. Run the program. This program gives you a chance to experiment with creating arcs. Enter starting and ending values from 0 through 6.28. (Put a minus sign in front of a number if you want QuickBASIC to draw a line from that point to the center of the circle.) Note that the starting value can be smaller than the ending value. Try several combinations of values just to see how the CIRCLE statement creates arcs.

A LAST LOOK AT BASIC GRAPHICS

We've covered quite a bit of ground here. BASIC (and in particular, the QuickBASIC Interpreter) offers some very powerful and useful tools. Regrettably, due to space constraints, we are unable to cover them all here. But the tools you've become acquainted with in this chapter should keep you busy for quite some time, and should enable you to add some spiffy graphics to your own programs.

NOTE: You can always check the on-line help system for more information on graphics. Experiment—it's the best way to learn!

INTRODUCTION TO PROGRAMMING WITH SOUND

You just learned how to use graphics to enliven your programs. Now you can learn how to jazz 'em up even more by using the sound capability of the QuickBASIC Interpreter.

The SOUND Statement Revisited

In Chapter 6, where you learned about loops, you had a brief introduction to the SOUND statement. Now is an appropriate time for a quick review.

The SOUND statement has the following syntax:

```
SOUND frequency, duration
```

frequency is an integer value from 37 through 32,767 that specifies the frequency, in hertz (cycles per second), of the desired tone. Low frequencies create low tones; high frequencies create high tones. Note that the range of human hearing is approximately 20 to 20,000 hertz and that tones with frequencies above 16,000 hertz are more audible to dogs than they are to most people.

The *duration* argument is a value that tells QuickBASIC how long to play the tone. The *duration* value specifies for how many "clock ticks" the note should play—there are 18.2 clock ticks per second, so a *duration* value of 9.1 would cause the QuickBASIC Interpreter to play the note for one-half second.

You must specify both a *frequency* and a *duration* value.

The sound effects in the sample programs you've seen so far generally were created with no particular tune in mind. However, you can choose *frequency* values that match musical notes. Figure 11-16 lists the standard *frequency* values and their associated notes as established by the American Standards Association in 1936. Because the smallest *frequency* value you

LEARN BASIC NOW

Note	Frequency	Note	Frequency	Note	Frequency
$D\#_1$	38.89	G_3	196.00	$A\#_5$	932.33
E_1	41.20	$G\#_3$	207.65	B_5	987.77
F_1	43.65	A_3	220.00	C_6	1046.50
$F\#_1$	46.25	$A\#_3$	233.08	$C\#_6$	1108.73
G_1	49.00	B_3	246.94	D_6	1174.66
$G\#_1$	51.91	C_4	261.63	$D\#_6$	1244.51
A_1	55.00	$C\#_4$	277.18	E_6	1328.51
$A\#_1$	58.27	D_4	293.66	F_6	1396.91
B_1	61.74	$D\#_4$	311.13	$F\#_6$	1479.98
C_2	65.41	E_4	329.63	G_6	1567.98
$C\#_2$	69.30	F_4	349.23	$G\#_6$	1661.22
D_2	73.42	$F\#_4$	369.99	A_6	1760.00
$D\#_2$	77.78	G_4	392.00	$A\#_6$	1864.66
E_2	82.41	$G\#_4$	415.30	B_6	1975.53
F_2	87.31	A_4	440.00	C_7	2093.00
$F\#_2$	92.50	$A\#_4$	466.16	$C\#_7$	2217.46
G_2	98.00	B_4	493.88	D_7	2349.32
$G\#_2$	103.83	C_5	523.25	$D\#_7$	2489.02
A_2	110.00	$C\#_5$	554.37	E_7	2637.02
$A\#_2$	116.54	D_5	587.33	F_7	2793.83
B_2	123.47	$D\#_5$	622.25	$F\#_7$	2959.96
C_3	130.81	E_5	659.26	G_7	3135.96
$C\#_3$	138.59	F_5	698.46	$G\#_7$	3322.44
D_3	146.83	$F\#_5$	739.99	A_7	3520.00
$D\#_3$	155.56	G_5	783.99	$A\#_7$	3729.31
E_3	164.81	$G\#_5$	830.61	B_7	3951.07
F_3	174.61	A_5	880.00	C_8	4186.01
$F\#_3$	185.00				

FIGURE 11-16.
Musical note frequencies ranging over approximately seven octaves.

can use with the SOUND statement is 37, the lowest note you can play is D#$_1$. (The American Standard pitch table actually begins at C$_0$, which has a frequency of 16.35.)

The subscript number to the right of each note name indicates the octave of that note. If you study Figure 11-16, you'll notice that to raise a note one octave you simply double its frequency—approximately. For example, C$_2$ has a frequency of 65.41 hertz, and C$_3$ has a frequency of 130.81—almost double the frequency of C$_2$. This fact can help you when you add music to your own programs—all you need do is double a particular frequency to raise that note one octave.

 Practice: Working with the SOUND statement

1. Load the SOUND-1.BAS program (Figure 11-17) from disk.

```
' SOUND-1.BAS
' This program demonstrates the SOUND statement.

CLS

INPUT "Please enter an octave value (1-7):  ", octave%

' play one octave

FOR i% = 1 TO 8
    READ note%                          ' read frequency of note
    note% = note% * (2 ^ octave%)       ' raise note to desired octave
    SOUND note%, 12                     ' play note
NEXT i%

' frequencies of the major notes in the second octave

DATA 65, 73, 82, 87, 98, 110, 123, 131
```

FIGURE 11-17.
SOUND-1.BAS: A program that plays a scale.

2. Run the program and then enter an octave value. Note that the table of frequencies in the DATA statement actually begins at C_2, so if you enter an octave value of 1, the program plays a major scale from C_2 to C_3. And because the SOUND statement accepts only integer values as frequencies, the DATA statement contains values that have been rounded to the nearest integer.

Musical Notation and BASIC

Most of us aren't used to dealing with musical notes in terms of each note's frequency. BASIC, however, requires that you tell it what notes to play by using their frequencies.

If you plan to add music to your programs—either a tune you wrote yourself or some sheet music you want to copy—you'll have to convert the notes to frequencies. You might want to make a "cheat sheet" to help you convert the notes more quickly.

Working from sheet music

Although it's beyond the scope of this book to explain musical notation in any detail, you might find the following tips helpful as you add music to your own programs. Take a look at Figure 11-18, which shows the names of the notes and their positions on the musical staff.

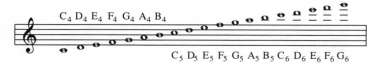

FIGURE 11-18.
The names of the notes on the musical staff.

If you take a piece of sheet music, match the positions of the notes to the notes in Figure 11-18, and look up the appropriate frequency values in Figure 11-16, you can write beside each note the proper values to use with the SOUND statement.

Another part of the SOUND statement concerns duration—that is, how long you want each note to last. Simply decide how long you want a whole note to be, and then divide that value by 2 for half notes, by 4 for quarter notes, and so on. Once you've established these values, you can go through your sheet music again and jot down a duration value beside each note.

After you've determined the frequency values and duration values for each note, you're ready to add a melody to your program.

Practice: Playing a song with BASIC

Figure 11-19 shows the music for the song "My Bonnie Lies Over the Ocean." We calculated the frequency value and duration value for each note and then wrote a short program to play the song.

FIGURE 11-19.
Music for "My Bonnie Lies Over the Ocean."

1. Load the SOUND-2.BAS (Figure 11-20) program from disk.

```
' SOUND-2.BAS
' This program demonstrates how to play a song in BASIC.

CLS

INPUT "Press Enter to begin...", dummy$

FOR i% = 1 TO 34
    READ note%, duration%
    SOUND note%, duration%
NEXT i%

'    My      bon-    nie     lies    o-      ver     the
DATA 392, 8,  659, 8,  587, 8,  523, 8,  587, 8,  523, 8,  440, 8

'    o-      cean,   My      bon-    nie     lies
DATA 392, 8,  330, 32, 392, 8,  659, 8,  587, 8,  523, 8

'    o-      ver     the     sea;    My      bon-    nie
DATA 523, 8,  494, 8,  523, 8,  587, 40, 392, 8,  659, 8,  587, 8

'    lies    o-      ver     the     o-      cean--  0
DATA 523, 8,  587, 8,  523, 8,  440, 8,  392, 8,  330, 32, 392, 8

'    bring   back    my      bon-    nie     to      me!
DATA 440, 8,  587, 8,  523, 8,  494, 8,  440, 8,  494, 8,  523, 32
```

FIGURE 11-20.
SOUND-2.BAS: A program that plays a song.

2. Run the program, and you'll hear the QuickBASIC Interpreter play the song. Note how the frequency values and the duration values are staggered in the DATA statements. Inside the FOR loop, the READ statement reads two values—one for the frequency and one for the duration—each time through the loop.

Experiment with the SOUND statement to see what kind of control you have over the values in the DATA statements. For example, try multiplying *note%* by 2 to raise the notes one octave, and try dividing *duration%* by 2 to see the effect on the tempo of the song.

SUMMARY

The QuickBASIC Interpreter contains a wide range of tools you can use to create graphics and sound—and here we've just touched on the basics. Once you've completed the book, however, take some time to experiment with the programs you've seen in this chapter. Or use the QuickBASIC Interpreter's on-line help to get more information. Graphics and sound programming, while not the easiest thing to master, is certainly one of the most rewarding aspects of BASIC programming.

QUESTIONS AND EXERCISES

1. What two components make up your computer's video equipment? What is the function of each component?

2. What is the difference between text mode and graphics mode?

3. What does the LOCATE statement do?

4. Write a short program that asks the user to enter a name and then displays the name at the left edge of the screen and ''moves'' it to the right edge of the screen.

5. What does the SCREEN statement do?

6. What do the PSET and PRESET statements do, and how do they differ?

7. What is the difference between absolute and relative coordinates?

8. True or False: You can use a LINE statement to create a filled box.

9. True or False: You can use a CIRCLE statement to create a filled circle.

10. Write a program that draws a circle near the left edge of the screen and then ''moves'' it to the right edge of the screen. (Hint: Don't forget to erase the previous circle.)

11. Convert the following tune into a BASIC program:

Debugging QuickBASIC Programs

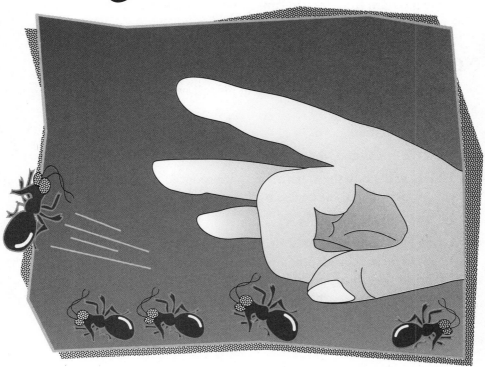

Remember your first BASIC program? You've come a long way since your output screen displayed *Ward, I'm worried about the Beaver*. Congratulations are definitely in order! But although you're on the road to being a BASIC programming whiz, the day will come when you'll find that a program you've written absolutely refuses to run. At such times you need to have confidence in your ability to diagnose and solve the programming problem. And this is where the skill of debugging comes in.

Debugging is the process of tracking down and fixing errors in a program. The ability to debug a problem program is one of the most important skills you can develop as a beginning programmer. Debugging requires you to think modularly—to analyze a program as a computer does, monitoring program execution each step of the way—in order to find the flaw that prevents the program from accomplishing its task.

Fortunately you're not alone. The Microsoft QuickBASIC Interpreter provides several powerful debugging commands that help you examine your programs. This chapter introduces these commands and describes how to program to avoid creating bugs in the first place. You'll also debug a sample program from start to finish to gain experience using the debugging commands.

THE PRACTICE OF DEBUGGING

When you debug a program, you repeat the following steps until your program runs successfully:

1. Run the program.

2. Observe errors and trouble spots.

3. Isolate and study the statements that produced each error, using programming tools as necessary.

4. Fix the errors.

If you have a printer, you'll likely want to print a copy of any program that needs to be debugged. Studying the code is a major part of debugging, and if you're like most people you'll find that reading and following a printout is easier than scrutinizing a program on screen.

Three Types of Errors

Three types of errors can occur in a BASIC program: *syntax errors,* *run-time errors,* and *logic errors.*

- A syntax error is a programming mistake that violates the rules of BASIC (such as a missing separator or a mis-spelled keyword). QuickBASIC points out syntax errors in your program as you type it in and won't let you run your program until each has been fixed.

- A run-time error is an error that causes a program to stop unexpectedly during execution. Run-time errors occur when an outside event or an unexpected syntax error forces a program to stop while it is running. Exceeding the bounds of an array or attempting to open a file with a bad filename are examples of run-time errors.

- A logic error is a human error—a programming mistake that makes the program produce the wrong results. Most debugging efforts are focused on tracking down logic errors introduced by the programmer.

Remember to use your on-line help resources when you encounter error messages produced by syntax errors or run-time errors.

QUICKBASIC MENU COMMANDS

The QuickBASIC Interpreter provides menu commands that help you track down bugs that surface when you run your program. The following sections list the debugging-related commands on the Run, Debug, View, and Options menus. For more detailed information about these commands, consult the on-line help.

The Run Menu

The Run menu contains three debugging-related commands:

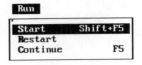

- Start (Shift-F5). Runs the currently loaded program from its beginning at full speed. Press Ctrl-Break to stop a program that is running.

- Restart. Resets all program variables and highlights the first executable statement in your program. Use Restart to move to the top of the program before you execute statements one at a time with the Step and Procedure Step commands on the Debug menu.

- Continue (F5). Runs the currently loaded program from the current line. Use Continue to continue full-speed execution of your program.

The Debug Menu

The Debug menu contains six debugging-related commands:

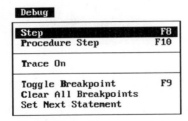

- Step (F8). Executes one program statement and highlights the next executable statement. Use Step to execute your program one instruction at a time.

- Procedure Step (F10). Executes one program statement and highlights the next executable statement. Unlike Step, Procedure Step executes an entire subprogram or user-defined function as one step.

- Trace On. A toggle command that prepares your program for slow-motion execution. When Trace On is active, programs run slowly and each statement is highlighted. When Trace On is inactive (the default), programs run at their normal speed.

- Toggle Breakpoint (F9). Sets or releases a breakpoint (a line where program execution will stop) in your program. If you have a color monitor, breakpoint lines appear in red by default.

- Clear All Breakpoints. Releases all breakpoints set by the Toggle Breakpoint command. Use Clear All Breakpoints to release multiple breakpoints at the same time.

- Set Next Statement. Sets the line the cursor is on as the next statement to be executed. Use Set Next Statement to rerun statements or to skip over program statements you don't want to execute.

The View Menu

The View menu contains one debugging-related command:

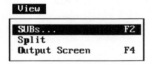

- Output Screen (F4). Displays the contents of the output screen. Use this command while you are stepping through your program, to see what your program has displayed on the output screen. To return to the editing environment, press any key.

The Options Menu

The Options menu contains one debugging-related command:

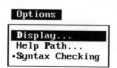

■ Syntax Checking. A toggle command that turns off Quick-BASIC's automatic syntax checker, which is on by default.

In addition to these debugging-related commands, you can use the F7 key to execute the current line and the lines between the current line and the cursor at full speed. Pressing this key is a shortcut for setting a breakpoint with the F9 key and executing from the current line to the breakpoint with the F5 key.

TRACKING VARIABLES WITH PRINT

Another helpful debugging tool is a statement you're already familiar with: the PRINT statement. By placing PRINT statements within a program, or by using them in the Immediate window, you can examine the contents of variables as a program executes. (You'll likely want to display the PRINT statements in a different color to differentiate them from program output.) After you use PRINT statements for debugging, remember to remove them from your program.

The following practice session uses PRINT to find a logic error in a program.

Practice: Using PRINT to track a changing variable

The BUGSHAKE.BAS program (Figure 12-1) is a simple guessing game that asks the user for the size in gallons of the largest milkshake ever made (an impressive record set in Ohio in 1988). Although the program runs without syntax errors, it doesn't operate properly: No matter what number the user enters, the program responds that the guess is too low. Can you find the logic error that causes the program to fail?

Load the BUGSHAKE.BAS program from the CHAP12 subdirectory on disk and run it.

```
' BUGSHAKE.BAS
' This program contains a logic error.  Can you find it?

CONST BIGSHAKE% = 174  ' constant equaling gallons in largest shake

CLS

PRINT "How many gallons were in the largest milkshake ever made?"
PRINT

DO WHILE (guess% <> BIGSHAKE%)         ' compare guess to largest shake
    INPUT ; "Guess:  ", guess          ' get guess from user

    COLOR 2                            ' set color to green for clue
    IF (guess% < BIGSHAKE%) THEN       ' determine if guess is high or low
        PRINT , "too low"              '   and print appropriate clue
    ELSEIF (guess% > BIGSHAKE%) THEN
        PRINT , "too high"
    ELSE
        PRINT
    END IF
    COLOR 7                            ' set color back to default white
LOOP

PRINT
PRINT "Correct!  A"; BIGSHAKE%; "gallon strawberry shake was mixed";
PRINT " in Ohio in 1988."
```

FIGURE 12-1.
BUGSHAKE.BAS: A guessing-game program containing a logic error.

You'll receive output similar to the following:

```
How many gallons were in the largest milkshake ever made?

Guess:  100    too low
Guess:  200    too low
Guess:  10000 too low
Guess:  174    too low
Guess:  Ctrl-C
```

No matter what value is entered (including the correct value of 174), the same message appears: *too low*. The program is stuck in an endless loop. The only way to terminate the program is to press Ctrl-C or Ctrl-Break.

Let's try to track down the error by using a PRINT statement to track the value of the one variable, *guess%*, which changes each time the user enters a new value in the DO loop.

1. Place the following statements (which display the value of the *guess%* variable in red) at the bottom of the DO loop, just above the LOOP statement:

    ```
    COLOR 4: PRINT "DEBUG:  guess% ="; guess%: COLOR 7
    ```

    When you do so your screen will look like this:

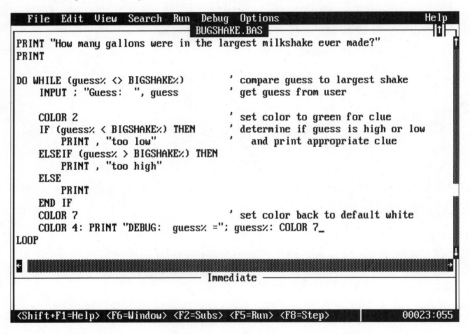

The PRINT statement is surrounded by two COLOR statements: The first changes the foreground color to red and the second changes it back to white. You might find this second color useful to distinguish the output of the program from the output of the debugging statements. If your monitor doesn't display color, omit the COLOR statements.

2. Run the program again. You'll receive output similar to the following, complete with debugging information:

```
How many gallons were in the largest milkshake ever made?
```

```
Guess:  10      too low
DEBUG:  guess% = 0
Guess:  30000 too low
DEBUG:  guess% = 0
Guess:  174     too low
DEBUG:  guess% = 0
Guess:  Ctrl-C
```

The result of the PRINT statement is interesting—it shows that for some reason the milkshake guess is not being assigned to the *guess%* variable. There are two explanations for this: Something is wrong with the INPUT statement, or the *guess%* variable has been modified somewhere along the line. Can you find the error?

If you examine the INPUT statement in the program closely, you'll discover that the problem is in the *guess%* variable—in the INPUT statement it's missing the % type-declaration character included in the rest of the program:

```
INPUT ; "Guess:  ", guess
```

As a result, BASIC considers *guess* and *guess%* to be two separate variables.

3. Fix the INPUT statement in the BUGSHAKE.BAS program by adding a % symbol after *guess* as follows:

```
INPUT ; "Guess:  ", guess%
```

4. Run the program again to be sure that it's running properly. If it is, remove the debugging statements you added in Step 1.

Common Programming Errors

The following logic errors pop up from time to time as the result of typing problems or design errors. Be on the lookout for them!

■ **Incorrect type assignments.** Be sure that data values aren't assigned to variables of the wrong type. Incorrect assignments can often slip by the QuickBASIC Interpreter and cause problems later in the program. Double-check the assignments in each INPUT, INPUT#, and READ statement in your program.

■ **Variable-name confusion.** Don't misspell variables or omit type-declaration characters. Also be on the lookout for potential confusion between local and global variables with the same name. Remember: You're on your own when you use variable names—BASIC doesn't check to ensure they're correct.

■ **Incorrect logical comparisons.** Check the logical comparisons made by relational operators in IF, SELECT CASE, and looping statements. Use sample programs or the Immediate window to verify that the comparisons work properly.

■ **Endless loops.** Beware of loops that can't end. Use the Immediate window to check the termination conditions of your loops.

■ **Garbled output.** Misuse of the PRINT, PRINT USING, LOCATE, and SCREEN statements can produce unclear or confusing screen output. Be sure your programs can handle whatever data the user might enter.

■ **Array troubles.** Don't confuse an array index with the value stored in the array. And to avoid the *Subscript out of range* error message, don't read or write past the end of an array.

DEBUGGING A PROGRAM STEP BY STEP

This section gives you additional experience in tracking down and fixing errors. You'll debug the DESSERT.BAS program, which uses an array to record your favorite desserts and the number of calories they contain.

A Bug-Free DESSERT.BAS

The DESSERT.BAS program is designed to prompt the user for a name and the number of desserts to be entered. The number is used to dimension a one-dimensional array of string values—the place the dessert names will be stored. A subprogram then supplies data to the array and totals the number of calories entered. The program then prints the contents of the array and displays the calorie total in flashing red.

When DESSERT.BAS runs properly, it produces output of the following form:

```
Welcome to the Dessert Program!

Please enter your name:  Mike

How many desserts would you like to enter, Mike? 2

    Dessert name:  Strawberries and cream
    Calories in dessert:  125

    Dessert name:  Chocolate fudge cake
    Calories in dessert:  310

The following is a list of Mike's favorite desserts:

    Strawberries and cream
    Chocolate fudge cake

The list contains a total of 435 calories!
```

Practice: Running the DESSERT.BAS program

But DESSERT.BAS (Figure 12-2) contains two logic errors. Load the DESSERT.BAS program from disk and run it to find out just what's wrong.

```
' DESSERT.BAS
' This program contains two logic errors.  Can you find them?

                                   ' declare GetData subprogram
DECLARE SUB GetData (array$(), num%, totalCalories%)

CLS
                                   ' print welcome message
PRINT "Welcome to the Dessert Program!"
PRINT                              ' get user's name
INPUT "Please enter your name:  ", userName$
PRINT                              ' get number of desserts
PRINT "How many desserts would you like to enter, "; userName$;
INPUT num%
PRINT

DIM desserts$(num%)                      ' dimension string array

GetData desserts$(), num%, totalCalories%  ' call subprogram

PRINT "The following is a list of "; userName$; "'s favorite desserts:"
PRINT

FOR i% = 1 TO num%
    PRINT "   "; desserts$(i%)          ' print array contents
NEXT i%

PRINT                              ' print total number of calories
PRINT "The list contains a total of"; '   with number in flashing red
COLOR 20: PRINT totalCalories%; : COLOR 7
PRINT "calories!"

END

SUB GetData (array$(), num%, totalCalories%)

' The GetData subprogram gets dessert information from the user.
```

FIGURE 12-2. *(continued)*
DESSERT.BAS: A program containing two logic errors.

FIGURE 12-2. *continued*

```
FOR i% = 1 TO num%      ' loop num% times (passed from main program)
   INPUT "  Dessert name:  ", array$(num%)      ' get dessert name
   INPUT "  Calories in dessert:  ", calories%  ' get calories
   PRINT
   totalCalories% = calories%                   ' keep running total
NEXT i%

END SUB                      ' return array$ and totalCalories% to main program
```

You'll receive output similar to the following:

```
Welcome to the Dessert Program!

Please enter your name:  Mike

How many desserts would you like to enter, Mike? 2

    Dessert name:  Strawberries and cream
    Calories in dessert:  125

    Dessert name:  Chocolate fudge cake
    Calories in dessert:  310

The following is a list of Mike's favorite desserts:


    Chocolate fudge cake

The list contains a total of 310 calories!
```

Note the two obvious problems: The program lists only one of the values stored in the *desserts$* array, and the program doesn't display the correct calorie total. With these general observations in mind you can begin debugging the program step by step.

Debugging the DESSERT.BAS Program

The introductory part of the program seems okay—it displays helpful information on the screen and obtains data from the user. Let's get past these statements by setting a breakpoint near the middle of the program and running the first section at full speed.

Setting a breakpoint

Complete the following steps to set a breakpoint and run the program:

1. Select the Restart command from the Run menu to prepare the program for execution at the beginning. The CLS statement, the first executable statement in the program, will be highlighted.

2. Move the cursor down to the 17th line of the program (the line containing the DIM statement) and select the Toggle Breakpoint command from the Debug menu (F9).

3. Select the Continue command from the Run menu (F5) to run the program to the breakpoint. Enter your own name at the first input prompt and the number 2 at the second input prompt. The program will stop when it reaches the breakpoint.

4. Select the Toggle Breakpoint command (F9) to clear the breakpoint—it's no longer needed.

Stepping through the *GetData* subprogram

Now that we're in bug land we'll be taking a slower pace through the code. Keep your eyes peeled—something that made sense to the person who wrote this program isn't working now. Complete the following steps:

1. Select the Step command from the Debug menu (F8) to execute the DIM statement that dimensions the *desserts$* array. *desserts$* should be large enough to hold all the dessert names the user types in—a number we know in advance and have stored in the *num%* variable. Note that *num%* appears in the DIM statement and the statement executes without error—looks like we're okay so far.

2. Select the Step command (F8) three times to enter the *GetData* subprogram and execute the first two statements in it. Enter *Cherry pie* at the dessert input prompt.

3. Take a long look at the contents of the *GetData* subprogram to determine if anything is out of order—sometimes a bug will jump out at you. An excellent way to examine the input process up to this point is to include a debug PRINT statement in the Immediate window. Let's do this now to see if the first dessert name is stored properly in the first element of *array$*. Press F6 to move to the Immediate window, and then enter the following line:

```
COLOR 4: PRINT "DEBUG:  array$(1) = "; array$(1): COLOR 7
```

The following debugging information is displayed on your screen in red:

```
DEBUG:  array$(1) =
```

The first element in the *array$* array (*array$(1)*) *should* contain the string *Cherry pie*—we just typed it in! Because it doesn't, something must be wrong with the INPUT statement; specifically, something must be wrong with the index element of the array assignment—it should evaluate to 1 the first time through the loop.

4. Press any key to return to the Immediate window.

Isolating the first logic error

We've found the symptom of our first logic error. Let's isolate its cause by taking a close look at the INPUT statement and its role in the FOR loop. A basic rule of thumb about array indexes and loops is that if the loop contains a counter variable and each element of the array needs to be accessed, the counter variable (or some derivative of it) should be used as the array index. The *GetData* subprogram has everything right but the array index: The INPUT statement should be using the counter variable *i%* for the array index, not the *num%* variable.

Fix the error by pressing F6 to return to the View window and then changing the INPUT statement as follows:

```
INPUT "   Dessert name:  ", array$(i%)
```

Testing the bug fix

The logic error has been corrected; now let's test it. Complete the following steps:

1. Leave the cursor on the line containing the dessert input line and select the Set Next Statement command from the Debug menu. The Set Next Statement command lets us rerun this statement to test our bug fix (saving the time it would take to run the program again from the beginning).

2. Press F8 to execute the new INPUT statement, and then enter *Cherry pie* again. To verify that *Cherry pie* is now stored in the first array element of *array$*, press F6 to move to the Immediate window, move the cursor up to the debug PRINT statement, and press Enter to execute it. This time the correct string value should appear on the screen. Press any key to return to the Immediate window, and then press F6 to return to the View window.

3. Continue your testing of the FOR loop by moving the cursor down to the line containing the END SUB statement—the last line in the subprogram. Select the Toggle Breakpoint command (F9) to set a breakpoint on this line, and then select the Trace On command from the Debug menu. These two steps let us view the remaining instructions in the FOR loop in slow motion. We specified two desserts at the top of the program, so the loop will be executed twice. Select the Continue command (F5) to start running the program in slow motion. As the loop executes, you'll be prompted to enter dessert data.

4. Looks like our bug fix did the trick—the program looped and stopped at the breakpoint without error. Select the Toggle Breakpoint command (F9) to remove the breakpoint, and then select the Trace On command again to return execution speed to normal.

Searching for the second bug

One down, one to go. Let's take it slow and search for the last bug in the program. Follow these steps:

1. Press F8 once to return to the main program and seven more times to display a few PRINT statements and the contents of the *desserts$* array (passed back to the main program by the *GetData* subprogram).

2. Press F4 to view the current output screen. The correct array elements are all here! Note that the output screen is starting to get a little messy with the debug messages and restarts we've been using. Don't worry too much about this—they won't show up in the final version of our program. Press any key to return to the View window.

3. Press F8 seven times to execute the statements that display the final calorie count on the screen and end the program. Press F4 to look at the results. The flashing red calorie count is impressive, but inaccurate: The number is completely wrong. Let's take a look at the *totalCalories%* variable with a PRINT statement. Press any key to return to the View window.

4. Move to the Immediate window, change the debug PRINT statement to the following, and press Enter.

    ```
    COLOR 4: PRINT "DEBUG:  totalCalories% ="; totalCalories%: COLOR 7
    ```

    The PRINT statement displays the last calorie count you entered! What's the deal here? Hasn't the *GetData* subprogram been keeping a running total of the calorie counts?

Isolating the second logic error

Let's return to the *GetData* subprogram to see if we can find the source of the error. The first thing we can examine is spelling—perhaps the variable has been misspelled in the code. Return to the View window, and then use the Find command from the Search menu to search for the *totalCalories%* variable. (The Find command is particularly useful when you're working with large programs.) The Find command locates the *totalCalories%* variable in the parameter list of the *GetData* subprogram. Select the Repeat Last Find command from the Search menu (F3) several times to find all occurrences of *totalCalories%* in the program. It appears six times—three times in *GetData* and three times in the main program.

Our problem is not a spelling error; these variable names are all spelled the same way. Let's check the statement in the *GetData* subprogram that keeps the running total of the calorie values. Press F2 and select *GetData* for editing. Examine the assignment statement at the bottom of the FOR loop:

```
totalCalories% = calories%
```

Does this statement properly update the *totalCalories%* variable to keep a running total?

Fixing the second logic error

The answer is *No!* As we've seen throughout the book, to update a running total you need to add the current total *and* the value to be added and then assign the result to the running total. To fix this assignment statement, change it to read as follows:

```
totalCalories% = totalCalories% + calories%
```

After this change is made, the program is ready to roll. Test the debugged program by running it from start to finish until you're sure it is completely bug-free. If you'd like to double-check your work, an error-free version of the program (named DESSERT2.BAS) is available on disk. It contains the corrections made in this chapter.

Avoiding Bugs

Now that you've learned how to track and fix bugs, here are some hints that will help you write bug-free programs in the future.

Plan your program carefully

Before you start typing, be sure you understand what you want your program to do and how you plan to write the program in BASIC. Think about the various algorithms your program will use, how program input and output will be organized, and how data will be stored and manipulated. Start simply and add complexity as you go.

Work one step at a time

Don't try to write your program all at once. Create and test your program one piece at a time. Isolate different tasks whenever possible by creating subprograms and functions.

Run your program often

Whenever you change your program, run it to ensure that your program still works. By following this rule, you can catch simple programming mistakes early on—before they compound themselves and become major programming problems.

Try new ideas in the Immediate window

Use the Immediate window to test small pieces of program code *before* you place them in the program.

Test your program rigorously

Test your program well each step of the way, and know how your program will respond to any type of input. Consider the following questions:

- What is the biggest number or string this program can handle?
- What is the smallest?
- What will cause this program to "crash"?
- How can I prevent a user from crashing this program?
- Will the user understand what this program does?

SUMMARY

This chapter contains a number of debugging tools, tips, and techniques. Debugging tools have come a long way in a few short years, and we're lucky to have such a powerful collection of them right here in the QuickBASIC Interpreter. But programmers learning how to debug their own programs (and, worst of all, other people's programs) need more than debugging tools to help them. Solutions come from thinking logically and creatively about your programs and by examining program execution step by step. The more you know about BASIC and its syntax rules, the better you'll be at detecting program errors and finding solutions for them.

QUESTIONS AND EXERCISES

1. What steps should you follow when isolating a bug in your program?

2. What is the difference between a syntax error and a run-time error?

3. If you were stranded on a desert island with only two commands from the Debug menu, which two commands would you want?

4. What does the F7 function key do?

5. What is the purpose of the Set Next Statement menu command?

6. What type of logic error do you find most difficult to track down and fix?

7. The following program (BADBEAR.BAS) contains two syntax errors. Load the program from the CHAP12 subdirectory on disk and fix them.

```
' BADBEAR.BAS
' This program contains two syntax errors.  Can you find them?

CLS

DIMM bears$(5)                           ' dimension string array

PRINT "Enter the names of your five favorite bears."
PRINT

FOR i% = 1 TO 5                          ' get 5 strings
    INPUT "Bear:  ", bears$(i%)
NET i%

PRINT
PRINT "You entered the following bears:"
PRINT

FOR i% = 1 TO 5                          ' print 5 strings
    PRINT bears$(i%)
NEXT i%
```

8. The following program (BADNAME.BAS) contains two logic errors. Load the program from the CHAP12 subdirectory on disk and use the debugging tools discussed in this chapter to find and fix them.

```
' BADNAME.BAS
' This program separates first and last names and prints them.
'   Can you find the two logic errors?

CLS

PRINT "Enter your first and last name in the following format:  ";
PRINT "Lastname, Firstname"
PRINT

INPUT "Name:  ", fullName$

commaLocation% = INSTR(1, fullName$, ",")

IF (commaLocation% < 0) THEN
    lastName$ = LEFT$(fullName$, commaLocation% - 1)
    firstName$ = RIGHT$(fullName$, LEN(fullName$) - commaLocation% - 1)

    PRINT
    PRINT "What a lovely name!  It's so nice to meet you, ";
    PRINT firstName$; " "; lastName$; "!"
ELSE
    PRINT
    PRINT "Name not in Lastname, Firstname format."
END IF
```

Learning More About BASIC

Congratulations! You've made it to the end of the line. Although this is the final stop on this particular journey, we hope that it's the jumping-off point for your own exploration of the BASIC language. This chapter reviews the topics covered in this book and introduces you to materials that can help you expand and enhance the BASIC programming skills you've developed here. In addition, it introduces you to the features of the Microsoft QuickBASIC Compiler, an advanced version of Quick-BASIC that you can purchase when you're ready for the next level of programming.

WHAT YOU HAVE LEARNED

You've come a long way in a short time. In fact, take a moment to reflect on your progress: Flip back through the introductory chapters and run a few of the early programs to see just how much you've learned about how the BASIC language works and how a computer goes about its business. Among other things, you've learned about the structure of a BASIC program and how to create a program using menu commands. You've learned how to store information in one place and use it in another and how to get input from a user and use it within your program. You've learned to program efficiently—to use loops for repetitive tasks and declare constants for values that never change. You've learned how to design your programs and fix them when they don't run correctly. You've even learned to use graphics and sound to make your programs both fun *and* functional. And the way you've learned these skills is by actually writing programs—an important fact to keep in mind as you continue your BASIC education.

As you work on your own programming projects, don't reinvent the wheel each time. Reuse the general-purpose parts of your programs whenever you can. Put together a folder with a printout of each program you write and keep it near your computer—you never know when your old programs will come in handy.

WHAT YOU HAVE YET TO LEARN

BASIC's methods of working with data, input and output, and repetitive operations—the methods you've learned about in this book—are the building blocks for each program you write. But there's plenty more to learn about BASIC. You'll likely find that as you continue to work with BASIC, you'll encounter situations that bring more specific types of questions to mind: How does BASIC work with the mouse attached to my system? How can I access the special capabilities of my printer? How do random-access files work? How can I use BASIC along with other programming languages? The following books may help you find the answers to such questions:

Craig, John Clark. *Microsoft QuickBASIC Programmer's Toolbox*. Microsoft Press, 1988. A collection of 250 subprograms and functions that let you extend the QuickBASIC language in your programs. Recommended for intermediate to advanced QuickBASIC programmers involved in longer programming projects. Includes information about mixed-language programming and using the mouse.

Hergert, Douglas. *Microsoft QuickBASIC*. 3d ed. Microsoft Press, 1989. An intermediate text about writing longer, task-oriented programs in QuickBASIC. Recommended for programmers with previous experience in BASICA or GW-BASIC. Includes information about random-access files and event trapping.

Jamsa, Kris. *Microsoft QuickBASIC*. Programmer's Quick Reference Series. Microsoft Press, 1989. A handy quick-reference guide to every QuickBASIC statement and function.

Lammers, Susan. *Programmers at Work*. Microsoft Press, 1989. Interviews with the personal computer programmers who built the industry, including Bill Gates, who wrote the first version of BASIC for a microcomputer in 1975.

Wolverton, Van. *Running MS-DOS*. 4th ed. Microsoft Press, 1989. A general introduction to personal computers and the MS-DOS operating system. Highly recommended for those interested in learning more about DOS commands and the operation of the IBM family of personal computers.

OTHER VERSIONS OF BASIC

The Microsoft QuickBASIC Interpreter supplied with this book is not the only software package available from Microsoft Corporation for BASIC programming. In terms of power, features, and cost, it actually falls near the low end of the list. Three of Microsoft's other BASIC language products are

- *The Microsoft QuickBASIC Compiler*
  A full-featured version of the QuickBASIC Interpreter, containing over two dozen additional menu options that support high-level debugging, file and procedure management, and modular programming. The major advantage of the QuickBASIC Compiler is that it can create libraries and stand-alone executable files, bringing it to the level of other full-featured programming language products. The QuickBASIC Compiler is the next logical step for those who want to continue programming with QuickBASIC.

- *Microsoft QuickBASIC for the Apple Macintosh*
  A BASIC compiler that runs on the Apple Macintosh family of personal computers. The Macintosh version of QuickBASIC is similar to the PC version but has been tailored to support the menu-driven, window-oriented operating environment of the Macintosh.

- *The Microsoft BASIC Compiler*
  An advanced BASIC compiler that addresses the needs of the professional BASIC programmer—including support for the OS/2 operating system and large programming projects. It comes with a copy of the Microsoft QuickBASIC Compiler to give you everything you should ever need to program anything in BASIC.

THE MICROSOFT QUICKBASIC COMPILER

The Microsoft QuickBASIC Interpreter included with this book is a solid and useful product for learning to program in BASIC and for developing your own applications. If you want more features, however, you might want to consider purchasing the Microsoft QuickBASIC Compiler. The Microsoft QuickBASIC Compiler has a number of advantages over the QuickBASIC Interpreter:

■ The ability to create stand-alone executable (.EXE) files

■ The ability to create libraries of often-used procedures

■ Enhanced debugging support

■ Support for multiple-module programs

■ Greater control over the programming environment

■ A number of other new menu options

Each of these features is integrated into the familiar QuickBASIC programming environment, so the programming skills you've already learned will be immediately applicable. In addition, the QuickBASIC programming language is identical in both products, so each of the programs you've already written will run without modification under the new compiler.

SUMMARY

This chapter makes a point of telling you what you have learned. But, more important, we hope that this chapter, along with the entire book, motivates you to explore further—to learn what you *haven't* learned. Maybe you picked up this book intending to write the world's greatest program someday. Or perhaps you simply wanted to get a handle on what programming is all about. No matter what your reason, the skills you've learned here will serve you well. In any case, be proud: You've taken the first exploratory steps into a new world. Embrace it! And program, program, program!

A

The QuickBASIC Interpreter Reference

This appendix serves as an at-a-glance reference. It is designed to help you perform some of the primary QuickBASIC tasks:

- Working with menus and commands
- Working with dialog boxes
- Working with keyboard commands
- Selecting text
- Getting help
- Printing

For more extensive coverage of these topics, refer to the Microsoft QBI Advisor and the QuickBASIC Express tutorial.

This appendix also contains information on several additional QuickBASIC topics:

- Changing display colors
- Using start-up options
- Converting 5¼-inch disks to 3½-inch disks

WORKING WITH MENUS AND COMMANDS

The QuickBASIC Interpreter contains eight drop-down menus that contain commands for file management, getting help, and editing, executing, and debugging programs. You can select menus and commands by using either the mouse or the keyboard.

With the Mouse...

1. Move the mouse pointer directly over the desired menu title and click the left mouse button to drop down the menu.

2. Move the mouse pointer to the command you want and click the left button again.

With the Keyboard...

1. Press the Alt key.

2. Press the key representing the first letter of the desired menu title.

3. Use the direction keys to highlight the desired command, and then press the Enter key. (Or simply press the letter highlighted in the command.)

WORKING WITH DIALOG BOXES

When QuickBASIC needs additional information before carrying out a command, it displays a *dialog box*. Figure A-1 shows the dialog box that appears when you select the Open command from the File menu. (The contents of your dialog box might be different.)

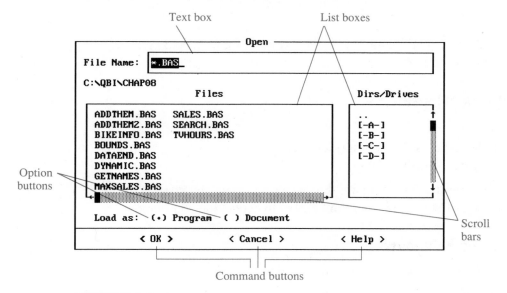

FIGURE A-1.
The elements of the Open dialog box.

A typical dialog box contains several fields:

- **Text boxes** receive information typed from the keyboard, such as filenames or search patterns.

- **List boxes** let you select one item (such as a filename, a directory name, or a color) from a number of choices. *Scroll bars* give you access to more information than can fit within boxes.

- **Check boxes** (not shown in Figure A-1) let you indicate whether an element is in effect or not by the presence of an "X" between square brackets.

- **Option buttons** are groups of buttons from which you can make only one selection.

- **Command buttons** control the operation of the dialog box. You use them to carry out a command, cancel a command, or get help.

You can fill in dialog boxes by using the mouse, the keyboard, or a combination of both.

With the Mouse...

1. Click on the field you want to modify.

2. Either type in the necessary information (in text boxes only) or click on the desired item.

3. Click on the *OK* command button to carry out the command, or click on the *Cancel* command button to cancel the command.

With the Keyboard...

1. Press the Tab key to move from field to field.

2. Either type in the necessary information (in text boxes only) or use the direction keys to select the desired item.

3. Press Enter to carry out the command, or press the Esc key to cancel it.

You can use the following keys within a dialog box:

Key(s)	Purpose(s)
Tab	Move to next field
Shift-Tab	Move to previous field
Direction keys	Select items in list box; select option button; toggle check box
PgUp/PgDn	Scroll list box several items at a time
Spacebar	Toggle check box; execute command button
F1	Get instructions for filling out dialog box
Enter	Carry out command
Esc	Cancel command

Scroll Bars

Scroll bars let a dialog box contain more text than is currently visible. Use the scroll bars to bring the hidden text into view.

Using scroll bars with the mouse

To use scroll bars with the mouse, click on the scroll bar arrows to view additional lines or rows of information and click in the area between the scroll bar arrows to move quickly through a list. You can also drag the scroll box to move to a specific location in the list.

Using scroll bars with the keyboard

To use scroll bars with the keyboard, press the direction keys to view additional lines or rows of information and press PgUp or PgDn to scroll many lines at a time.

You can also move directly to items starting with a particular letter by pressing the corresponding letter. Continue pressing it to cycle through all list entries beginning with that letter.

KEYBOARD EQUIVALENTS OF MENU COMMANDS

The QuickBASIC Interpreter provides shortcut keys for most menu commands and for a number of commands that have no menu equivalent. The following table describes these shortcut keys and their uses.

Key(s)	Purpose	Menu/Command
F1	Display specific help	Help/Topic
Shift-F1	Display general help	Help/Help
F2	Display procedure list	View/SUBs
Shift-F2	Display next procedure	None
Ctrl-F2	Display previous procedure	None
F3	Find next occurrence of search string	Search/Repeat Last Find
F4	Display output screen	View/Output Screen
F5	Continue program execution	Run/Continue
Shift-F5	Execute program from start	Run/Start
F6	Make next window active	None
Shift-F6	Make previous window active	None
F7	Execute program to cursor	None
F8	Execute next statement (step)	Debug/Step
F9	Toggle breakpoint	Debug/Toggle Breakpoint
F10	Execute next statement (step over procedure)	Debug/Procedure Step
Ctrl-F10	Toggle between full screen and multiple windows	None

KEYBOARD COMMANDS FOR EDITING

Along with the editing commands on the Edit menu, QuickBASIC supports a number of keyboard editing commands, most of which have WordStar equivalents. The following table describes the most significant of these commands.

Key(s)	WordStar keys	Purpose
←	Ctrl-S	Move one character left
→	Ctrl-D	Move one character right
Ctrl-←	Ctrl-A	Move one word left
Ctrl-→	Ctrl-F	Move one word right
↑	Ctrl-E	Move one line up
↓	Ctrl-X	Move one line down
Home	Ctrl-QS	Move to first character in line
End	Ctrl-QD	Move to last character in line
Ctrl-Enter	Ctrl-J	Move to beginning of next line
Ctrl-Home	Ctrl-QR	Move to top of procedure
Ctrl-End	Ctrl-QC	Move to bottom of procedure
Ins	Ctrl-V	Toggle insert mode
Shift-Ins	None	Paste contents of Clipboard at cursor
Shift-Del	None	Cut selected text (place in Clipboard)
None	Ctrl-Y	Cut current line (place in Clipboard)
None	Ctrl-QY	Cut from cursor to end of line (place in Clipboard)
Del	Ctrl-G	Delete selected text or character at cursor
None	Ctrl-T	Delete word at cursor
Shift-Tab	None	Delete one indentation level for selected lines
Ctrl-Ins	None	Copy selected text to Clipboard
PgUp	Ctrl-R	Scroll one page up
PgDn	Ctrl-C	Scroll one page down

SELECTING TEXT

Selecting text is the process of highlighting a block of text with the keyboard or the mouse. Selected text can be used in a number of QuickBASIC commands, including the following:

Menu/Command	Key(s)	Purpose
Edit/Cut	Shift-Del	Delete selected text (place in Clipboard)
Edit/Copy	Ctrl-Ins	Copy selected text to Clipboard
Edit/Paste	Shift-Ins	Paste contents of Clipboard at cursor
File/Print	None	Print selected text
Search/Find	None	Search for selected text
Search/Change	None	Search for and change selected text
Edit/New SUB	None	Use selected text as name for new subprogram
Edit/New Function	None	Use selected text as name for new function

The next sections describe selecting text with the mouse and keyboard.

 NOTE: Be cautious with selected text. If you type any character (even a space) while a line of text is selected, whatever you type replaces all selected text (which is permanently lost). To cancel a selection (to "unselect" it), click the left mouse button or press a direction key.

With the Mouse...

To select text with the mouse, follow these steps:

1. Place the mouse pointer on the first character you want to select. (The first character depends on which direction you move the mouse—see the following table.)

2. Hold down the left mouse button.

3. Move the mouse pointer to the last character you want to select.

4. Release the mouse button.

Mouse movements have the following effects when you select text:

Movement	Effect
Double-click	Select word mouse pointer is on
Right one column	Select character mouse pointer is on
Left one column	Select character to left of mouse pointer
Up one line	Select line mouse pointer is on and line above*
Down one line	Select line mouse pointer is on and line below†

* If the mouse pointer starts in the first column, only the line above the starting point is selected.

† If the mouse pointer starts in the first column, only the line containing the starting point is selected.

With the Keyboard...

To select text with the keyboard, follow these steps:

1. Move the cursor to the first character you want to select.

2. Hold down the Shift key.

3. Move the cursor to the last character you want to select. (See the following table for hints on using direction keys.)

4. Release the Shift key.

The direction keys have the following effects when you select text:

Direction key(s)	Effect
→	Select character cursor is on
←	Select character to left of cursor
↑	Select line cursor is on and line above*
↓	Select line cursor is on and line below†
PgUp	Select line cursor is on and one screenful up
PgDn	Select line cursor is on and one screenful down
Home	Select from character to left of cursor to beginning of line
End	Select from cursor to end of line
Ctrl-Home	Select from cursor line to beginning of procedure
Ctrl-End	Select from cursor line to end of procedure

* If the cursor starts in the first column, only the line above the starting point is selected.

† If the cursor starts in the first column, only the line containing the starting point is selected.

GETTING HELP

The QuickBASIC Interpreter contains useful on-line documentation for BASIC keywords and language elements, menu commands, error messages, and general programming topics. You can get on-line help in one of three ways:

■ For help with your program, place the cursor on the keyword or language element you want documentation for and press the F1 key. If you're using a mouse, click the right mouse button on the keyword or language element.

■ For help with a menu command or an error message, press F1 when the menu command is highlighted or when the error message is displayed.

■ For help with a general programming topic or the help system itself, press Alt-H to choose the Help menu, and then select one of the following commands:

    ☐ *Index* An alphabetic listing of BASIC keywords and subjects

    ☐ *Contents* A list of general programming topics including using the QuickBASIC Interpreter, BASIC language elements, and technical information about QuickBASIC

    ☐ *Topic* On-line documentation for the BASIC keyword the cursor is on

    ☐ *Help on Help* Information about the help system

The QuickBASIC help system, called the Microsoft QBI Advisor, is made up of interconnected elements: Each help dialog box contains *hyperlinks,* which let you reference other parts of the help system. To select one of these hyperlinks with the mouse, double-click on it. To select with the keyboard, press Tab until the cursor is on the desired hyperlink, and then press Enter.

If the text in the Help window is longer than one screen, use PgUp and PgDn or the scroll bars to view the parts that are off the screen. When you're finished working with the help system, press Esc to quit.

NOTE: If your computer beeps when you press F1, no on-line help exists for the word your cursor is on.

Copying Programs from the QBI Advisor

To copy sample code from the help system into your program, follow these steps:

1. Locate the sample code you want to copy, and select it.

2. Select Copy from the Edit menu.

3. Press Esc to close the Help window.

4. Move the cursor to the line where you want the program code to appear.

5. Select Paste from the Edit menu.

PRINTING

If a printer is attached to your system, you can print all or part of your program with the Print command on the File menu.

1. Select the Print command. The following dialog box appears:

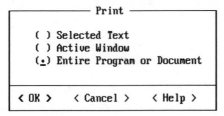

2. Select the appropriate option:

   □ *Selected Text* Prints only the selected text. (Before you can use this option, you must select the desired portion of your program.)

   □ *Active Window* Prints the contents of the active window only—useful in printing the contents of the main program, a procedure, or the contents of the Immediate window.

   □ *Entire Program or Document* Prints the entire program, including all subprograms and functions.

3. Press Enter or click on *OK* to carry out the Print command.

Printing Portions of the Help System

You can also use the Print command to print selections from the help system.

1. Enter the help system and locate the entry you want to print.

2. Select the Print command. The following dialog box appears:

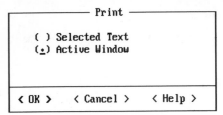

3. Select the appropriate option:

    ☐ *Selected Text* Prints only the selected text. (Before you use this option you must select the desired portion of documentation.)

    ☐ *Active Window* Prints the entire help entry.

4. Press Enter or click on *OK* to carry out the Print command.

CHANGING DISPLAY COLORS

The QuickBASIC Interpreter lets you change the foreground and background colors on the screen and modify other characteristics of the environment to suit your personal preferences. (Your video adapter and monitor dictate which colors you can use. See Chapter 11, "Working with Graphics and Sound," for more information.)

1. Select the Display command from the Options menu. (Figure A-2 shows the dialog box that appears.) The Display dialog box lets you change the foreground and background colors for three text elements on the screen:

    ☐ *Normal text* The regular screen text

    ☐ *Current statement* The next statement to be executed by QuickBASIC

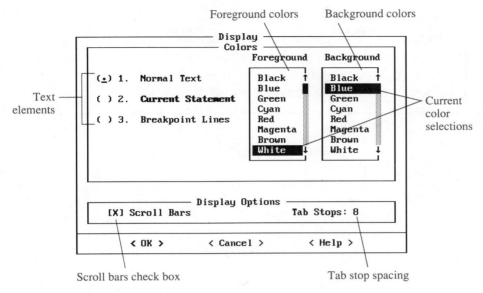

FIGURE A-2.

The elements of the Display dialog box.

□ *Breakpoint lines* The lines designated as breakpoints by the Debug Toggle Breakpoint command

2. Select the text element for which you want to choose colors.

3. Select the desired colors for the foreground and background.

4. Press Enter or click on *OK* to carry out the Display command.

NOTE: If you choose color settings other than the default values supplied by QuickBASIC, resist the temptation to combine bright or contrasting colors. In time, your eyes will thank you for your restraint!

The Display Options portion of the dialog box gives you the options of removing scroll bars from the screen and adjusting the spacing of your tab stops. By removing the scroll bars, you can see more of your program at one time; by changing *Tab Stops* to a value less than 8, you can fit more code on the screen and in your printouts (assuming you use the Tab key to indent your program lines).

START-UP OPTIONS

When you start the QuickBASIC Interpreter you can have it perform several special tasks simply by adding some extra information, known as *command-line options,* to the standard QBI command. The following is a partial list of these options. (For a complete list, refer to the help system.)

Option	*Description*	*Example*
`program`	Causes QuickBASIC to load the named program	`qbi bowling`
`/run program`	Causes QuickBASIC to load and run the named program before displaying the code	`qbi /run welcome`
`/b`	Runs the QuickBASIC Interpreter in black-and-white mode	`qbi /b`

CONVERTING 5¼-INCH DISKS TO 3½-INCH DISKS

If you have an IBM PS/2 or other computer that requires 3½-inch disks, you can order 3½-inch disks containing the Microsoft QuickBASIC Interpreter and the programs in this book directly from Microsoft Press, or you can copy the three 5¼-inch disks supplied with this book to two 3½-inch disks on your own.

Copying the disks requires that you have access to a computer with both a 3½-inch and a 5¼-inch drive. Your best chance at finding this type of machine is by checking around at work, at school, or at the store where you bought your computer. A number of computer hardware and software outlets will do disk conversions for free or for a nominal charge (provided you supply the disks).

Ordering 3½-Inch Disks

To order 3½-inch disks directly from Microsoft Press, send your original 5¼-inch disks along with $9.98 (plus sales tax for your state) to Microsoft Press, Attn: Learn BASIC Now Disks, 16011 NE 36th Way, Box 97017, Redmond, WA 98073-9717. You can pay by check or money order (payable to Microsoft Press; U.S. funds only).

For information on 3½-inch disk availability in the U.K., contact Microsoft Press, 27 Wrights Lane, London W8 5TZ.

Copying the Disks

When you find a computer that has both 3½-inch and 5¼-inch drives, determine which drive letters correspond to the drives. On a typical IBM PC or compatible computer, the 5¼-inch drive will be drive A and the 3½-inch drive will be drive B. On a typical IBM PS/2, the 3½-inch drive will be drive A and the 5¼-inch drive will be drive B. To find out for sure, insert disks into both drives, type *A:*, and press Enter. The drive whose light comes on will be drive A.

The copying process described here transfers the contents of the first two 5¼-inch disks to the first 3½-inch disk and then transfers the contents of the third 5¼-inch disk to the second 3½-inch disk. The following procedures assume drive A is a 3½-inch disk drive and drive B is a 5¼-inch disk drive. If this is not the case, switch the drive letters in the following commands.

Complete the following steps:

1. Put a blank, formatted 3½-inch disk in drive A.

2. Put Disk 1 in drive B.

3. Enter the following command at the system prompt:

```
xcopy b:\*.* a:\ /s
```

The contents of Disk 1 will be copied to the 3½-inch disk.

4. Remove Disk 1 from drive B and put Disk 2 in drive B.

5. Enter the following command at the system prompt:

    ```
    xcopy b:\*.* a:\ /s
    ```

    The contents of Disk 2 will be copied to the 3½-inch disk.

6. Remove the first 3½-inch disk from drive A and label it *Learn BASIC Now Disks 1 and 2*. Put the second blank, formatted 3½-inch disk in drive A.

7. Remove Disk 2 from drive B and put Disk 3 in drive B.

8. Enter the following at the system prompt:

    ```
    xcopy b:\*.* a:\ /s
    ```

    The contents of Disk 3 will be copied to the second 3½-inch disk.

9. Remove the second 3½-inch disk from drive A and label it *Learn BASIC Now Disk 3*.

10. Remove the 5¼-inch Disk 3 and store it in a safe place with the other two 5¼-inch disks. Make a backup copy of the new 3½-inch disks when you get back to your computer.

Installing the 3½-Inch Version

The INSTALL.BAT program on Disk 1 is designed to copy the contents of the three 5¼-inch disks to the \QBI directory on drive C. INSTALL will not copy the contents of the new 3½-inch disks to your hard disk. Rather than using INSTALL, copy the 3½-inch disks onto your hard disk by following these steps:

1. Put the combination Disk 1 and 2 in drive A.

2. Enter the following command at the system prompt:

    ```
    xcopy a:\*.* c:\qbi\ /s
    ```

    The contents of the first 3½-inch disk will be copied to the \QBI directory on drive C.

3. Remove the first disk from drive A and put Disk 3 in drive A.

4. Enter the following command at the system prompt:

```
xcopy a:\*.* c:\qbi\ /s
```

The contents of the second 3½-inch disk will be copied to the \QBI directory on drive C.

5. Remove the second disk from drive A and put it in a safe place with the first disk.

The QuickBASIC Interpreter is now installed on your system and is ready for use. If you want to execute the QuickBASIC Interpreter programs from any drive or directory, consult your DOS documentation for how to include the C:\QBI directory in the PATH command in your AUTOEXEC.BAT file.

B

ASCII and IBM Extended Character Sets

Between them, Tables B-1 and B-2 show the 256 characters available on most personal computers that run DOS: Table B-1 is the ASCII character set, and Table B-2 is the IBM extended character set. You can display most of these characters by using PRINT and other BASIC statements, and you can compare them by using BASIC relational operators. (Chapter 9 describes both the display and compare techniques in detail.)

Some of the ASCII characters (0 through 32, as well as 127) are called *control characters*. You use them to carry out special tasks such as sounding the computer's "bell" or advancing the paper in the printer. Table B-3 lists the most frequently used control characters.

Table B-1: The ASCII character set (codes 0–127)

Symbol	ASCII code	Symbol	ASCII code	Symbol	ASCII code
	0	←	27	6	54
☺	1	⊢	28	7	55
☻	2	↔	29	8	56
♥	3	▲	30	9	57
♦	4	▼	31	:	58
♣	5	\<space\>	32	;	59
♠	6	!	33	\<	60
•	7	"	34	=	61
▫	8	#	35	\>	62
○	9	$	36	?	63
◙	10	%	37	@	64
♂	11	&	38	A	65
♀	12	'	39	B	66
♪	13	(	40	C	67
♫	14	)	41	D	68
☼	15	*	42	E	69
►	16	+	43	F	70
◄	17	,	44	G	71
↕	18	-	45	H	72
‼	19	.	46	I	73
¶	20	/	47	J	74
§	21	0	48	K	75
▬	22	1	49	L	76
↨	23	2	50	M	77
↑	24	3	51	N	78
↓	25	4	52	O	79
→	26	5	53	P	80

(continued)

TABLE B-1. *continued*

Symbol	ASCII code	Symbol	ASCII code	Symbol	ASCII code
Q	81	a	97	q	113
R	82	b	98	r	114
S	83	c	99	s	115
T	84	d	100	t	116
U	85	e	101	u	117
V	86	f	102	v	118
W	87	g	103	w	119
X	88	h	104	x	120
Y	89	i	105	y	121
Z	90	j	106	z	122
[	91	k	107	{	123
\	92	l	108	¦	124
]	93	m	109	}	125
^	94	n	110	~	126
_	95	o	111	△	127
`	96	p	112		

Table B-2: The IBM extended character set (codes 128–255)

Symbol	ASCII code	Symbol	ASCII code	Symbol	ASCII code
Ç	128	ô	147	ª	166
ü	129	ö	148	º	167
e	130	ò	149	¿	168
â	131	û	150	⌐	169
ä	132	ù	151	¬	170
à	133	ÿ	152	½	171
å	134	Ö	153	¼	172
ç	135	Ü	154	¡	173
ê	136	¢	155	«	174
ë	137	£	156	»	175
è	138	¥	157	░	176
ï	139	₧	158	▒	177
î	140	ƒ	159	▓	178
ì	141	á	160	│	179
Ä	142	í	161	┤	180
Å	143	ó	162	╡	181
É	144	ú	163	╢	182
æ	145	ñ	164	╖	183
Æ	146	Ñ	165	╕	184

(continued)

441

TABLE B-2. *continued*

Symbol	ASCII code	Symbol	ASCII code	Symbol	ASCII code
╣	185	╤	209	Θ	233
║	186	╥	210	Ω	234
╗	187	╙	211	δ	235
╝	188	╘	212	∞	236
╜	189	╒	213	∅	237
╛	190	╓	214	∈	238
┐	191	╫	215	∩	239
└	192	╪	216	≡	240
┴	193	┘	217	±	241
┬	194	┌	218	≥	242
├	195	█	219	≤	243
─	196	▄	220	⌠	244
┼	197	▌	221	⌡	245
╞	198	▐	222	÷	246
╟	199	▀	223	≈	247
╚	200	α	224	°	248
╔	201	β	225	•	249
╩	202	Γ	226	·	250
╦	203	π	227	√	251
╠	204	Σ	228	η	252
═	205	σ	229	²	253
╬	206	μ	230	▪	254
╧	207	τ	231		255
╨	208	Φ	232		

Table B-3: Commonly used ASCII control characters

ASCII code	Control character	Description
7	Bell	Sounds computer's bell
8	Backspace	Backs up one character on screen
9	Tab	Moves right one tab stop on screen
10	Linefeed	Advances printer one line
12	Formfeed	Advances printer one page
13	Carriage return	Advances cursor to next line on screen

QuickBASIC
Statements
and Functions

This appendix lists the name of each statement and function available in the QuickBASIC Interpreter. To get complete documentation for each of these items, including reference material and sample programs, start QuickBASIC, type the name of the item, and press the F1 key.

STATEMENTS

BEEP	DO...LOOP	LOCK...UNLOCK
BLOAD	DRAW	LPRINT
BSAVE	END	LPRINT USING
CALL	ENVIRON	LSET
CALL ABSOLUTE	ERASE	MID$
CHAIN	ERROR	MKDIR
CHDIR	EXIT	NAME
CIRCLE	FIELD	ON ERROR
CLEAR	FILES	ON
CLOSE	FOR...NEXT	OPEN
CLS	FUNCTION	OPTION BASE
COLOR	GET	OUT
COM	GOSUB	PAINT
COMMON	GOTO	PALETTE
CONST	IF...THEN...ELSE	PCOPY
DATA	INPUT	PEN
DATE$	INPUT#	PLAY
DECLARE	IOCTL	PMAP
DEF	KEY	POKE
DEFDBL	KILL	PRESET
DEFINT	LET	PRINT
DEFLNG	LINE	PRINT USING
DEFSNG	LINE INPUT	PRINT# USING
DEFSTR	LINE INPUT#	PSET
DIM	LOCATE	PUT

(continued)

STATEMENTS. *continued*

RANDOMIZE	SEEK	TIME$
READ	SELECT CASE	TIMER
REDIM	SHARED	TROFF
REM	SHELL	TRON
RESET	SLEEP	TYPE
RESTORE	SOUND	UNLOCK
RESUME	STATIC	VIEW
RETURN	STOP	WAIT
RMDIR	STRIG	WHILE...WEND
RSET	SUB	WIDTH
RUN	SWAP	WINDOW
SCREEN	SYSTEM	WRITE

FUNCTIONS

ABS	CVSMBF	INPUT$
ASC	DATE$	INSTR
ATN	ENVIRON$	INT
CDBL	EOF	IOCTL$
CHR$	ERDEV	LBOUND
CINT	ERDEV$	LCASE$
CLNG	ERL	LEFT$
COMMAND$	ERR	LEN
COS	EXP	LOC
CSNG	FILEATTR	LOF
CSRLIN	FIX	LOG
CVD	FRE	LPOS
CVDMBF	FREEFILE	LTRIM$
CVI	HEX$	MID$
CVL	INKEY$	MKDMBF$
CVS	INP	MKD$

(continued)

FUNCTIONS. *continued*

MKI$	SADD	STRING$
MKL$	SCREEN	TAB
MKSMBF$	SEEK	TAN
MKS$	SETMEM	TIME$
OCT$	SGN	UBOUND
PEEK	SIN	UCASE$
PEN	SPACE$	VAL
POINT	SPC	VALPTR
POS	SQR	VALSEG
RIGHT$	STICK	VARPTR
RND	STR$	VARPTR$
RTRIM$	STRIG	VARSEG

D

Answers
to Questions
and Exercises

This appendix contains answers to the questions and exercises at the ends of Chapters 2 through 12. The programs listed in this appendix are in the APPNDX-D subdirectory on disk.

CHAPTER 2

1. Type *qbi* at the system prompt.

2. False.

3. The View window contains your program and is the primary window in the QuickBASIC Interpreter. The Immediate window lets you test program lines before you use them in your program.

4. The New command clears the View window and prepares the QuickBASIC Interpreter for a new program. The Open command uses the Open dialog box to load an existing program from disk.

5. The View window displays the program you are working on. The output screen displays the output of the program when you run the program.

6. The Cut command deletes a selected block of text from the View window and places it in the Clipboard. The Copy command places a copy of the selected block of text in the Clipboard without removing the original from the View window.

7. Text can be deleted from a program in the following ways:

   ☐ With the Cut command on the Edit menu (selected text)

   ☐ With the Del key (single character or selected text)

   ☐ With the Backspace key (single character)

   ☐ With the Ctrl-Y key combination (line)

8. The insert cursor adds text to a line without overwriting the existing characters. The overstrike cursor replaces existing characters with the new characters you type. The visual difference between the two is that the insert cursor appears as a blinking underscore and the overstrike cursor appears as a blinking rectangle. Change back and forth between the two cursors by pressing the Ins key.

9. Eight.

10. The following filenames are invalid:

Invalid filename	Reason
PRINTNAME.BAS	Too long (PRINTNAME is nine characters long)
BIG+BAD.BAS	+ character not allowed
BIG RED.BAS	Space not allowed
HI-AND-LO.BAS	Too long (HI-AND-LO is nine characters long)
PROG[1].BAS	[and] characters not allowed
1ST*PROG.BAS	* wildcard character not allowed

11. Select Exit from the File menu to quit the QuickBASIC Interpreter. If your file contains unsaved changes, QuickBASIC displays a dialog box with the following options: *Yes* (save the program), *No* (discard unsaved changes), *Cancel* (return to QuickBASIC), and *Help* (display help).

CHAPTER 3

1. A statement operates in a straightforward manner, usually producing results that are obvious or tangible (such as displaying characters on the screen). A function generally does its work behind the scenes and returns a value to the program that can be used as an argument to a statement.

2. BEEP — statement
   CLS — statement
   DATE$ — function
   PRINT — statement
   TIME$ — function

3. An item in square brackets is optional. The ¦ character means that you can choose only one of the values in the brackets.

4. An argument is a piece of information supplied to a statement or function.

5. A string is a collection of characters (including letters, numbers, or symbols) surrounded by double quotation marks. A numeric expression is a number or a numeric variable (discussed in Chapter 4).

6. The output of the two PRINT statements is the same.

7. A semicolon or comma at the end of a PRINT statement causes output from subsequent PRINT statements to be displayed on the same line. A semicolon prints the next PRINT statement's output immediately after the output from the current PRINT statement. A comma prints the next PRINT statement's output in the next print zone.

CHAPTER 4

1. Regular integer, long integer, single-precision floating-point, and double-precision floating-point. They differ in the type and size of number they can hold and in their type-declaration characters.

2. To reserve a space for a minus sign if the number is negative.

3. An invalid comma likely appeared within a QuickBASIC number.

4. A number outside the range of a numeric data type was assigned to a variable.

5. a. Integer

    b. Single-precision floating-point

    c. Single-precision floating-point

    d. Double-precision floating-point

    e. Integer or single-precision floating-point

    f. Single-precision floating-point

    g. Long integer

    h. Double-precision floating-point

    i. Single-precision floating-point

6. Regular division returns an integer and a remainder; integer division returns only an integer; remainder division returns only a remainder.

7. Exponentiation (^); multiplication and division (*, /, \, MOD); addition and subtraction (+, −).

8. 300.

9. One possible solution to this problem is the CALC.BAS program:

```
' CALC.BAS
' This program calculates and prints four formulas.

CLS

PRINT "ABS(-10) + 5 ="; ABS(-10) + 5
PRINT "SQR(36) ="; SQR(36)
PRINT "SQR(4) ^ 2 ="; SQR(4) ^ 2
PRINT "COS(3.14) ="; COS(3.141592654#)
```

10. One possible solution to this problem is the CIRCLE.BAS program:

```
' CIRCLE.BAS
' This program displays the circumference of a circle when
'   the radius is supplied by the user.

CONST PI# = 3.141592654#               ' declare constant

CLS                                     ' clear screen

PRINT "This program calculates the circumference of a circle ";
PRINT "from its radius."
PRINT                                   ' get input from user
INPUT "Enter the radius of the circle:  ", radius!

circum! = 2 * PI# * radius!             ' calculate circumference

PRINT                                   ' print result
PRINT "The circumference of the circle is"; circum!
```

CHAPTER 5

1. A numeric expression uses mathematical operators and yields a numeric result. A conditional expression uses conditional operators and yields a true or false result.

2. b, c, f, i, j, k.

3. True.

4. AND requires that both conditions be true before an action is taken; OR requires that only one condition be true before an action is taken.

5. ELSE lets you execute a block of statements when a conditional expression in an IF statement evaluates to false. ELSE is the opposite of THEN.

6. ELSEIF lets you evaluate another condition if the previous IF or ELSEIF statement has evaluated to false. The THEN keyword must appear on the same line as ELSEIF.

7. One possible solution to this problem is the QUESTION.BAS program:

```
' QUESTION.BAS
' This program asks the user a question about programming in BASIC.

CLS

INPUT "Do you like programming in BASIC so far (Y,N)?  ", reply$
PRINT

IF (reply$ = "Y") OR (reply$ = "y") THEN
    PRINT "Great!  There's more fun to come!"
ELSEIF (reply$ = "N") OR (reply$ = "n") THEN
    PRINT "Sorry to hear that.  Don't worry--it gets better!"
ELSE
    PRINT "Please run the program again."
    PRINT "Enter 'Y' for Yes or 'N' for No at the prompt."
END IF
```

8. QuickBASIC evaluates the expression that appears after SELECT CASE and then checks the following CASE clauses for a matching value. If a match is found, QuickBASIC executes the statements that follow.

9. CASE ELSE lets you specify a block of statements that will be executed if all the CASE conditions in a SELECT CASE statement evaluate to false.

10. IS lets you use a conditional expression in a CASE statement. TO lets you specify a range of numeric values in a CASE statement.

11. One possible solution to this problem is the STATES.BAS program:

```
' STATES.BAS
' This program displays information about one of three states.

CLS

PRINT "Which of the following states would you like to know about?"
PRINT
PRINT "   1) Washington"
PRINT "   2) Virginia"
PRINT "   3) Minnesota"
PRINT
INPUT "State (1-3):  ", reply%
PRINT

SELECT CASE reply%
    CASE 1
        PRINT "** Washington **"
        PRINT "    Population in 1980:  4,538,000"
        PRINT "    Capital:  Olympia"
        PRINT "    Statehood year:  1889"
    CASE 2
        PRINT "** Virginia **"
        PRINT "    Population in 1980:  5,346,818"
        PRINT "    Capital:  Richmond"
        PRINT "    Statehood year:  1788"
```

(continued)

continued

```
    CASE 3
        PRINT "** Minnesota **"
        PRINT "    Population in 1980:  4,075,970"
        PRINT "    Capital:  St. Paul"
        PRINT "    Statehood year:  1858"
    CASE ELSE
        PRINT "Please run the program again and select a number ";
        PRINT "between 1 and 3."
END SELECT
```

CHAPTER 6

1. The counter variable identifies the *value* of the loop—an integer between the *start* and *end* limits of the loop.

2. *start* and *end* can be numeric constants, numeric variables, or numeric expressions.

3. 4.

4. The SOUND statement causes your computer's speaker to emit a tone of the specified frequency and duration.

5. A nested loop is a FOR, WHILE, or DO loop inside another FOR, WHILE, or DO loop.

6. Putting the condition at the top of a DO loop ensures that the condition must be met before the loop is executed. Putting the condition at the bottom of a DO loop ensures that the statements in the loop will be executed at least once.

7. Use a FOR loop when you want to execute a block of statements a specific number of times. Use a WHILE or DO loop to execute a block of statements based on the value of a condition.

8. One possible solution to this problem is the GASCASH.BAS program.

```
' GASCASH.BAS
' This program uses a FOR loop to track weekly gasoline expenses.

CLS

PRINT "For each of the seven days of the week, enter the amount ";
PRINT "you spent on gasoline."
PRINT

FOR day% = 1 TO 7
    PRINT "  Cash spent on day"; day%;
    INPUT "--> $", dayTotal!
    weekTotal! = weekTotal! + dayTotal!
NEXT day%

PRINT
PRINT "Wow!  $"; weekTotal!; "on gas in one week!"
```

9. One possible solution to this problem is the SOUNDER.BAS program:

```
' SOUNDER.BAS
' This program plays a note based on frequency and duration values
'    entered by the user.

CLS

PRINT "Enter frequency and duration values for the sound you want"
PRINT "to hear.  To quit, enter -999 for frequency."
PRINT

DO
    INPUT "Frequency (37-32767):  ", frequency%
    IF (frequency% <> -999) THEN
        INPUT "Duration (0-65535):  ", duration&
        SOUND frequency%, duration&
        PRINT
    END IF
LOOP UNTIL (frequency% = -999)
```

10. One possible solution to this problem is the HIROLLER.BAS program:

```
' HIROLLER.BAS
' This program rolls one simulated die 10 times and displays the
'   message "Nice Roll!" if the die shows 6.

CLS

INPUT "Press Enter to roll the die 10 times.  Think six...", dummy$
PRINT

RANDOMIZE TIMER

FOR i% = 1 TO 10
    roll% = INT(RND * 7)
    PRINT "Roll: "; roll%,
    IF (roll% = 6) THEN
        COLOR 2
        PRINT "Nice Roll!"
        COLOR 7
    ELSE
        PRINT
    END IF
NEXT i%
```

CHAPTER 7

1. All are advantages.

2. The *EnterName$* subprogram name has a string type-declaration character (*$*). This is incorrect—only functions are marked for the type of data they will return. The correct SUB statement would be as follows:

   ```
   SUB EnterName (firstName$, lastName$)
   ```

3. F2.

4. The Procedure Step command on the Debug menu (F10).

5. `COMMON SHARED total%`

6. Subprograms let you carry out a number of tasks or send a number of values to the main program. Functions let you carry out smaller, more specific tasks, and they return one value to the main program.

7. The *GetCarFacts* subprogram can be written as follows:

```
SUB GetCarFacts (make$, model$, year%, color$)

PRINT "Please enter information about your car"
PRINT
INPUT "  Car make:  ", make$
INPUT "  Car model:  ", model$
INPUT "  Model year:  ", year%
INPUT "  Car color:  ", color$

END SUB
```

A statement that calls *GetCarFacts* can be written as follows:

```
GetCarFacts carMake$, carModel$, carYear%, carColor$
```

8. The *FindLarger%* function can be written as follows:

```
FUNCTION FindLarger% (int1%, int2%)

IF (int1% >= int2%) THEN
    FindLarger% = int1%
ELSE
    FindLarger% = int2%
END IF

END FUNCTION
```

A statement that calls *FindLarger%* can be written as follows:

```
PRINT "The larger integer is"; FindLarger%(first%, second%)
```

9. One possible solution to this problem is the SHAPES.BAS program.

```
' SHAPES.BAS
' This program displays a shape filled with your favorite character.

' declare constants used as arguments to the COLOR statement

CONST CYAN% = 3
CONST WHITE% = 7

' declare subprograms before they are used; subprogram names and
'    parameters should match those in the subprograms

DECLARE SUB GetShape (symbol$, choice%)
DECLARE SUB PrintLine (char$)
DECLARE SUB PrintRectangle (char$)
DECLARE SUB PrintTriangle (char$)

CLS

' call GetShape subprogram to get desired character and shape

GetShape character$, shape%    ' pass two arguments to GetShape

PRINT
PRINT
COLOR CYAN%

' use CASE statement to call the requested subprogram

SELECT CASE shape%
    CASE 1            ' if shape% = 1, display a triangle
        PrintTriangle character$
    CASE 2            ' if shape% = 2, display a rectangle
        PrintRectangle character$
    CASE 3            ' if shape% = 3, display a line
        PrintLine character$
END SELECT

COLOR WHITE%

END
```

(continued)

continued

```
SUB GetShape (symbol$, choice%)

' The GetShape subprogram prompts the user for a symbol and a shape
'    and returns them to the main program in the symbol$ and choice%
'    variables.

PRINT "This program prints a collection of characters in the ";
PRINT "shape you specify."
PRINT
INPUT "What character would you like to use?  ", symbol$
PRINT
PRINT "What shape would you like to see?"
PRINT
PRINT "     1) Triangle"
PRINT "     2) Rectangle"
PRINT "     3) Line"
PRINT

DO          ' prompt the user until choice% is in the right range
    INPUT "Shape (1, 2, or 3):  ", choice%
LOOP WHILE (choice% < 1) OR (choice% > 3)

END SUB    ' subprogram complete--return to the main program

SUB PrintLine (char$)

' The PrintLine subprogram receives an argument from the main
'    program and uses it to print a line 30 characters long.

CONST LENGTH% = 30      ' set the length of the line at 30 characters

FOR i% = 1 TO LENGTH%  ' display the character 30 times
    PRINT char$;         ' use semicolon to print them one after another
NEXT i%

PRINT

END SUB
```

(continued)

continued

```
SUB PrintRectangle (char$)

' The PrintRectangle subprogram receives an argument from the main
'   program and uses it to print a rectangle 50 characters long by
'   7 characters high.

CONST LENGTH% = 50          ' set length of rectangle at 50 rows
CONST HEIGHT% = 7           ' set height of rectangle at 7 lines

FOR i% = 1 TO HEIGHT%       ' for each of the 7 rows in the rectangle,
    FOR j% = 1 TO LENGTH%   '   display 50 characters one after another
        PRINT char$;
    NEXT j%
    PRINT                   ' print a carriage return after each row
NEXT i%

END SUB

SUB PrintTriangle (char$)

' The PrintTriangle subprogram receives an argument from the main
'   program and uses it to print an equilateral triangle.  The Tab
'   function moves the cursor to the correct column location.

CONST ROWS% = 10        ' set the number of rows to 10
left% = ROWS%           ' use left% to build left side of triangle
right% = ROWS% + 1      ' use right% to build right side of triangle

FOR rowCount% = 1 TO ROWS%              ' for each row in the triangle
    FOR i% = left% TO ROWS%
        PRINT TAB(i%); char$;           ' display left side of row
    NEXT i%

    FOR i% = ROWS% + 1 TO right% - 1    ' display right side of row
        PRINT TAB(i%); char$;
    NEXT i%
```

(continued)

continued

```
    PRINT                  ' print carriage return at end of row
    left% = left% - 1      ' first character in next row will start one
    right% = right% + 1    '   space closer to left margin and extend
NEXT rowCount%             '   one space closer to the right margin

END SUB
```

CHAPTER 8

1. READ statements come first.

2. DATA, READ, and RESTORE work best for data in the following categories:

   ☐ Data you know about in advance (before the program is run)

   ☐ Data that always appears in the same order

   ☐ Data that can be cycled through repeatedly, such as hours in the day

3. One possible solution to this problem is the BEAV.BAS program:

```
' BEAV.BAS
' This program reads the names of Beaver Cleaver and his friends from
'   a DATA statement.

CLS

FOR i% = 1 TO 7
    READ pal$
    PRINT pal$
NEXT i%

DATA Beaver, Wally, Lumpy, Whitey, Gus, Eddie, Larry
```

4. False.

5. `DIM numbers!(99)`

6. An end-of-data marker is a number or string indicating that no more data items exist in a list.

7. One possible solution to this problem is the BANZAI.BAS program:

```
' BANZAI.BAS
' This program uses a one-dimensional dynamic string array to store names
'   of characters from the movie "The Adventures of Buckaroo Banzai."

OPTION BASE 1                    ' set array base at 1

CLS

PRINT "** This program collects character names from the film ";
PRINT "'Buckaroo Banzai' **"
PRINT
INPUT "How many names would you like to enter?  ", names%

DIM characters$(names%)        ' dimension array

PRINT                            ' fill dynamic array
FOR i% = 1 TO names%
    INPUT "  Name:  ", characters$(i%)
NEXT i%

PRINT
PRINT "You entered the following names:"
PRINT

FOR i% = 1 TO names%             ' print contents of array
    PRINT characters$(i%)
NEXT i%
```

8. An out-of-range error occurs when your program attempts to reference an element that does not exist in an array.

9. One possible solution to this problem is the BASEBALL.BAS program.

```
' BASEBALL.BAS
' This program keeps score for a nine-inning baseball game with a
'    two-dimensional array named scoreboard%.

OPTION BASE 1              ' set first array element at 1
DIM scoreboard%(2, 9)      ' dimension 2x9 array for baseball scoreboard


' get team and mascot names

visitor$ = "Boston": visitorMascot$ = "Red Sox"
home$ = "Seattle": homeMascot$ = "Mariners"


CLS


PRINT "Enter runs scored by each team in a nine-inning baseball game."
PRINT


FOR inning% = 1 TO 9      ' get number of runs scored in each inning
    PRINT "Inning"; inning%; "-->    "; visitor$;
    INPUT ; ": ", scoreboard%(1, inning%)
    PRINT "    "; home$;
    INPUT ": ", scoreboard%(2, inning%)
                            ' ...and keep running total for each team
    visitorScore% = visitorScore% + scoreboard%(1, inning%)
    homeScore% = homeScore% + scoreboard%(2, inning%)
NEXT inning%


' determine the winner of the game and display results


PRINT
COLOR 2    ' set foreground color to green for "News Flash"

IF (visitorScore% > homeScore%) THEN
    PRINT "News Flash:  "; visitorMascot$; " beat "; homeMascot$;
    PRINT visitorScore%; "to"; homeScore%
ELSEIF (homeScore% > visitorScore%) THEN
    PRINT "News Flash:  "; homeMascot$; " beat "; visitorMascot$;
    PRINT homeScore%; "to"; visitorScore%
```

(continued)

continued

```
ELSE
    PRINT "News Flash:  "; visitorMascot$; " tie "; homeMascot$;
    PRINT visitorScore%; "to"; homeScore%
END IF

COLOR 7    ' set foreground color to white

' display the final scoreboard

PRINT
PRINT "Inning         1   2   3   4   5   6   7   8   9"
PRINT "-----------------------------------------------------"

FOR team% = 1 TO 2          ' for each team in the game
    IF (team% = 1) THEN PRINT visitor$,  ELSE PRINT home$,
    FOR inning% = 1 TO 9 ' ...and for each inning in the game...
        PRINT scoreboard%(team%, inning%); "  ";
    NEXT inning%            ' print the number of runs scored
    PRINT
NEXT team%
```

CHAPTER 9

1. True.

2. False. The correct declaration does not have the $ type-declaration character:

   ```
   DIM lastName AS STRING * 20
   ```

3. ONETWOTHREE

4. a, b, c, d.

5. A value of 0 from INSTR means one of the following:

   ☐ *searchstring* was not found in *basestring*

   ☐ *start* is greater than the length of *basestring*

   ☐ *basestring* contains no characters

6. H

7. 77.

8. One possible solution to this problem is the GETNAMES.BAS program:

```
' GETNAMES.BAS
' This program gets first and last names from the user and displays
'    them in uppercase.

CLS

INPUT "First name:  ", firstName$
INPUT "Last name:   ", lastName$
PRINT
PRINT UCASE$(lastName$); ", "; UCASE$(firstName$)
```

9. One possible solution to this problem is the REVERSE.BAS program:

```
' REVERSE.BAS
' This program reverses the order of the characters in a string.

CLS
                                     ' get string from user
INPUT "Enter a string of characters to be reversed:  ", inString$
numOfChars% = LEN(inString$)         ' find length of string

FOR i% = numOfChars% TO 1 STEP -1    ' step backwards through string
    tempChar$ = MID$(inString$, i%, 1)   ' extract one letter at a time
    reverse$ = reverse$ + tempChar$  ' build new string
NEXT i%

PRINT                                ' display new string
PRINT "The characters in reverse order are "; reverse$
```

10. One possible solution to this problem is the DIVIDE.BAS program.

```
' DIVIDE.BAS
' This program divides a string into three parts.

CONST BLANK$ = " "                   ' declare string constant
char$ = ""                           ' initialize variables
charCount% = 1
nameCount% = 0


CLS                                  ' clear screen

PRINT "Enter name in the following format:  First Middle Last"
INPUT "Name:  ", fullName$           ' get 3-part name from user
nameLength% = LEN(fullName$)          ' determine length of name

' loop until the entire three-part string has been stepped through

DO WHILE (charCount% <> nameLength% + 1)

'    read characters one at a time until a blank or end of string
'       is encountered; assign characters to name$ variable

    DO WHILE (char$ <> BLANK$) AND (charCount% <> (nameLength% + 1))
        char$ = MID$(fullName$, charCount%, 1)
        name$ = name$ + char$
        charCount% = charCount% + 1   ' track number of character read
    LOOP

    char$ = ""                       ' reset char$
    nameCount% = nameCount% + 1       ' increment nameCount%

    SELECT CASE nameCount%            ' assign string to name variables
        CASE 1                        '    based on value of nameCount%
            firstName$ = name$
        CASE 2
            middleName$ = name$
        CASE 3
            lastName$ = name$
    END SELECT
    name$ = ""                       ' reset name$
LOOP
```

(continued)

continued

```
PRINT
PRINT "Results of separation process:"
PRINT
PRINT "First name is "; firstName$     ' display results
PRINT "Middle name is "; middleName$
PRINT "Last name is "; lastName$
```

CHAPTER 10

1. OUTPUT deletes the contents of the existing file; APPEND adds to the end of the existing file.

2. d.

3. False.

4. LINE INPUT# is more useful than INPUT# when you need to read long lines of string data or lines containing commas from a file.

5. A literal argument to the SHELL statement must be enclosed in quotation marks. The correct statement would be as follows:

```
SHELL "copy test.txt test2.txt"
```

6. Search string found!

7. One possible solution to this problem is the CITY.BAS program:

```
' CITY.BAS
' This program stores a list of cities in a sequential file.

OPEN "CITY.TXT" FOR OUTPUT AS #1      ' open file in current drive/dir

CLS

PRINT "This program stores city names on disk in a file named CITY.TXT."
PRINT "Enter your favorite cities and type END to quit."
PRINT
```

(continued)

continued

```
DO WHILE (city$ <> "END")                ' until user enters END
    INPUT "  City name: ", city$      '   get names from user
    IF (city$ <> "END") THEN PRINT #1, city$    ' write names to file
LOOP

CLOSE #1                                  ' close file

PRINT
INPUT "Press Enter to see the cities you entered.  ", dummy$
PRINT

OPEN "CITY.TXT" FOR INPUT AS #1       ' open file for input

DO WHILE (NOT EOF(1))                 ' until end of file is reached
    INPUT #1, city$                   '   get names
    PRINT city$                       '   print names
LOOP

CLOSE #1                              ' close file
```

8. One possible solution to this problem is the SORTLIST.BAS program:

```
' SORTLIST.BAS
' This program gets names and addresses from the user, sorts
'    them alphabetically by last name, and stores them in the
'    sequential file NAMES.TXT.

DECLARE SUB AddNamesToFile ()          ' declare procedures
DECLARE FUNCTION NumberOfNamesInFile% ()
DECLARE SUB CopyFileToArrays (names$(), addresses$(), numOfItems%)
DECLARE SUB ShellSort (names$(), addresses$(), numOfElements%)
DECLARE SUB CopyArraysToFile (names$(), addresses$(), numOfItems%)
DECLARE SUB DisplayNewFile ()

OPTION BASE 1                          ' set base of arrays to 1
```

(continued)

continued

```
CLS                                   ' clear screen

AddNamesToFile                        ' call sub to get input from user
numOfNames% = NumberOfNamesInFile%    ' call function to get num of names

DIM names$(numOfNames%)               ' dimension array to hold names
DIM addresses$(numOfNames%)           ' dimension array to hold addresses

' copy names and addresses in file to arrays in preparation for sorting
CopyFileToArrays names$(), addresses$(), numOfNames%

' sort names$ and addresses$ arrays alphabetically by last name
ShellSort names$(), addresses$(), numOfNames%

' copy sorted arrays back to file
CopyArraysToFile names$(), addresses$(), numOfNames%

' display new file on screen
DisplayNewFile

END

SUB AddNamesToFile

OPEN "NAMES.TXT" FOR APPEND AS #1     ' open for append so we don't lose
                                      '   any existing names and addresses
PRINT "This program adds names and addresses to the file NAMES.TXT"
PRINT "and then sorts the file alphabetically."
PRINT
PRINT "Enter names in Lastname, Firstname format.  Type END to quit."
PRINT

DO WHILE (fullName$ <> "END")         ' get names until user enters END
```

(continued)

continued

```
     LINE INPUT "  Name (Last, First):  "; fullName$
     IF (fullName$ <> "END") THEN     ' use LINE INPUT to allow commas
         PRINT #1, fullName$              ' write data to file
         LINE INPUT "  Address:  "; address$
         PRINT #1, address$
     END IF
     PRINT
LOOP

CLOSE #1

END SUB

SUB CopyArraysToFile (names$(), addresses$(), numOfItems%)

OPEN "NAMES.TXT" FOR OUTPUT AS #1    ' open for output to overwrite
                                     '    out-of-order entries
FOR i% = 1 TO numOfItems%
    PRINT #1, names$(i%)                 ' write array contents to file
    PRINT #1, addresses$(i%)
NEXT i%

CLOSE #1

END SUB

SUB CopyFileToArrays (names$(), addresses$(), numOfItems%)

OPEN "NAMES.TXT" FOR INPUT AS #1    ' open for input to get file data

FOR i% = 1 TO numOfItems%
    LINE INPUT #1, names$(i%)        ' read file contents
    LINE INPUT #1, addresses$(i%)
NEXT i%

CLOSE #1

END SUB
```

(continued)

continued

```
SUB DisplayNewFile

INPUT "Press Enter to view NAMES.TXT.  ", dummy$
PRINT

OPEN "NAMES.TXT" FOR INPUT AS #1     ' open for input to get file data

DO WHILE (NOT EOF(1))                ' until end of file is reached,
    LINE INPUT #1, fullName$              ' read file data
    LINE INPUT #1, address$
    PRINT fullName$; " -- "; address$        ' and display on screen
LOOP

CLOSE #1

END SUB

FUNCTION NumberOfNamesInFile%

OPEN "NAMES.TXT" FOR INPUT AS #1     ' open for input to read file data

count% = 0                          ' counter tracks number of name-and-
                                    '   address items
DO WHILE (NOT EOF(1))               ' until end of file is reached,
    LINE INPUT #1, fullName$             '   read name and address
    LINE INPUT #1, address$
    count% = count% + 1             ' increment item counter
LOOP

CLOSE #1

NumberOfNamesInFile% = count%       ' return item count to main program

END FUNCTION

SUB ShellSort (names$(), addresses$(), numOfElements%)
```

(continued)

continued

```
' A discussion of the Shell Sort can be found in Chapter 9.
' Note that this version sorts two arrays based on the contents
'    of names$().

span% = numOfElements% \ 2

DO WHILE (span% > 0)
    FOR i% = span% TO numOfElements% - 1
        j% = i% - span% + 1
        FOR j% = (i% - span% + 1) TO 1 STEP -span%
            IF names$(j%) <= names$(j% + span%) THEN EXIT FOR

            ' swap array elements that are out of order
            SWAP names$(j%), names$(j% + span%)
            SWAP addresses$(j%), addresses$(j% + span%)
        NEXT j%
    NEXT i%

    span% = span% \ 2
LOOP

END SUB
```

9. One possible solution to this problem is the VIDEO.BAS program. Because of its length, we have not reproduced the program here. You can find VIDEO.BAS on disk in the APPNDX-D subdirectory.

CHAPTER 11

1. The two components are the video adapter and the monitor. The video adapter determines the screen modes, generates the text and graphics to be displayed, and generates the colors. The monitor simply displays whatever the video adapter sends it.

2. In text mode, the graphics adapter can display only alphanumeric characters. In graphics mode, the video adapter can display both text and graphic shapes (pixels, lines, boxes, circles, etc.).

3. LOCATE lets you position the text cursor on the output screen.

4. One possible solution to this problem is the MOVENAME.BAS program:

```
' MOVENAME.BAS
' This program "moves" a name across the screen.

CONST DELAY% = 400

CLS

INPUT "Please enter your first name:  ", name$
LOCATE 10, 1
PRINT name$

FOR i% = 2 TO 70
    LOCATE 10, i% - 1
    PRINT SPACE$(10)
    LOCATE 10, i%
    PRINT name$

    FOR j% = 1 TO DELAY%            ' delay loop
    NEXT j%

NEXT i%
```

5. SCREEN changes your video adapter's mode and determines the screen resolution and (if applicable) the number of colors your video adapter can display.

6. The PSET and PRESET statements set individual pixels on the screen at specified locations. The PSET statement sets the pixel in the current foreground color; the PRESET statement sets the pixel in the current background color.

7. Absolute coordinates are calculated using a starting point of (0, 0), which is the upper-left corner of the screen. Relative coordinates use the last plotted point as the starting point for calculation.

8. True, provided you use the B and F options.

9. False.

10. One possible solution to this problem is the CIRCMOVE.BAS program:

```
' CIRCMOVE.BAS
' This program "moves" a circle across the screen.

CONST DELAY% = 50

SCREEN 1                 ' change this value as needed for your adapter

CIRCLE (20, 100), 20

FOR i% = 21 TO 299       ' assumes 320 x 200 resolution
    CIRCLE (i% - 1, 100), 20, 0      ' erase previous circle
    CIRCLE (i%, 100), 20             ' draw new circle

    FOR j% = 1 TO DELAY%             ' delay loop
    NEXT j%

NEXT i%
```

11. One possible solution to this problem is the ANTHEM.BAS program:

```
' ANTHEM.BAS
' This program plays the opening bars of "The Star-Spangled Banner."

CLS

INPUT "Press Enter to begin...", dummy$

FOR i% = 1 TO 12
    READ note%, duration%
    SOUND note%, duration%
NEXT i%

DATA 349, 4, 294, 4, 233, 8, 294, 8, 349, 8, 466, 16
DATA 587, 4, 523, 4, 466, 8, 294, 8, 330, 8, 349, 16
```

CHAPTER 12

1. a. Run your program.

    b. Observe errors and trouble spots in program execution.

    c. Study the statements that produced the error using printouts, programming tools, and your knowledge of BASIC syntax.

    d. Fix the error and test the program.

2. A syntax error is a programming mistake that violates the rules of BASIC. A run-time error is an error that causes a program to stop unexpectedly during execution.

3. No one correct answer here. Our favorites are the Step and Toggle Breakpoint commands.

4. The F7 function key executes the current line and the lines between the current line and the cursor at full speed.

5. Set Next Statement sets the line the cursor is on as the next statement to be executed.

6. Again, no one correct answer here (especially with so many to choose from!). Our picks for the worst are logic errors resulting from incorrect arithmetic or faulty conditional expressions.

7. DIM and NEXT are misspelled. Here is the correct version (GOODBEAR.BAS):

```
' GOODBEAR.BAS
' This program is the corrected version of BADBEAR.BAS.

CLS

DIM bears$(5)                           ' dimension string array

PRINT "Enter the names of your five favorite bears."
PRINT

FOR i% = 1 TO 5                         ' get 5 strings
    INPUT "Bear:  ", bears$(i%)
NEXT i%
```

(continued)

continued

```
PRINT
PRINT "You entered the following bears:"
PRINT

FOR i% = 1 TO 5                                    ' print 5 strings
    PRINT bears$(i%)
NEXT i%
```

8. The INPUT statement should be a LINE INPUT statement to handle the comma in the user's input, and the conditional expression in the IF statement should use a greater-than operator (>) instead of a less-than operator (<). Here is the correct version (GOODNAME.BAS):

```
' GOODNAME.BAS
' This program separates first and last names and prints them.

CLS

PRINT "Enter your first and last name in the following format:  ";
PRINT "Lastname, Firstname"
PRINT

LINE INPUT "Name:  ", fullName$

commaLocation% = INSTR(1, fullName$, ",")

IF (commaLocation% > 0) THEN
    lastName$ = LEFT$(fullName$, commaLocation% - 1)
    firstName$ = RIGHT$(fullName$, LEN(fullName$) - commaLocation% - 1)

    PRINT
    PRINT "What a lovely name!  It's so nice to meet you, ";
    PRINT firstName$; " "; lastName$; "!"
ELSE
    PRINT
    PRINT "Name not in Lastname, Firstname format."
END IF
```

Index

Note: Italicized page numbers refer to entries in programs or figures.

Special characters

Michael Halvorson

Michael Halvorson received his B.A. in computer science from Pacific Lutheran University, Tacoma, Washington, in 1985, and has been employed as a programmer, technical editor, and community college instructor. He is currently senior technical editor of Microsoft Press. Michael is coeditor (with JoAnne Woodcock) of *XENIX at Work,* published in 1986 by Microsoft Press.

David Rygmyr

David Rygmyr got started in computers in 1977 by preparing daily feedings of paper tape and punch cards for a room-sized UNIVAC computer. He has since received instruction in computer science, electronics, and digital control/robotics. David is currently technical manager of Microsoft Press, which he joined in 1984.

The manuscript for this book was prepared and submitted to Microsoft Press in electronic form. Text files were processed and formatted using Microsoft Word.

Cover design by Greg Hickman
Interior text design by Darcie S. Furlan
Illustrations by Becky Geisler-Johnson
Principal typography by Ruth Pettis

Text composition by Microsoft Press in Times Roman with display in Times Roman Bold, using the Magna composition system and the Linotronic 300 laser imagesetter.

NOTE TO VGA OWNERS
The Microsoft QuickBASIC Express tutorial (LEARN.COM) on Disk 2 does not work with all VGA cards. If your VGA card is not 100 percent IBM VGA compatible, we regret that you may be unable to use the tutorial. You can, however, make full use of the Microsoft QuickBASIC Interpreter and all the sample programs and utilities on disk.

A Word About Microsoft® QuickBASIC

When you're ready to move up to the professional programming environment of the Microsoft QuickBASIC Compiler, Microsoft Press has the books to help you make the transition smoothly and quickly. *(You'll find more information on the Microsoft QuickBASIC Compiler in Chapter 13.)*

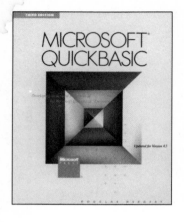

MICROSOFT® QUICKBASIC, 3rd ed.
Developing Structured Programs in the Microsoft QuickBASIC Environment

Douglas Hergert

"No matter what your level of programming experience, you'll find this book irreplaceable when you start to program in QuickBASIC." **Online Today**

Learn structured programming techniques through a collection of realistic and useful application programs. MICROSOFT QUICKBASIC includes six full-length programs that highlight exciting language elements and demonstrate how to work with large programs. They include programs that use data types and data structures, decision and looping structures, sequential data files, random-access file handling, the powerful graphics commands, and event trapping. You'll find that the tutorial programs are practical applications that you can use as is or customize for special projects. Updated to address the new QuickBASIC user-interface enhancements of version 4.5.
400 pages, softcover 7 ³⁄₈ x 9 ¹⁄₄ $21.95 Order Code 1-55615-236-1

MICROSOFT® QUICKBASIC PROGRAMMER'S TOOLBOX
An Essential Library of More than 250 Functions, Routines, and Utilities for Supercharging QuickBASIC Programs

John Clark Craig

If you want to increase the power and speed of your QuickBASIC programs, this resource is an unrivaled collection of more than 250 helpful subfunctions, functions, and utilities designed for both novice and intermediate programmers. The subprograms are easily referenced and address both common and unusual programming tasks: ANSI.SYS screen control, printer control, mouse interface routines, pop-up windows, fonts, graphics, editor routines, and more. Each subprogram and function is creative and practical, and each takes maximum advantage of QuickBASIC's capabilities. MICRO-SOFT QUICKBASIC PROGRAMMER'S TOOLBOX is complete with a detailed section on interlanguage calling techniques with examples and is a solid reinforcement of programming techniques that will enhance your skills.
512 pages, softcover 7 ³⁄₈ x 9 ¹⁄₄ $22.95 Order Code 1-55615-127-6

MICROSOFT® QUICKBASIC: PROGRAMMER'S QUICK REFERENCE
Covers Microsoft QuickBASIC for MS-DOS® through version 4.5

Kris Jamsa

Now you can have instant answers at your fingertips! This handy guide—in alphabetic format—is an instructive look at every QuickBASIC statement and function. Jamsa provides information on exact syntax and calling sequences gives you concise descriptions of each statement and function, along with notes, comments, and cautions. This convenient guide is sure to be a frequent reference.
144 pages, softcover 4 ³⁄₄ x 8 $6.95 Order Code 1-55615-204-3

Available wherever books and software are sold. Or order directly from Microsoft Press.

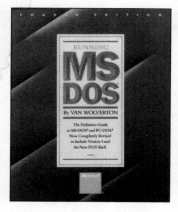

From the DOS experts...

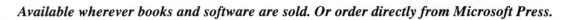